OXFORD
UNIVERSITY PRESS

ASPIRE
SUCCEED
PROGRESS

Complete
Computer Science
for **Cambridge IGCSE® & O Level**

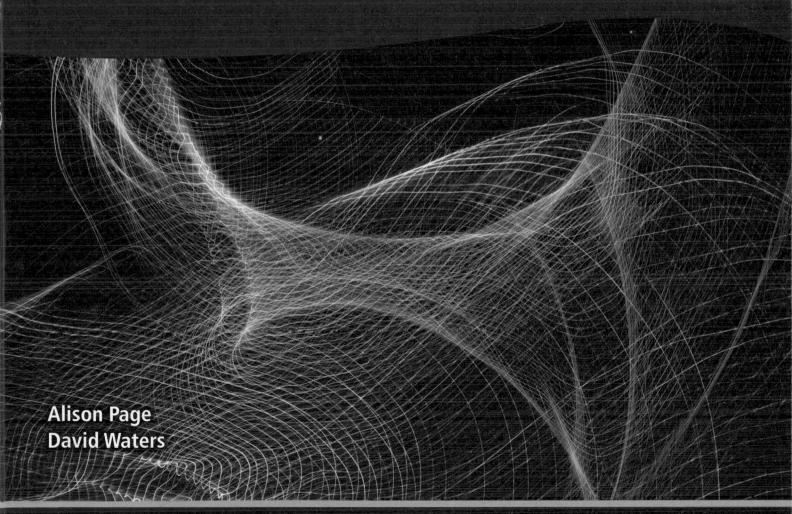

Alison Page
David Waters

Oxford excellence for Cambridge IGCSE & O Level   OXFORD

OXFORD
UNIVERSITY PRESS

Great Clarendon Street, Oxford, OX2 6DP, United Kingdom

Oxford University Press is a department of the University of Oxford. It furthers the University's objective of excellence in research, scholarship, and education by publishing worldwide. Oxford is a registered trade mark of Oxford University Press in the UK and in certain other countries

© Oxford University Press 2016

The moral rights of the authors have been asserted

First published in 2016

British Library Cataloguing in Publication Data
Data available

978-0-19-836721-5

3 5 7 9 10 8 6 4 2

Paper used in the production of this book is a natural, recyclable product made from wood grown in sustainable forests. The manufacturing process conforms to the environmental regulations of the country of origin.

Printed in India by Manipal Technologies Ltd

Acknowledgements

®IGCSE is the registered trademark of Cambridge International Examinations.

The questions and example answers that appear in this book were written by the authors.

The publishers would like to thank the following for permissions to use their photographs:

Cover image: John Lund/Getty images; p1: Sashkin/Shutterstock; p2: Rusm/iStockphoto; p4: Image Courtesy of The Advertising Archives; p5: Giorgio Rossi/Shutterstock; p9: From Computer Science Unplugged (csunplugged.org); photo by Jack Morgan; p15: SwEviL/ Shutterstock; p16: Anna Danilkova/Shutterstock; p21: Icedesigner/ Shutterstock; p20: Alison Page; p24: Alison Page; p25: Yayayoyo/ Shutterstock; p26: CreativeAct - Technology Series; p27: Ingvar Bjork/Shutterstock; p28: Mjf99/Shutterstock; p31: Nature Capture Realfoto/Shutterstock; p35(T): ChezBriand/iStockphoto; p35(B): S1001/Shutterstock; p36: DJMphoto/Shutterstock; p37: Maodoltee/ Shutterstock; p43: Incamerastock/Alamy Stock Photo; p44: Barrett Lyon/The Opte Project; p46: Frederic Sierakowski/Rex Shutterstock; p47: Rose Carson/Shutterstock; p48(L): Alison Page; p48(R): Alison Page; p50(L): Alison Page; p50(R): Alison Page; p55: Childnet www. childnet.com; p58: M. Timothy O'Keefe/Alamy Stock Photo; p61: Photocreo Michal Bednarek/Shutterstock; p93: Nikkytok/ Shutterstock; p94: Rozbyshaka/Shutterstock; p95(T): Tatiana Popova/ Shutterstock; p95(B): Insago/Shutterstock; p95(C): Alydv/iStockphoto; p96: Gareth Boden; p97(T): Umberto Shtanzman/Shutterstock; p97(B): Rogulin Dmitry/ITAR-TASS Photo/Corbis; p100: Vartanov Anatoly/ Shutterstock; p101(L): Bloomua/Shutterstock; p101(R): Aleph Studio/ Shutterstock; p102: Constantine Pankin/Shutterstock; p103: Images of Africa Photobank/Alamy Stock Photo; p104: Pashkov Andrey/ Alamy Stock Photo; p105(L): Oliver Berg/DPA/Corbis; p105(R): Hilippe Lissac/Godong/Corbis; p107: Handout/Corbis; p109: Twins/fstop/ Corbis; p110: D. Hurst; p111: Singkham/Shutterstock; p113: Tomertu/ Shutterstock; p115(T): Rezachka/Shutterstock; p115(B): Purestock; p116: Christian Delbert/Shutterstock; p117: Alexander Kirch/ Shutterstock; p118: Moso Image/Shutterstock; p119: Cultura/Rex Shutterstock; p121: Ruslan Kudrin/Shutterstock; p122: Alison Page; p123: Alison Page; p126: Kitch Bain/Shutterstock; p127(T): Surapong Naowasate/Shutterstock; p127(B): Claudio Divizia/Shutterstock; p128: Roman Sigaev/Shutterstock; p130: Christophe Testi; p131: Natalia Siverina/Shutterstock; p132(L): Iandagnall Computing/Alamy Stock Photo; p132(R): Nirut Rupkham/Shutterstock; p136: Vjom/ Shutterstock; p139: Grzegorz Knec/Alamy Stock Photo; p149: Andrey Popov/Shutterstock; p150: Goodluz/Shutterstock; p153: Rawpixel/ Shutterstock; p154: Scyther5/Shutterstock; p156(T): Gerald Martineau/ The Washington Post/Getty Images; p156(B): Ian Waldie/Getty Images; p157: WithGod/Shutterstock; p164: Sjscreens/Alamy Stock Photo; p165: Nakophotography/Shutterstock; p173(R): We Are Anonymous by Parmy Olsen. Copyright © 2002, 2003 by Henry Louis Gates, Jr. By permission of Grand Central Publishing; p173(L): AF Archive/Alamy Stock Photo; p177(L)-251: Alison Page; p135: Dencg/Shutterstock; p147: Mikser45/Shutterstock; p167: Marekuliasz/Shutterstock; p175: Dencg/Shutterstock; p219: Tele52/Shutterstock; p253: Stickasa/ Shutterstock. Artwork by Q2A Media Services Pvt. Ltd. and OUP.

Introduction

If you are studying Computer Science for Cambridge IGCSE® or O Level, then this book is designed for you. Its purpose is to help you achieve your best in the course and examination, equipping you with the knowledge you need to study the subject at a higher level.

The book follows the latest syllabuses and consists of ten chapters: chapters 1-7 cover the first section of the syllabus (Theory of Computer Science), while chapters 8-10 cover the second section (Problem-solving and programming).

Each chapter consists of topics that map to the sub-sections of the syllabus; each topic consists of several two-page units called spreads. To help you make the most of this student book, the following features are used to organise the content:

Syllabus reference

The explicit syllabus reference allows you to frame your learning and build connections between different topics.

Introduction

The short introduction will make it clear what you will learn in each lesson.

The material marked with a line on the side goes beyond the requirements of the syllabus and will not be tested in the examination. It's intended to give you a broader understanding of computer science and hopefully you'll find it interesting!

Test yourself & Learning activity

The "Test yourself" and "Learning activity" questions will help you check your understanding after each lesson and give you further opportunities to practise what you have learnt.

Key terms and interesting facts

These key terms, interesting facts and tips will extend your understanding of the subject.

The review page at the end of each chapter highlights the new key terms you've learnt in that chapter and proposes further project work.

Programming

In this student book, Python is used as an example programming language. There are many other programming languages and your teacher might have chosen a different one. However, the features you will learn about are found in almost all languages.

Contents

What's on your kerboodle ?

The *Complete Computer Science for Cambridge IGCSE and O Level Kerboodle* is an online learning platform, specifically designed to accompany this student book. If your school has a subscription, you will be able to access a bank of resources to support your learning, help you prepare for the examination and achieve your best.

Your resources

The *Complete Computer Science for Cambridge IGCSE and O Level Kerboodle* consists of three main modules:

1. The Lessons module contains lesson presentations and is a teacher-only area.

2. The Resources module is where you will find hundreds of worksheets and interactive activities to help you practise and develop your knowledge and skills.

3. The Assessment module is where you will see all the quizzes assigned to you by your teacher.

On Your Marks

The interactive **On Your Marks** are designed to help you build your skills and confidence when answering examination questions. Covering a range of question types, there is one activity for each of the topics covered in the student book. Each activity is split into two separate parts, allowing you to take a step-by-step approach:

- **Understand and prepare** (found in the Resources module of Kerboodle) gives you the opportunity to analyse an examination question and three sample student answers. It will then ask you to look at examiner feedback for those answers. Finally, you will have to give each sample answer a mark.

- **Test** (found in the Assessment module of Kerboodle, only available once your teacher assigns it to you) allows you to answer the question for yourself, and receive feedback and a mark from your teacher.

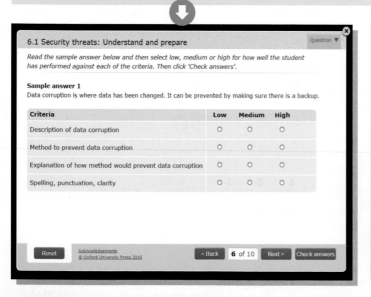

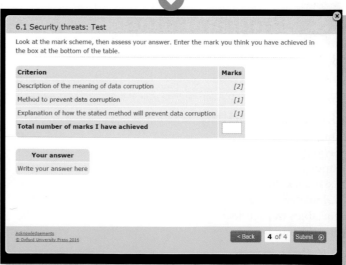

WebQuest

The **WebQuest** mini projects allow you to research specific aspects of the topics covered in the student book. Besides strengthening your understanding of the subject, they will help you develop skills such as communication and teamwork.

Interactive activities

There is a **starter** activity for each spread of the student book, specifically designed to consolidate your understanding of key concepts in computer science.

2.2 What is the Internet?: Activity

Solve the clues to complete the crossword.

Across

3 The Internet is the world's biggest computer _____.

4 Data transmission can be wired or _____.

6 To share data across the Internet computers must use the same rules or _____.

7 The Internet can be very useful and helpful but it can also be _____.

Down

1 About half the people on Earth have used the _____.

2 Data _____ allows computers to share data.

5 We connect to the Internet through an

Reset   Acknowledgements
© Oxford University Press 2016   Check answers

Worksheets

There is an **extension** worksheet for each spread of the student book, to extend your understanding and inspire further study of the subject.

WebQuest

4.3 Using storage devices and media

Introduction

Storage devices form a category of computer hardware. This WebQuest is concerned with secondary storage devices, which are the ones that allow you to make more permanent copies of your files and data. Each type of storage device has different strengths and weaknesses which makes it more suited to specific purposes. Not every storage device is suitable for every task.

What storage devices are there and how do they work? What is the difference between a storage device and storage medium, and which medium goes with which device? For which purposes are these storage systems best suited in the real world?

Task

Do some research to find out about a range of storage devices and media. Some examples are hard disk drives (fixed and removable), solid state drives, DVD, CD, Blu-ray disc and USB flash memory. Your teacher may ask each group to research a different category of storage device.

First, find out how each device works, and if appropriate, what storage medium it uses. Try to discover the main benefits and drawbacks of each type of storage device and medium. You will then describe how each device is used in real life scenarios.

Create a presentation of about five minutes' duration for the rest of your class. Your presentation should be informative, concise and include pictures of the devices and, if relevant, their associated media.

Process

Step 1: Roles

A useful way to organise this task would be for each group to be allocated a category of storage device and medium to research. Your group should decide how to tackle the task you have been assigned. One method would be for each member of the group to initially look at a particular type of storage device and medium, and where it may be used, gathering as much useful information as possible. Once this is done, the group as a whole will create the final presentation.

Step 2: Research

Carry out the research on your specific storage device(s) and any associated media, and find as much as you can about how it works, and its good and bad points. Make sure you have a picture of it. Then find out and explain how and where it can be used in real life situations.

© Oxford University Press 2016
www.oxfordsecondary.com/acknowledgements   1

Extension Worksheet

4.1 Sensors

A Building Management System, or BMS, is a computerised system that works in a building to monitor and control major parts of that building's environment. Some of the things a BMS controls are:

- temperature and ventilation
- lighting
- electrical power
- fire systems
- access systems (for example, entry and exit doors).

The top floor of a school needs to be brought into the Building Management System. You have been asked to plan where sensors will be installed. This is what you have been asked for:

1. temperature control sensors in every room

2. smoke sensors in all rooms plus three in the corridor to link into fire alarm system

3. motion sensors in every room to control lights and link into security alarm system

4. light sensors in every room to close blinds automatically in direct sunlight.

The money available for this work is £4,750.

The table below shows the cost of installing each type of sensor and what it will cost if you meet all four of the requirements above in full. You will see straight away that you will not have enough money.

	Cost per sensor	Number of sensors	Total cost	Your suggested number	Your cost
Temperature	£200	7	£1400		
Smoke	£75	10	£750		
Motion	£250	7	£1750		
Light	£400	7	£2800		
		Total	£6700	Total	

1. Suggest how the number of sensors can be reduced so that the cost is equal to or less than £4,750. For each of the four types of sensor, think about where they are really needed. For example, does the school really need to maintain a constant temperature in a store room? Do they need to have automatic light control in rooms that are in constant use? Use the plan below to help you think about this problem and use the table above to record your suggestions.

Hint: The compass might help you make some savings!

© Oxford University Press 2016
www.oxfordsecondary.com/acknowledgements   1

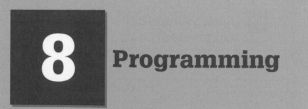

8 Programming

Java

7

Java and Visual Basic programming support

If you are learning to program in Java or Visual Basic rather than Python, these PDF booklets will bring you all the material on the programming spreads in the student book, but with specific Java or Visual Basic syntax and examples.

Summative quizzes

One for each topic, these **multiple choice quizzes** allow you to test your knowledge and identify any areas of improvement.

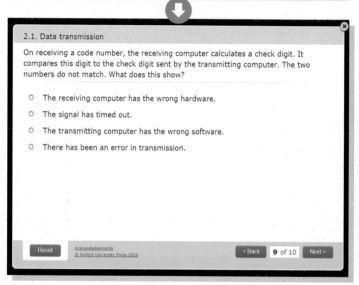

2.1. Data transmission

On receiving a code number, the receiving computer calculates a check digit. It compares this digit to the check digit sent by the transmitting computer. The two numbers do not match. What does this show?

○ The receiving computer has the wrong hardware.

○ The signal has timed out.

○ The transmitting computer has the wrong software.

○ There has been an error in transmission.

Reset   Acknowledgements   © Oxford University Press 2016   < Back   **9** of 10   Next >

Practice Paper 2A

Section A

You are advised to spend no longer than 40 minutes answering this section.

Here is a copy of the pre-release material.

DO NOT attempt tasks 1, 2 and 3 now.

Use the pre-release material and your experience from attempting the tasks before the examination to answer Question 1.

Pre-release material

As a school exercise you will be storing the heights and genders of all the students in your class at the start of the year and then at regular intervals to find out how much they have grown.

Write and test a program for your class.

Your program must include appropriate prompts for the entry of data.

Error messages and other output must be set out clearly.

All variables, constants and other identifiers are expected to have meaningful names.

You will need to complete these **three** tasks. Each task must be fully tested.

TASK 1 – Setting up the base data

The initial heights, as well as genders of the students in the class, must first be entered and stored using arrays. Assuming the class has 30 students, write a program that will allow you to:

- input and store the height of each student
- input and store the gender of each student
- calculate the average height of all students in the class
- calculate the average height of all males in the class
- calculate the average height of all females in the class.

TASK 2 – Setting up the first comparison data

Input and store the heights of the students in the class after three months have passed. Ensure that the new height and previous height can be identified as belonging to the same student. It should be possible to calculate the average heights from the new data, as in task 1.

TASK 3 – Work out statistics

Modify the program so that it will calculate and store the height changes for each student. It should be possible for the following data to be output:

- initial height, new height and height change for each student
- the average height change for all students
- the average height change for males
- the average height change for females
- the largest height change in the class
- the largest height change for males
- the largest height change for females
- the smallest height change in the class
- the smallest height change for males
- the smallest height change for females

2

Exam preparation

These exam-style practice papers will test your understanding of theory (**Paper 1**) and assess your problem-solving and programming skills (**Paper 2 and pre-release materials**).

1 Data representation

Syllabus reference

1.1.1 Binary systems

Learners should be able to show understanding of why computers use binary systems.

See also:

3.3 Inside the CPU

1.1 Binary systems

Binary data

> ### Introduction
>
> In this section you will learn what a computer does. You will learn why computers use binary data.

What is a computer?

A computer is an electronic machine for processing data. "Data" is a general term for facts and figures. All types of data can be processed by a computer. Computers can work with numbers, words, images, sounds, and video, and they can control physical processes. All of these types of data can be stored inside a computer. The computer processes the data. That means it turns the data into something more useful. The useful output of the computer is often called "information".

⬆ Data is processed to make useful information

A computer processes data to make useful information. Computers are made by people, to be useful to people. There is no point in using a computer unless it does something you want.

Inside the computer

Inside every computer is a processor. The processor stores and processes data. The processor stores the data using electrical switches that can either be on or off. A switch that is on will conduct electricity. A switch that is off will not carry an electric signal.

"Binary" means anything that can be in one of two different states. A switch that can be on or off is binary. There are exactly two choices – no more, no less. The data inside a computer is stored in a binary format.

➡ A flashlight can be in one of two states – either on or off

A computer can process data of many different kinds, but all types of data must first be turned into binary data so the computer can use it. That is why this chapter – the first in the book – teaches you about binary data.

Representing binary data

When we want to show binary data we write it as a "binary number": that is, a number made of 1s and 0s. We can also call this "base 2". For example:

01001110

Of course, if you opened up a computer and looked in the processor you would not see 1s and 0s. That is just a convenient way of representing the on and off electrical signals.

Test yourself

Use the information on these pages to answer the following questions.

1. The computer does not have 1s and 0s inside its memory. Why do we sometimes represent computer data in that form?

2. Explain in your own words why data must be converted into binary form when it is input to a computer.

3. On this page a flashlight is given as an example of something that is binary (has two different states). Think of another example, from outside computer science.

4. Why are computers useful?

Binary

Anything that can exist in two different states, and only two, is called binary.

Data

Facts and figures of any kind are known as data. Facts and figures are stored inside the computer as binary data.

Learning activity

On this page, five different types of data are mentioned: numbers, words, images, sounds and video. Search on the Internet for a short example of each type of data. Store a sample of each type of data in your own storage area of the computer system.

Syllabus reference

1.1.1 Binary systems

Learners should be able to: show understanding of the concept of a byte and how the byte is used to measure memory size; use binary in computer registers for a given application.

See also:

1.3 Data storage
3.3 Inside the CPU

Bits and bytes

Introduction

You have learned that data is held in the computer in binary form. In this section you will learn how the size of computer memory is measured as the amount of binary data it can hold.

Bits and bytes

Binary numbers are made up of the digits 1 and 0 (one and zero). We abbreviate the term "binary digit" to "bit". Therefore, in computer science, one bit is a 0 or a 1. One bit is the smallest piece of computer memory. A bit represents a single on/off switch inside the computer's electronic memory.

Inside the computer, on/off bits are organised into groups of eight. A group of eight bits is called a "byte".

For this reason we usually write binary numbers in groups of eight bits. That matches the way a computer organises bits. If the number is less than eight bits long, we put extra 0s on the left of the digits to make it up to 8 bits. For example, the binary number 1 1 0 1 would be represented by this byte:

0 0 0 0 1 1 0 1

Measuring memory

The area of the computer processor that stores data as on/off electrical signals is called the memory (random-access memory or RAM). We measure the size of RAM by how many bytes it can hold.

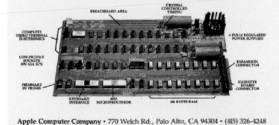

⬆ This old advert boasts that a memory card will add 16K (kilobytes) to your computer's RAM

We measure memory in kilobytes, megabytes and gigabytes:

- A kilobyte is 1024 bytes. That will store about half a page of text.
- A megabyte is 1024 kilobytes. A picture may be 3 megabytes.
- A gigabyte is 1024 megabytes. A movie may be 4 gigabytes.

When computers are advertised they often say how many bytes of RAM there are in the computer processor.

RAM and Computer Speed

The computer processor makes changes to the data in RAM. That is called processing the data. It is very quick and easy for the processor to access the contents of RAM. The processing will be quick.

If there isn't enough room in RAM, then some of the data must be stored outside of RAM. It is slower for the processor to access this data. That means the computer will go more slowly.

Adding more RAM to a computer will help it process data more quickly.

Registers

There may be 8 gigabytes of RAM in the main memory of a computer.

Processing does not happen in the main memory though. Data that is ready to be processed is copied into a much smaller area of memory called a register. Registers are normally measured by the number of bits they can hold, for example an 8-bit register or a 32-bit register.

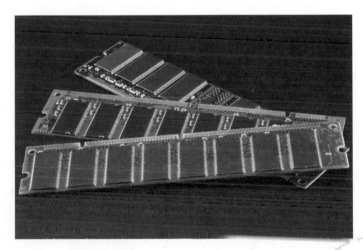

A processor often contains several kinds of registers, each used for a different purpose. Computers with large registers can work on more data at a time than those with small registers, so they usually work more quickly.

Test yourself

1. Explain the difference between a bit and a byte.
2. Work out exactly how many bytes there are in a megabyte.
3. Roughly how many pictures could be stored using 1 gigabyte of data?
4. Explain two factors that increase the speed of a computer.

Learning activity

Using magazines and the Internet, collect adverts for computers currently for sale. What does each advert say about the computer? How big is the RAM?

Syllabus reference

1.1.1 Binary systems

Learners should be able to: recognise the use of binary data in computer systems; convert positive binary integers into denary.

Binary and denary

Introduction

You have learned that the computer stores data as binary numbers. In this section you will compare binary to denary (our normal number system).

The denary system

The number system that you are familiar with in everyday life uses ten different digits. We can also call this "base 10". Every number that exists can be represented using these ten digits:

0 1 2 3 4 5 6 7 8 9

Something that can be in ten different forms is known as denary. Our number system uses ten different digits, so it is a denary system. Another name for it is 'decimal'. It can also be referred to as "base 10".

How do we represent every number, using just ten digits? The answer is we use the position of a digit to change its meaning. Look at these numbers:

702

720

207

Each of these denary numbers uses the digit 2. In the first case it means two. In the next example it means twenty. In the final example it means two hundred. The difference is the position of the digit in the number.

Start at the right of a number. The digit on the right stands for single units. As we move to the left each digit has a value that is ten times bigger.

1000 (thousands)	100 (hundreds)	10 (tens)	1 (units)
0	7	2	0

In this example we have seven hundreds, two tens and no units. That is the meaning of 720 in denary.

The binary system

Binary numbers are made of the binary digits 1 and 0 (also called bits). Every number that exists can be represented using just 1s and 0s.

As with the denary system, the position of the bit tells you its value. Start at the right of a number. The bit on the right stands for single units. As we move to the left each bit has a value that is two times bigger. Here is an example: the binary number 1 0 1.

8 (eights)	4 (fours)	2 (twos)	1 (units)
0	1	0	1

In this example we have one four, no twos and one unit. Adding the values together makes 5. Therefore, 1 0 1 in binary is 5 in denary.

Invention of the denary system

The denary number system that we use today was developed in India, probably in the 3rd century BCE (2,300 years ago). It was better for doing complex maths than any other number system that existed at that time.

This number system was adopted in the Arabic world, and spread beyond India. Around 850 CE, the Persian mathematician Al-Khwarizmi and the Arab mathematician Al-Kindi wrote books that explained the denary number system.

Later, Europeans learned this system from Arabic mathematicians. In Europe, denary digits are still sometimes called 'Arabic numerals'.

Invention of the binary system

Binary number systems were developed much later. A German philosopher called Gottfried Leibniz set out the idea of binary numbers, made with 1s and 0s, in 1679. In the 19th century, a British mathematician called Ada Lovelace wrote notes about how binary numbers could be used in digital processing.

Test yourself

1. Why is our normal number system called a denary system?

2. Explain why a digit such as 9 can hold many different values in a denary number.

3. How many bits are there in the binary number 0010?

4. In the binary number 0010 what value does the 1 stand for?

Denary

Anything that can exist in ten different states is known as denary. Our usual number system is denary.

Learning activity

Complete this table by replacing the question marks with number values. Remember each value is twice as big as the one before.

?	?	?	?	8	4	2	1
0	0	1	0	0	1	0	1

Talking about binary numbers

When you talk about binary numbers, never use denary words. For example, the binary number

1 0 1

Is **not** "one hundred and one". It is "one zero one" or "one 'oh' one".

Syllabus reference

1.1.1 Binary systems

Learners should be able to recognise the use of binary data in computer systems.

Counting in binary

Introduction

You have learned about binary and denary numbers. In this section you learn how to count in binary, and how it compares to counting in ordinary (denary) numbers.

Counting in denary

To count up from zero in ordinary, denary, numbers you start at 0. You count in the "units" column. The digit in the "units" column gets 1 bigger each time:

> 00
>
> 01
>
> 02

When you get to 9, you have run out of digits:

> 09

How can you add more? You return the "units" column back to 0, and add 1 to the next column along. In denary that is the "tens" column:

> 10

You then start again, counting upwards in the "units" column. When you reach 9:

> 19

You reset the units column to 0 and add 1 in the "tens" column:

> 20

In this way you can count up to any number using denary.

Counting in binary

When you count in binary it is the same. Start with 0:

> 0

Then add 1:

> 1

You have used 0 and 1 and there are no more binary digits. Therefore, you return the "units" column to 0, and add 1 in the column to the left:

> 10

Continue to count. Add 1 in the "unit" column:

> 11

Now you have run out of digits in both columns, so you reset them both to 0, and add a 1 in the column to the left:

> 100

In this way you can count up to any number in binary. However, the numbers can get quite long.

Group learning activity

Form a group of eight students. Sit in a row on eight chairs. Each student will be one of the bits in a byte. The rest of the class can watch. Later, everyone will get a turn.

The teacher is going to count up in the normal way. The students are going to act out binary counting.

- A student who is sitting down means 0.
- A student who is standing up means 1.

The chair on the right of the line represents the "units" column. The student in this chair has the most work to do. Every time the teacher counts, the student in this chair has to change position. If you are that student, you have to follow these rules:

- If you are sitting down, stand up.
- If you are standing up, turn and nod to the person next to you, and sit down.

The students in the other chairs don't move. They wait and watch the person to their right. If you are one of these students and the person to your right nods to you:

- If you are sitting down, stand up.
- If you are standing up, turn and nod to the person next to you, and sit down.

If you follow these rules carefully you can count through every binary number from 0 to 255.

⬆ Students carrying out the "count binary" activity.

Notes for the teacher

Make sure you count slowly. The students will do their best to keep up.

Variations on this activity

Instead of using standing and sitting to represent 1 and 0 you could hold up cards with 1s and 0s on them or you could use flashlights that you turn on and off. The boys in this picture are turning around to display a 0 on their back or a 1 on their front.

Syllabus reference

1.1.1 Binary systems

Learners should be able to convert positive binary integers into denary (a maximum of 16 bits will be used).

Convert binary to denary

Introduction

You have learned about binary and denary numbers. In this section you will learn how to turn binary numbers into denary form.

Position values

You have seen that the value of a bit in a binary number depends on the position of the bit in the number. This table shows the position value of the eight bits that make up a byte.

128	64	32	16	8	4	2	1

To convert a binary number into denary, you write the number into a table like this one. Make sure the number ends in the column on the right. Any empty columns should be at the left of the table. Put a 0 in any empty column.

Here is an example: the binary number 11010.

128	64	32	16	8	4	2	1
0	0	0	1	1	0	1	0

To turn this number into a denary number:

- find all the columns that have a 1 in them
- add the column values together.

The columns are 16, 8 and 2:

$$16 + 8 + 2 = 26$$

This shows that the binary number 11010 is the denary number 26.

16-bit numbers

The example on this page shows a number that uses up to eight bits (a single byte). One byte of data can hold any number from 0 to 255. Of course a computer can process numbers that are much larger than this. To do this the computer links several bytes together to make a large enough storage space.

You should learn how to convert numbers as large as 16 bits (two bytes). Remember that as you move to the left of a number, each bit has a value twice as big as the one before it.

Here are the position values of the bits in a 16-bit number.

32 768	16 384	8192	4096	2048	1024	512	256	128	64	32	16	8	4	2	1

You do not have to remember all these values. If you ever need to find the value of a 16-bit number you can work out the position values by starting at 1 in the right-hand column, and doubling the value as you count to the left (using a calculator).

To convert a 16-bit number into denary, create this table. Enter the 16-bit number into the table. Then add together the values of any column with a 1 in it.

Test yourself

1. Convert these 8-bit binary numbers into denary:

00011001

01010000

10010011

11111111

2. Here is the biggest number you can make with 16 bits. Convert this number to denary:

1111111111111111

Learning activity

Write a handout or a presentation to teach young learners how to convert 8-bit binary numbers into denary.

Syllabus reference

1.1.1 Binary systems

Learners should be able to convert positive denary integers into binary.

Convert denary to binary

Introduction

You have learned to convert binary numbers into denary. In this section you will learn how to turn denary numbers into binary.

Converting denary to binary

There is more than one way to convert denary numbers into binary. You will learn a method that uses the position values table.

Start with the denary number you want to convert. For example, let us convert the number 40 to binary. Next look at the table of position values. What is the largest value you can subtract from 40 (without making a minus number)?

128	64	32	16	8	4	2	1

The largest value you can subtract is 32, so you write a 1 in the "32" column.

128	64	32	16	8	4	2	1
		1					

Now take away the value. In this example 40 – 32 = 8.

What is the next largest value you can take away? It is 8, so you write a 1 in the "8" column.

128	64	32	16	8	4	2	1
		1		1			

8 – 8 = 0, so the conversion is complete. Write a 0 in every other column.

128	64	32	16	8	4	2	1
0	0	1	0	1	0	0	0

This shows that 40 in denary is 00101000 in binary.

Simplify the process

To simplify the process, complete all the subtractions and then transfer the values to the position table.

For example, let us convert the denary number 99 into binary:

$$99 - 64 = 35$$
$$35 - 32 = 3$$
$$3 - 2 = 1$$
$$1 - 1 = 0$$

Now mark the numbers you have taken away in the position table. Write a 0 in every other column.

128	64	32	16	8	4	2	1
0	1	1	0	0	0	1	1

This shows that 99 in denary is 01100011 in binary.

Summary of the method

To convert a denary number to binary, you must remember the column values of the binary table. Start with the largest value you can subtract from the number without going below zero.

Take the remainder from this subtraction. Continue to subtract numbers and take the remainder, until you have got to 0.

Look at all the numbers you have subtracted. Put a 1 in the matching columns of the binary table. Put a 0 in all the other columns.

Q

Test yourself

1. Convert these denary numbers into 8-bit binary numbers:

31

55

70

101

2. Convert 500 into 16-bit binary.

Q

Learning activity

Make a class handout to tell young learners how to convert denary numbers into binary.

Syllabus reference

1.1.2 Hexadecimal

Learners should be able to show understanding of the reasons for choosing hexadecimal notation to represent numbers.

1.2 **Hexadecimal**

What is hexadecimal?

> **Introduction**
>
> You have learned about the binary and denary number systems. In this section you will learn about the hexadecimal number system. It is based on the number 16.

Hexadecimal digits

You have learned that binary numbers are made using two digits (0 and 1). We can also call this "base 2". Denary uses ten different digits. We can also call it "base 10". Hexadecimal is a number system that uses 16 different digits, which is why we can also call it "base 16".

The 16 hexadecimal digits are:

0 1 2 3 4 5 6 7 8 9 A B C D E F

These 16 digits stand for the numbers 0 to 15. Digits 0 to 9 are just the same as denary. The next six digits stand for the numbers 10 to 15:

A means 10

B means 11

C means 12

D means 13

E means 14

F means 15.

Position values

Just as with binary and denary numbers, the hexadecimal digits have different values in different positions. Many of the hexadecimal numbers you will look at have just two digits. As with all numbers, the right-hand column stands for units (1s). Because hexadecimal is base 16, the next column is 16 times greater in value. Digits in the second column stand for 16s.

16 (sixteens)	1 (units)

Let us look at one example. Here is the hexadecimal number 2B.

16	1
2	B

There is a 2 in the 16s column. This has the value:

2 × 16 = 32

There is a B in the units columns. In the hexadecimal system, B stands for 11:

11 × 1 = 11

Adding the two values together:

32 + 11 = 43

Therefore, hexadecimal number 2B means 43 in denary. You will soon learn more about converting hexadecimal to denary (see pages 16–17).

Why do we use hexadecimal?

You have learned that the computer processes all data in binary form. Binary numbers are very useful in computer science, but they have disadvantages:

- It is hard for people to read and understand binary numbers.
- When you write a binary number it is easy to make a mistake.
- It is hard to spot and fix errors in binary numbers.
- Writing a binary number takes a lot of space.

People wanted numbers that were easier to understand and work with. Denary notation wasn't suitable because converting binary to denary is difficult.

The hexadecimal notation was chosen for these reasons:

- It is very easy to turn hexadecimal into binary.
- It is very easy to turn binary into hexadecimal.
- Hexadecimal is much easier to read than binary.
- Hexadecimal numbers take up much less space than binary numbers.

Using hexadecimal notation is an easy way to work with binary numbers. Learn more about converting hexadecimal to binary on pages 18–19.

↑ Hexadecimal numbers can be used to represent binary data

Test yourself

1. Explain the difference between a hexadecimal digit and a hexadecimal number.

2. What is the biggest hexadecimal digit and what is its value?

3. What value does the hexadecimal number A0 have?

4. Can you have a hexadecimal number that doesn't have letters in it? Explain your answer.

Learning activity

Make an advertising poster for your computer room at school that aims to persuade why hexadecimal is better than binary.

Spot the hexadecimal

Hexadecimal numbers do not always have letters in them. Letters are used in some hexadecimal numbers, but not all.

Syllabus reference

1.1.2 Hexadecimal

Learners should be able to: represent positive numbers in hexadecimal notation; convert positive hexadecimal integers to and from denary (a maximum of four hexadecimal digits will be required).

⬆ Why do people count in denary (base 10)?

Hexadecimal and denary

Introduction

You have learned that hexadecimal is base 16. In this section you will learn how to convert between hexadecimal and denary numbers.

Convert hexadecimal to denary

In the previous section you saw how hexadecimal numbers are made. Hexadecimal numbers use 16 different digits. The value of the digit depends on its position. Each column has a value 16 times greater than the column to its right. A two-digit hexadecimal number is easy to convert.

16 (sixteens)	1 (units)
7	C

You multiply the first digit by 16. Then you add the value of the second digit. Remember that in hexadecimal notation, C stands for 12, so the answer is:

$$7 \times 16 = 112$$
$$112 + 12 = 124$$

Longer hexadecimal numbers

Converting longer hexadecimal numbers uses the same method. You may need to add more columns to the left of the position table. Each column is 16 times bigger than the one to its right. Here is a four-column hexadecimal table. You don't need to remember these column headings. You can work them out by multiplying by 16, using a calculator.

4096	256	16	1

Once you have made the table of column headings, put the hexadecimal number into the table. Here is an example, using the number 1A00.

4096	256	16	1
1	A	0	0

Now multiply each digit by its position value, and add the values together.

First digit: the digit 1 is in the largest column. The column value is 4096:

$$4096 \times 1 = 4096$$

Second digit: the digit A is in the next column. The column value is 256. The digit A in hexadecimal stands for 10:

$$256 \times 10 = 2560$$

Complete the calculation: you have worked out the value of each digit, now add the values together:

$$4096 + 2560 = 6656$$

The calculation looks difficult, but it is easy with a calculator.

Convert denary to hexadecimal

To turn denary numbers into hexadecimal:

- Divide the denary number by 16.

- The result goes in the 16s column.

- The remainder goes in the units column.

For example, to convert 59 into hexadecimal:

$$\frac{59}{16} = 3 \text{ remainder } 11$$

11 is B in hexadecimal, so the answer is 3B.

16	1
3	B

This method works for all numbers up to 255.

Convert larger denary numbers

For numbers bigger than 255, you will have to use the larger hexadecimal column values. They are 256 (16 × 16) and 4096 (256 × 16).

Let us call the denary number we want to convert into hexadecimal X. Carry out the following process:

- Find the largest column that is smaller than X.

- Divide X by this column value.

- Take the remainder and divide by the next smallest column value.

- Continue until you reach the units column.

For example, let's convert the number 602 to hexadecimal:

- The largest column value that is smaller than 602 is 256

- Divide 602 by 256:

$$\frac{602}{256} = 2 \text{ remainder } 90$$

- The remainder is 90.

- Divide 90 by the next column value, which is 16:

$$\frac{96}{16} = 5 \text{ remainder } 10$$

- We have reached the units column.

- 10 is A in hexadecimal.

- Put these answers in the columns.

4096	256	16	1
0	2	5	A

This shows that 602 in denary is 25A in hexadecimal.

Syllabus reference

1.1.2 Hexadecimal

Learners should be able to convert positive hexadecimal integers to and from binary (a maximum of 16-bit binary numbers will be required).

Hexadecimal and binary

Introduction

You have learned to convert between hexadecimal and denary numbers. In this section you will learn how to convert between hexadecimal and binary numbers. It is much easier.

Exact match

On pages 8–9 you learned how to count up in binary. There is an exact match between the first 16 binary numbers and the 16 hexadecimal digits.

Hexadecimal	Binary
0	0000
1	0001
2	0010
3	0011
4	0100
5	0101
6	0110
7	0111
8	1000
9	1001
A	1010
B	1011
C	1100
D	1101
E	1110
F	1111

You can use this table to convert between hexadecimal and binary. Every number converts exactly. There are no subtractions or remainders to worry about.

Match and convert hexadecimal

It is very easy to use the table above to turn hexadecimal into binary. For example think of the hexadecimal number A1B7. Refer to the table above and simply write in the four-bit binary number that matches each digit.

A	1	B	7
1010	0001	1011	0111

This shows that the answer in binary is 1010 0001 1011 0111. By using the table you can get the answer in a few seconds.

Match and convert binary

Using the table of matching numbers you can convert any binary number into hexadecimal. Just put the bits into groups of four. If the bits don't divide equally into fours, then add some 0s at the start of the number.

For example, take the binary number 1010111001100. There are 13 bits in this number. We have to add three 0s at the start, then we can arrange the bits into four groups of four bits:

0001 0101 1100 1100

Next use the table to turn each group of four bits into a hexadecimal digit.

0001	0101	1100	1100
1	5	C	C

The answer in hexadecimal is therefore 15CC.

Make the conversion table

Sometimes you need to convert between hexadecimal and binary, but you do not have the conversion table. It is easy to make it for yourself:

- Write down the first 16 hexadecimal numbers from 0 to F, down the page, each on a new line
- Count the first 16 binary numbers from 0000 to 1111, writing them down the page next to their hexadecimal equivalent.

When you get used to this conversion, you will find you won't even need the table: you'll be able to do it in your head.

Test yourself

1. Convert the hexadecimal number ABCD into binary.
2. Convert the binary number 1010 1111 1010 0000 into hexadecimal.
3. Convert your age into binary and hexadecimal.
4. Explain why it is more convenient to use hexadecimal than denary for people who need to work with binary values.

Learning activity

Create a large and colourful version of the table that matches hexadecimal and binary digits.

"Nibble"

When you do binary to hexadecimal conversion you put the bits into groups of four. There are eight bits in a byte, so four bits is half a byte. Computer scientists use the word "nibble" or "nybble" to mean a four-bit binary number. Can you guess why they chose that word?

Syllabus reference

1.1.2 Hexadecimal

Learners should be able to:
represent numbers stored in
registers and main memory as
hexadecimal; identify current
uses of hexadecimal numbers in
computing.

See also:

1.3 Data storage
3.3 Inside the CPU
5.2 Computer languages

How hexadecimal is used

Introduction

You have learned that it is very easy to convert binary numbers directly
into hexadecimal. For this reason hexadecimal is used in many computer
activities. In this section you will learn about some of them.

Binary data

Every item of data or information inside the computer is held in binary form.
Everything within the computer has to be a binary number. That includes:

- text (letters and other characters)
- colours
- sounds
- software instructions.

The computer uses different coding systems to turn all the different types of
data into binary numbers. When human users work with this binary data they
almost always use hexadecimal instead. This is because hexadecimal:

- converts easily and directly into binary
- is much easier to read, write, check and understand than binary.

Uses of hexadecimal

Main memory and the registers

RAM is made of "bits" of data. The bits are arranged in bytes. Every location
in RAM has its own "address". Memory addresses are binary numbers.
Therefore, everything about RAM can be represented by binary numbers.
The data that is stored is binary. The address where it is stored is binary.
We use hexadecimal to make it easier to read and write this information.

Colours

Nowadays the most common way to store colour information is in "24-bit
colour". Every colour is made of a mix of red, blue and green. Three bytes
of data are used. One byte stores the amount of red, another byte stores the
amount of blue, and
the third stores the
amount of green. By
mixing the three primary
colours together in
different proportions,
over 16 million different
colours can be made.
Each colour can be
written as a hexadecimal
number. The picture
shows some of these.

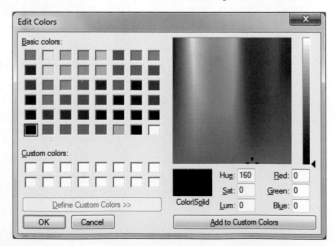

Machine code and assembly language

Machine code is a number code system that turns all software instructions into binary numbers. Programmers who write in machine code almost always turn these numbers into hexadecimal. We can also represent machine code instructions using a simple word code called assembly language.

Programmers use hexadecimal to represent binary data and binary addresses. This makes it much easier to write machine code and assembly language. It also makes it easier to debug (fix errors). Error messages are often displayed using a hexadecimal code.

Q

Test yourself

1. Why is the colour system that uses red, blue and green called 24-bit colour?

2. Why do programmers use hexadecimal instead of denary to represent binary codes?

3. Apart from colours, identify two different types of information that are stored in the computer using binary codes.

4. What is an error message and how does it help with debugging?

Q

Learning activity

Create a hexadecimal colour chart like the one shown on this page. You can investigate different examples of hexadecimal colour codes.

Debug

To debug means to find errors in software. It is much easier to debug software using hexadecimal because it is easier to read than binary.

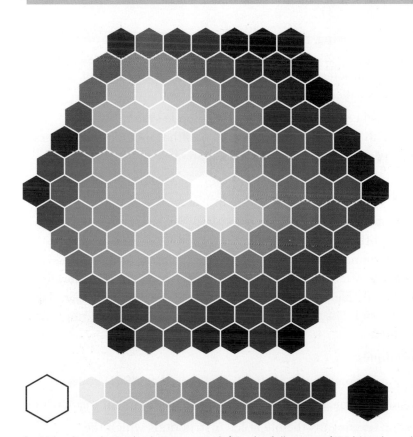

⬆ Using hexadecimal values we can define the full range of 24-bit colour choices

Syllabus reference

1.1.3 Data storage

Learners should be able to show understanding that text and numbers are stored in different formats.

See also:

3.3 Inside the CPU
4.3 Memory and storage

1.3 Data storage

Digital data

Introduction

Computers work with all types of data, including numbers, text, images and sound. All these different types of data must be held in binary form inside the computer. When data is held in binary form it is called digital data.

Number values

You have learned about binary numbers. All number values are processed as binary numbers inside the computer. One byte of storage can store all the whole numbers from 0 to 255. A whole number is called an integer. By combining several bytes together, the computer can store bigger integers.

The computer can also store fractions. In denary, all fractions can be represented as a number with a decimal point. For example, one quarter is 0.25. Binary fractions are stored in a similar way. The computer uses an extra byte of data to store the position of the point. These numbers are sometimes called floating point numbers.

Text

The computer stores text using a number code. Every letter of the alphabet is given a code number. There are different codes for upper and lower case letters and the other characters on the keyboard such as punctuation. The basic character code is called ASCII.

Since 1988, ASCII has been extended into a bigger code system called Unicode. Unicode is an international character code that includes characters from other alphabets such as Arabic, Hindi and Japanese.

File types

The different ways of storing digital data are called formats. Different types of computer file use different data formats. You can tell the format of a file by looking at the file name. Every computer file has a name. At the end of the name is a full stop. After the full stop is a short file extension – generally three or four letters. The file extension tells you what type of data is stored in the file. The file extension lets the computer know what data format to expect when it reads the file.

Here are some examples:

- The file extension .txt means the file holds text stored as ASCII code.
- The file extension .doc means the file holds text plus document formatting.
- The file extension .exe means the file holds instructions which the computer can execute (carry out).

Problems with file formats

Although all files contain binary numbers, the meaning of the numbers is different in different file formats. The computer must detect the file format, so it knows what the numbers mean.

In some cases, you need a particular software application in order to open a file format. For example the extension .xlsx means the file is a spreadsheet. It can only be opened by spreadsheet software.

Numbers as characters and values

Numbers can be stored in two ways: as number values, or as text characters. The two types of number will look the same. But the computer will process them differently. If a number is stored as a set of text characters the computer will not be able to do calculations with it.

It is important to choose the right format for numerical data.

ASCII	**Digital**
ASCII stands for "American Standard Code for Information Interchange". This is a number code that represents all standard keyboard characters.	"Digital" means something that has a precise value and that can be represented as a number. Digital data is data with a precise value. Binary data inside a computer is digital because the values are distinct, a pattern of on/off switches.

Test yourself

1. Why does a computer store letters of the alphabet using a digital (number) code?

2. Look at your computer keyboard. As well as letters of the alphabet, identify three other characters that are represented in ASCII code.

3. Why is Unicode preferred to ASCII in modern computer systems?

4. You see a file called holiday.jpeg. What is the file extension? Find out what kind of data is held in this type of file.

Learning activity

Find out the ASCII code number for each letter of the alphabet. Write a message in ASCII code. Swap messages with another student, and decode each other's work.

To set the other student a bigger challenge, turn the ASCII code into hexadecimal or binary numbers before sending it.

Syllabus reference

1.1.3 Data storage

Learners should be able to show understanding that pictures are stored in different formats.

See also:

1.2 Hexadecimal (How hexadecimal is used)

1.3 Data storage (Compression)

⬆ Close up you can see a bitmap image is made of pixels

Digital graphics

> ## Introduction
>
> You have learned that text and numbers are held in binary form in the computer's memory. In this section you will learn how images are stored.

Images

Pictures (also called images) are held in digital form inside the computer. The computer can display the image on the screen, or print it. A computer image is made up of millions of tiny dots called pixels (short for "picture elements"). A pixel represents one point of light on the screen, or one dot of ink on the paper.

The software that makes images is called graphic software. Different types of graphic software make different types of image. Two common methods are used to store images in digital form: bitmap and vector graphics.

Bitmap graphics

A bitmap file stores the position and colour of every pixel that makes up an image. The image is made of millions of pixels and the colour of each pixel is stored using a number code. That means a bitmap file has a lot of data. A bitmap file can be very large, consisting of many megabytes.

Bitmap files hold an image in full dot-by-dot detail. All the details and varied colours of real life can be stored. A bitmap is a good way to store photographs and other realistic images.

Some images are made of lots of very small pixels. That makes the image sharp and detailed. This is called a "high resolution" image. An image with fewer, larger, pixels is called "low resolution"; a low resolution image takes up less space.

As bitmap files are very large, they are often compressed to make them smaller. Read more about file compression on page 28.

Vector graphics

A vector image is made of shapes constructed from lines. The computer stores mathematical formulas that tell it how to draw the shapes and lines. This is less information than storing every single pixel in the image. In practice, this means that a vector file is smaller than a bitmap file. When you want to display or print the image, the computer creates it from the stored mathematical formulas.

Vector graphics are good for images made of simple lines and shapes, for example cartoons, diagrams and graphs. Vector graphics are not a good way to store photographs.

File extensions

Different file extensions are used for different graphics formats:

- The file extension .bmp is used for bitmap graphics files. Other extensions are used for compressed bitmap formats.

- The file extension .svg is an example of a vector graphic file. There are many others.

Learn more about compressed file extensions on page 29.

Pixelation

A bitmap image is made of dots. If the image is made larger, all the dots get bigger and the image looks distorted. We say it is "pixelated". Pixelation does not affect vector images. They are drawn to the correct size using the stored mathematical formulas.

BITMAP **VECTOR**

⬆ Vector images are not affected by pixelation

Colour depth

You have learned that a bitmap file stores the position and colour of every pixel in the image. There are different ways of storing the colour of each pixel. The number of colours that can be used in an image is called "colour depth". A greater colour depth allows more varied and subtle colours.

On page 20 you saw that 24-bit colour uses three bytes of data to store a colour code. This gives 16 million different colours. The file uses three bytes for every pixel in the image, allowing for varied and realistic colours.

There are other colour formats:

- Monochrome: each pixel is either black or white and uses just one bit (a 0 or 1).

- 16-colour: each pixel is half a byte (4 bits gives the numbers 0–15 in binary).

- 256-colour: each pixel is one byte (8 bits gives the numbers 0–255).

These options use less storage space, but give fewer colours.

File name:	Untitled.bmp
Save as type:	24-bit Bitmap (*.bmp;*.dib)

Monochrome Bitmap (*.bmp;*.dib)
16 Color Bitmap (*.bmp;*.dib)
256 Color Bitmap (*.bmp;*.dib)
24-bit Bitmap (*.bmp;*.dib)
JPEG (*.jpg;*.jpeg;*.jpe;*.jfif)
GIF (*.gif)
TIFF (*.tif;*.tiff)
PNG (*.png)

⬆ When you save an image you can choose between different formats

Test yourself

1. What is a pixel?

2. An architect wants to create a precise blueprint for a bridge. The blueprint may have to be expanded and printed on very large sheets of paper. What is the best graphics choice for this image, bitmap or vector? Explain your answer.

3. A photographer wants to edit a photograph by making tiny changes to individual dots of colour. Would a bitmap or a vector representation be best for this image? Explain your answer.

4. Would a bitmap or a vector image take up more space in computer memory? Explain your answer.

Learning activity

Research the different graphics applications that are available for free or to buy.

Find out whether each one creates bitmap or vector graphics.

For extra stretch and challenge create images using at least one of the applications.

Syllabus reference

1.1.3 Data storage

Learners should be able to: show understanding that sound (music) and video is stored in different formats; show understanding of the concept of musical instrument digital interface (MIDI) files, MP3 and MP4 files.

See also:

7.1 Ethics (Copyright)

⬆ Most people listen to digital music on MP3 players

Digital sound and video

Introduction

As well as text and images, computers store many other types of data. In this section you will learn how computers store sound and video in digital formats.

Audio formats

Sound content including music can be stored using a range of different formats. The different formats have different uses:

- WAV – this digital format stores music very accurately and with high quality. It is used by radio broadcasters. The disadvantages of WAV files are that they very large. That means they use a lot of space and take a long time to copy. For this reason, WAV files not suitable for use on websites or personal music players.

- MP3 – this digital format uses much less storage than WAV. It is a common audio format for websites, and digital audio players such as the iPod. MP3 format has worse sound quality than WAV. It is widely used because it is suitable for Internet download and storage on portable devices.

- MIDI – this format works like a piece of sheet music. It stores instructions to send to an audio synthesizer, to generate the notes from the different instruments required. MIDI uses very little storage compared to true audio formats.

Typically, a band in a recording studio will record their song onto a separate WAV track for each instrument and for each voice. These tracks will be edited and combined into a single stereo WAV file, used for making CDs and playing on the radio. The WAV file is reduced to a lower-quality MP3 file for download onto personal music players.

Editing audio files

Computers can process and edit MIDI files. This gives music producers a lot of control over the sound. For example, producers can use a computer feature called auto-tune. Auto-tune is a computer process that changes the pitch of each note. By using auto-tune the producer can make sure the singer always hits the right note.

A good producer is important for the success of a record. Other edits that music producers use nowadays include:

- making a long track by repeating a short clip over and over again
- changing the speed of the track
- "borrowing" samples from other musicians.

Borrowing samples sometimes causes disagreements between musicians. Read more in *7.1 Ethics (Copyright)*.

Video formats

Video files are much larger than audio files. A video file stores millions of images. When the images are viewed in sequence, the effect is of a single moving image. A common format for video is MPEG-4, also called MP4. MP4 is a "container" format. That means an MP4 file is a way of holding other digital formats. It can hold video, audio, image or text files. As MP4 is a container format, it does not use a standard method to format the content it holds. MP4 can be used by a wide range of devices, which gives it a significant advantage over other video formats. A disadvantage of MP4 is that it can only contain pre-recorded (archived) content. It cannot be used to live-stream broadcasts.

Although they have similar names, MP3 and MP4 formats were developed by different organisations. They work in different ways.

↑ YouTube is a site where people can share long and short video clips

File size

The number of bits used to store one second of sound or video is called "bit rate". The bit rate of a sound recording depends on:

- sample rate (number of times the sound changes per second)
- number of channels (mono, stereo, quad etc.)
- bit depth (range of sound frequencies used).

The bit rate of video also depends on all those factors, as well as the visual quality of the video. High resolution images use more storage space.

File quality

High quality sound and video has a high bit rate. For example, full CD-quality audio:

Feature	Rate
Sample rate	44 100 samples per second
Number of channels	2 (2-track stereo)
Bit depth	16 bits per sample

So the storage size for one second of high-quality audio is:

$$44,100 * 2 * 16 = 1\ 411\ 200 \text{ bits} = 176\ 400 \text{ bytes}$$

Formats that use less storage provide lower quality sound. The lowest quality is used in landline phones. Imagine listening to music over the phone. The quality is low.

"Believe"

"Believe", recorded by Cher in 1998, was the first song to use auto-tuning.

Q Test yourself

Explain the advantages, disadvantages and main uses of these four file formats:

- WAV
- MIDI
- MP3
- MP4.

Q Learning activity

Investigate what a podcast is and listen to an example of a podcast on the subject of technology. Write and record a sound file discussing audio formats.

Syllabus reference

1.1.3 Data storage

Learners should be able to: show understanding of the principles of data compression (lossless and lossy) applied to music and video, photographs and text files; show understanding of the concept of JPEG files.

See also:

4.3 Memory and storage

Compression

Introduction

You have learned that digital files can be very large. In this section you will learn about methods to reduce the size of digital files. Making a file smaller is called compression.

Why compression is important

A computer stores text, audio, image and video data in digital format. The data files can be very large. The disadvantages of large files are that they:

- use a lot of the computer's electronic memory, making the computer go more slowly
- take up a lot of space in storage, such as a DVD or a flash drive
- are slow to send, for example over the Internet.

Compressed files store the same data, or approximately equivalent data, but using fewer bytes.

Lossless or lossy?

There are many different compression methods. The different methods are described as lossless or lossy:

- Lossless compression reduces the size of a data file. There is no loss of data quality. Perfect lossless compression is hard to achieve.
- Lossy compression produces a bigger reduction, but data quality is reduced. Some of the detail of the file is lost. For example, an image might become more blurred.

Compressed image files

There are a number of ways to compress an image file. These produce different image formats.

Reducing image quality

The size of an image file depends on the number of pixels and the number of bytes used to store each pixel. File size can be reduced by:

- using fewer, larger, pixels to make the image, which reduces image resolution
- using fewer bytes to store the colour code, which reduces the depth of colour.

These are lossy compression methods.

Remove repetition

An image file can be simplified by removing repetition. This makes the file smaller. For example, an image may include a large group of pixels that are all the same colour. In an uncompressed bitmap file, each pixel is stored separately. In a compressed file, the colour is stored once, with a number to say how often that colour is repeated. Storing the colour only once uses far fewer bytes. Depending on the type of image there may be little loss of quality.

⬆ Lossy compression means a lower-quality data file

File formats

One of the most common image formats is JPEG (pronounced "jay-peg"). The file extension is usually .jpg or .jpeg. JPEG is a lossy compression method. Websites often use the JPEG format. JPEG is used a lot for digital photographs. It works well for images with realistic shading of colour. JPEG is not so good for images with sharp lines and hard edges between colours. Other compressed image formats include TIFF, GIF and PNG.

Compressed sound

The bit rate of a sound recording means the number of bits used to store one second of sound (see page 27). Sound compression reduces the bit rate of the recording. For example:

- using fewer channels (eg. Stereo becomes Mono)
- lower sample rate (fewer sound changes per second)
- reduced bit depth (fewer bits to store each sample by removing higher and lower sounds).

Sound compression does produce a reduction in sound quality. WAV files are high quality. But most listeners find MP3 format good enough for day to day listening.

Compressed video

Modern high definition TV (HDTV) uses a lot of storage space. Video compression means reducing the bit rate. To do this you can reduce:

- the number of audio channels
- the sample rate
- the image quality (for example the number of pixels per image).

In compressed video, the image may be less sharp and the movement less smooth.

Test yourself

1. What are the advantages and disadvantages of file compression?

2. Explain the difference between lossless and lossy compression in your own words.

3. List four different compressed file formats.

4. A high-resolution image is made of lots of small pixels. What do you think are the advantages and disadvantages of high-resolution image files?

Learning activity

Find a photograph on the Internet. Copy it into a graphics package such as Microsoft Paint. Save it using several different file formats. See how this affects the size of the file and the quality of the image.

Review

Key terms

Binary
: Anything that can exist in two different states, and only two, is called binary. The binary number system uses two digits: 1 and 0.

Bit
: Binary numbers are made up of the digits 1 and 0 (one and zero). We abbreviate the term "binary digit" to "bit".

Bitmap
: A bitmap file stores the position and colour of every pixel that makes up an image.

Byte
: Inside the computer, on/off bits are organised into groups of eight. A group of eight bits is called a "byte".

Data
: Facts and figures of any kind are known as data. Facts and figures are stored inside the computer as binary data.

Debug
: To debug means to find errors in software.

Digital
: "Digital" means something that has a precise value that can be represented as a number. Data which is stored as binary numbers is an example of digital data.

Hexadecimal
: Hexadecimal is a number system based on 16. It has 16 digits. Each column-value is worth 16 times more than the previous column.

Unicode
: Inside the computer text characters are coded in digital form. Unicode is an international code used to represent text characters.

Vector
: A vector image is made of shapes constructed from lines. The computer stores mathematical formulas that tell it how to draw the shapes and lines.

Project work

On page 9 you learned a binary counting activity. Practice this activity again as a class. When you are very good at doing it without any mistakes, make a video of the activity. There are a number of ways you could do this:

- Your teacher could use the equipment, and act as a film director
- This might be a project for those students in your school studying media or film
- You could do the task as a class, working the digital recording equipment yourselves

If you do not have access to the right equipment, or this is not possible, there are some alternatives. For example, you could make a sound recording explaining some of the key facts you have learned while working on this chapter or you could take photographs of students doing the activities from this chapter, such as binary counting or completing the binary to hexadecimal quiz.

Complete the project by writing about the experience of doing this task. You have learned how to work with digital data of different types (video, audio or photographic).

2 Communications and the Internet

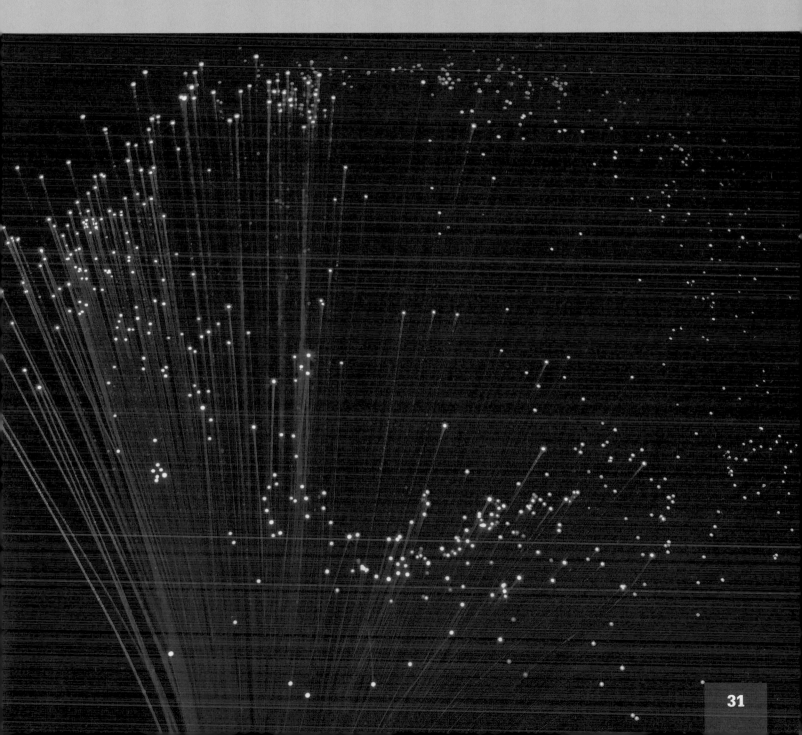

Syllabus reference

1.2.1 Data transmission

Learners should be able to: show understanding of what is meant by transmission of data; distinguish between simplex, duplex and half-duplex data transmission; show understanding of the need to check for errors.

See also:

1.1 Binary systems (Bits and bytes)

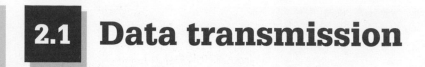

2.1 Data transmission

How data is transmitted

Introduction

In Chapter 1 you learned how data is held in a digital electronic format inside a computer. In this chapter you will learn how data is shared and communicated between computers.

Data transmission

Computers hold data in binary form, using on/off switches. Each on/off signal represents one bit of data. Computers can turn this binary data into a stream of on/off signals which can be transmitted. That means the signals are sent from one place to another. The signals can be:

- electrical pulses that travel down metal cables
- pulses of light that travel down a fibre-optic cable
- wireless signals – radio signals, microwave and infrared waves – when the bits are sent as electromagnetic waves that move through space, and also air and many other materials (including human beings, who are not affected by them).

Whatever system is used to carry the on/off signals, it is known as the transmission medium.

Long or short distance

Data transmission is used to link computers. The computers can share and send data. The Internet is based on long-distance communication links.

Data transmission is also used over short distances. The different parts of a computer transmit data to each other. When you send your work to a printer, that requires data transmission.

Bluetooth is an example of a short distance wireless data link. Bluetooth can be used to link an earpiece (headset) to a mobile phone.

Simplex
one direction only

⬆ Simplex communication

Simplex and duplex

Communication links can be simplex, duplex or half-duplex.

- Simplex communication is a one-way link. The signal can only go in one direction. An example of a simplex communication is the signal from a closed-circuit TV camera to a security guard's monitor. The security guard can see on the monitor what the camera sends, but cannot send anything back to the camera.

- Duplex communication is a two-way link. The signal can go both ways. A phone conversation is an example of duplex communication. Both people can talk. Both people can listen.

- Half-duplex means the link can only carry signals in one direction at a time. The two sides have to take turns to send a signal. A walkie-talkie system is half-duplex.

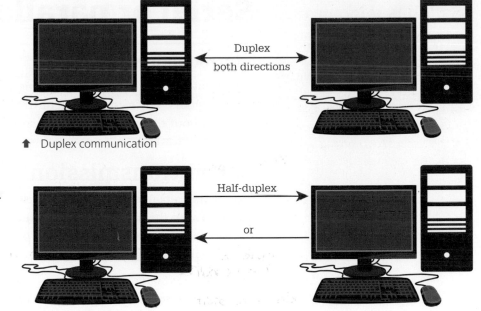

↑ Duplex communication

↑ Half-duplex communication

Types of cable

Cables connect devices together. Signals are sent along the cable. These are the main types of cable:

- Twisted pair cable: this is made of pairs of copper wires, individually insulated then twisted together. It is inexpensive, flexible and convenient, but it is not suitable for a long-distance link. Electrical interference can cause errors in the data. It is used for short-distance links.

- Coaxial cable: this is a metal cable, surrounded by a layer of insulation then another layer of metal. It is protected against electrical interference. It is more expensive than twisted pair, and it is not as flexible. It is used where cables need to go close to electrical and radio equipment.

- Fibre-optic cable is fairly expensive but it has many advantages over the other types of cable. It is not affected by electrical interference. It is suitable for long-distance links.

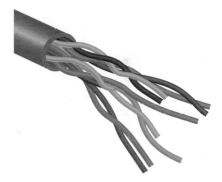

↑ Twisted pair cable

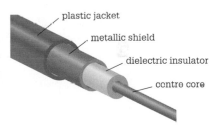

plastic jacket
metallic shield
dielectric insulator
centre core

↑ Coaxial cable

Test yourself

1. What is the alternative to using cables for data transmission?

2. What is the difference between the content of a transmission and the transmission medium?

3. A computer is not connected to the Internet or any other computer. However, it still uses data transmission. Explain why.

4. I have a radio receiver but not a transmitter. What type of communication link is this?

5. Draw a diagram to show the difference between simplex, duplex and half-duplex communication.

Learning activities

You have seen that wireless communication can use different forms of signal: radio, microwave and infrared. Investigate examples of each type of wireless signal being used for communication.

Find examples of how the three types of cable are used.

↑ Fibre-optic cable

Syllabus reference

1.2.1 Data transmission

Learners should be able to: show understanding of what is meant by transmission of data; distinguish between serial and parallel data transmission; show understanding of the reasons for choosing serial or parallel data transmission.

See also:

Chapter 1 Data representation

Serial or parallel?

Introduction
You have learned that data transmission happens when bits are turned into signals. The signals are sent from one place to another. Now you will learn about the types of data transmission.

Serial transmission

Most data transmission is serial transmission. In serial transmission, the bits that make up the data are sent one at a time. The bits all travel along the same transmission medium, one after the other, in a series. The signals are sent down a single wire, or as a wireless signal. The bits arrive at the other end one at a time.

Serial transmission is the most reliable method of data transmission. The bits are kept separate from each other. They arrive in the same order that they were sent. Serial transmission is used for long-distance communication, for example an Internet connection.

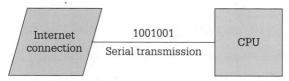

⬆ Serial transmission – the eight bits are sent one after the other down the same wire

Parallel transmission

You have learned that bits are held in groups of eight called bytes.

Some communication links use several wires at the same time. Each wire carries one bit, so several bits can be sent at the same time. Some parallel systems have eight wires. This means that all the bits in a byte can be sent at once. Each bit goes down a different wire. All the bits arrive at the same time.

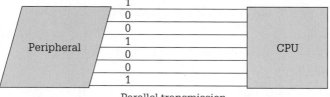

⬆ Parallel transmission – the eight bits are sent at the same time along different wires

Advantages and disadvantages

Parallel transmission is quicker than serial transmission. Several bits are transmitted at the same time, so it takes less time to send the data.

However, there are risks when you use parallel transmission. There is more chance of an error in the signal. Microscopic differences in the wires might mean that they transmit signals at slightly different speeds. Over a long distance that might turn into a big difference. The bits won't all arrive at the same time. The signal will not be transmitted accurately. For this reason, parallel transmission is only used for short-distance communications, for example to connect a monitor to the computer.

Serial transmission can take longer, because the bits are sent one at a time, but it is more reliable over a long distance.

Long or short distance?

Some connections are long distance. For example, Internet connections link computers all over the world. For these connections we would use serial transmission. Some connections are very short distance, for example connections between components inside the computer. For these, we might use parallel transmission.

Other connections are between these extremes, for example the connection between a computer and a printer in the same room. In this case either serial or parallel transmission can be chosen.

Serial and parallel ports

Old personal computers used to be equipped with both serial ports and parallel ports, and you could see the difference between them by looking at the pins on their connectors.

A serial port used only a few pins, with just one reserved for transmitting data and another for receiving. Other pins might be used to control the port, but they weren't used for data.

⬆ A serial port

Test yourself

1. What is the main advantage of parallel transmission?

2. Explain why parallel transmission may not be reliable over long distances.

3. What is the visual difference between serial and parallel cable?

4. What is a port on a computer?

⬆ A parallel port

Learning activity

Use graphics software to draw a diagram showing both serial and parallel transmission.

Complete this table to show the advantages and disadvantages of the different types of transmission

	Advantages	Disadvantages	Uses
Serial			Long distance
Parallel			Short distance

Syllabus reference

1.2.1 Data transmission

Learners should be able to: show understanding of the use of serial and parallel data transmission, in universal serial bus (USB) and integrated circuit (IC).

See also:

3.3 Inside the CPU

⬆ The lines on the circuit board are actually thin copper wires acting as data buses

Data bus

Introduction

You have learned about data transmission between computers. In this section you will learn about data transmission within a single computer system. This is how the different parts of a computer "talk to" each other.

Integrated circuits

Data in the computer is stored using on/off electronic switches. An integrated circuit (IC) is a collection of microscopic electronic circuits, sealed into a single plastic or ceramic package. Different ICs are used for different tasks inside the computer. Many ICs are used for data storage. One of the ICs, the central processing unit (CPU), contains the computer's processor and registers. All these parts must be connected together. We will talk more about the CPU in *3.3 Inside the CPU*.

The different ICs are linked by wired connections called data buses. Some ICs, particularly CPUs, have internal buses too, made from metallic layers within the IC. Each part of the IC works very quickly. The speed of a whole computer is strongly affected by how quickly the buses can transmit data between the different parts.

Parallel data bus

The buses inside the CPU, and between CPU and RAM, use parallel transmission, which has advantages and disadvantages:

- The advantage of parallel transmission is speed. The speed of each data bus strongly affects the performance of the computer system.

- The disadvantage of parallel transmission is that it needs more wires, so it takes up more of the very limited space available inside the IC or on the circuit board.

Connecting peripherals

The processor is at the centre of the computer. That is where the work of the computer takes place. A computer needs other devices such as a screen, a keyboard and a mouse. These additional devices are called peripherals. The peripherals have to be connected to the processor. Buses are used to connect the peripherals to the processor.

There are several ways to join a peripheral to the processor. It can be done using:

- permanent wiring, for example the keyboard of a laptop is permanently wired into the computer casing

- a plug-in cable, for example a monitor can be plugged in to the computer

- a wireless connection, for example a wireless mouse.

In each case, a bus is needed to complete the connection.

Peripherals work more slowly than the processor. For example, when you type data into the computer, your typing comes much more slowly than the computer works. A very fast connection is not so important. A serial bus is often used to connect a peripheral to the processor. A serial bus is slower than a parallel bus, but it is fast enough, and it is less expensive because it needs hardware for only a single signal.

Universal serial bus (USB)

Peripherals are made by many different companies. The manufacturers want people to buy their peripherals. They want to make it easy to connect the peripheral to a computer. They want the peripheral to work with all types of computer.

Nowadays most companies that make peripherals use a standard connection. It is called a USB (which stands for "universal serial bus"). It is a serial connection. It is called universal because it can be used in most modern computers.

Almost all modern computers have one or more USB ports. That means devices from many different manufacturers can be used with those computers.

↑ A USB connection

Test yourself

1. What is meant by a data bus and why is bus speed so important?

2. Each part of the CPU works very fast. Explain why parallel transmission is suitable for use within the CPU.

3. A peripheral works much more slowly than the CPU. Explain why serial transmission is used to connect peripherals to the CPU.

4. A friend sets up a company making keyboards for computers. Write a short note to him, explaining why he should make keyboards that have a USB connection.

Learning activity

Investigate the computer where you are sitting. What peripherals does it have? What connections does it have? Is there a wireless connection? Write a short report giving your findings.

Syllabus reference

1.1.3 Data representation

Learners should be able to identify and describe methods of error detection and correction, such as automatic repeat request (ARQ).

Transmission errors

Introduction

Data transmission means sending bits and bytes from one location to another. It is important that the data is transmitted in full and without errors. In the rest of this chapter you will learn about ways to detect errors.

Transmission errors

Data is transmitted through a medium, which may use a cabled or a wireless connection. The transmission media carries bits in the form of electrical, radio or optical (light) pulses. All types of transmission media can be affected by errors.

Errors can be caused by flaws in the transmission medium, such as imperfections in a copper wire. Errors can be caused by external factors, such as electrical fields. We can design systems to reduce errors. For example, wires can be shielded by an outer conductive layer, to prevent electrical interference. Despite this, errors can still occur.

Transmission errors can have serious effects. Every bit in a signal is important. Changing one bit alters the value of the binary number. The whole signal will be wrong. For this reason it is important to check for errors in transmitted data. If the data has an error, it can be sent again.

Types of error

Errors in transmission can mean that:

- some of the bits are lost from the data stream
- extra bits are added to the data stream
- 1 bits change to 0, or 0 bits change to 1.

If a human operator is involved, for example someone typing the data, the person can also make errors. An error made in copying data, for example when typing it, is called a transcription error. An error where two letters or numbers are in the wrong order is called a transposition error.

Transmitter and receiver

Data transmission involves a transmitter and a receiver.

- The transmitter is the device that has the data to start with, and sends it.
- The receiver is the device that gets the data, after transmission.

Typically these devices are computers, but they could be a computer and its peripherals. The receiver will check the accuracy of the data sent by the transmitter. If an error is found, the receiver will ask the transmitter to send the data again.

Ways to detect errors

On the next few pages you will learn about ways the computer can check a transmission for errors. Parity checks are discussed on pages 40–41. Check digits are discussed on pages 42–43.

Automatic Repeat reQuest (ARQ)

The error checks methods are used in a process called automatic repeat request (ARQ). This is a method to ensure correct transmission of data. It works like this:

- The transmitter sends some data (called a packet).
- When the receiver gets the data packet, it checks it for errors.
- If the receiver finds no errors, it will send an acknowledgement.
- If the transmitter doesn't receive an acknowledgement, it sends the data again.

The transmitter will keep on sending the data packet until it receives an acknowledgement. There is usually a time limit. Once the time is up, the transmitter will stop trying to send the package. The signal has timed out.

Test yourself

1. Give the meanings of transmission errors, transposition errors and transcription errors.
2. What changes can occur to data bits as the result of transmission errors?
3. How does shielding help to prevent transmission errors?
4. Explain the roles of the transmitter and receiver devices in the ARQ process.

Types of error

If two digits or letters are accidentally swapped around, this is called a **transposition error**. It is one of the most common types of **transmission error**.

Syllabus reference

1.2.1 Data transmission

Learners should be able to explain how parity bits are used for error detection.

1.1.3 Data representation

Learners should be able to identify and describe methods of error detection and correction, such as parity checks.

Parity check

Introduction

You have learned that it is important to detect errors in data transmission. In this section you will learn about parity checks. A parity check is one way to check data for errors. Make sure you know the difference between the role of receiver and transmitter.

Parity

"Parity" is a term from mathematics. It means whether a number is odd or even. Parity is used to check whether data has errors in it. The most common type of parity check is known as an even parity bit.

Before the data is sent, the transmitter counts how many 1s there are in each byte. The transmitter then adds an extra bit to the end of each byte:

- If there is an even number of 1s in the byte, the parity bit is set to 0.
- If there is an odd number of 1s in the byte, the parity bit is set to 1.

This extra bit makes sure the number of 1s transmitted is an even number.

After the data is received:

- The receiver counts how many 1s there are in each byte plus its parity bit.
- Each byte plus parity bit should have an even number of 1s.

If any of the bytes with its parity bit has an odd number of bits, the receiver will know there was an error during transmission. The data must be sent again.

Even parity bit

In the example on this page, the even parity bit is shown at the right of the transmitted number. In practice it may not be stored in this location.

Worked example

The transmitter got ready to send this signal.

| 0 | 1 | 1 | 0 | 0 | 0 | 1 | |

There are three 1s in the data. That is an odd number, so the parity bit was set to 1. Now there are four 1s in the byte – an even number. The parity bit is highlighted.

| 0 | 1 | 1 | 0 | 0 | 0 | 1 | 1 |

Next the signal was transmitted. There was an error during transmission. One of the bits was altered by an error in transmission. The error is highlighted. The signal has gone wrong.

| 0 | 1 | 0 | 0 | 0 | 0 | 1 | 1 |

The computer that received the data added up the number of 1s in the signal. There were three 1s in the signal. That is an odd number, so there must have been a transmission error.

In conclusion: the error has been spotted. The data has to be sent again.

Odd parity

Some communication systems use "odd parity". In this system the number of 1s in each byte is an odd number. Otherwise it works just the same as even parity. Of course, the transmitter and receiver must both use the same system.

Which bit?

Data is normally stored and sent in groups of eight bits:

- In some cases, seven of the bits are used to send the data. The eighth bit is a parity bit. The parity bit is part of the byte.
- In other cases all eight bits are used to send the data. The parity bit is sent as an extra signal following the byte.

Limitations

The parity method is not perfect:

- If there are two errors in a byte (or any even number of errors) then the parity check will fail.
- If two bits get swapped round (transposition error) then the parity check will not spot the error.

For this reason other data checks are used as well as a parity bit.

Test yourself

Here is a block of data to be transmitted.

```
0 0 0 1 1 0 0
1 1 1 0 1 1 0
1 0 1 0 1 0 0
1 1 1 1 0 0 0
1 0 0 0 1 1 0
1 0 0 1 1 1 0
0 0 0 1 0 0 1
```

Assume that you are using even parity and add a parity bit to each row.

Learning activity

This is an extension activity. You will work with the block of data from the last question. You have added an even parity bit in each row. Now look at each column of data. Assume that you are using even parity and add a parity bit to the bottom of each column.

Now the data has a parity bit at the end of each row and the bottom of each column. This gives an additional check. It overcomes the two limitations mentioned on this page.

Syllabus reference

1.2.1 Data transmission

Learners should be able to identify and describe methods of error detection and correction, such as check digits and checksums.

Check digit and checksum

Introduction

Parity checks are error checks for binary data. In this section you will learn about error checks that can be used for denary numbers. These checks can detect transmission errors, and human errors such as typing (transcription) errors.

Check digit

A check digit is similar to a parity bit. It is added to the end of a denary number. The check digit is worked out from the digits in the number.

A check digit is used in the same way as a parity bit:

- A computer works out the check digit before transmission, and sends it with the number.
- The receiving computer works out the check digit after transmission, and compares it to the original.
- The two check digits should match.
- If they do not match there has been an error in transmitting the number.

Calculate the check digit

There is more than one way to work out the check digit from a denary number.

Simple method

This is the simplest way to work out the check digit:

- Add up all the digits in the number to give the sum of the digits.
- Divide the sum by 10.
- The remainder from this division is used as the check digit.

The remainder when dividing a value by 10 is called the value modulo 10, or the value mod 10. Sometimes a check digit uses modulo 11, where the sum is divided by 11. If the remainder is 10, the letter X is used as the check digit.

A simple check digit cannot identify a transposition error. That is when two digits get swapped around. That is because a transposition of two digits will not change the overall sum of the digits.

Other methods

For this reason, other ways to calculate a check digit have been invented. The digits in different positions in the number are multiplied by different values. Then the numbers are added together and the check digit is calculated in one of the following ways:

- using the Luhn method, every second digit is multiplied by 2 and the total must be an exact multiple of 10.
- using the ISBN-10 method, every digit is multiplied by its position in the number: the first digit by 1, the next by 2 and so on. The check digit is the total mod11.

Sum

In mathematics the sum is the result of adding together a group of numbers.

Modulo (mod)

In mathematics the modulo is the remainder that is left after a division has been carried out. It is shortened to "mod".

These methods are more complex, but they have a big advantage. If a digit is accidentally transmitted in the wrong position, the sum will change. The check digit will change. That means these methods will detect transposition errors.

⬆ Every credit card has a number on it which includes a check digit

Checksum

Using a checksum is a way of checking a group of numbers:

- The transmitter adds up the total of a group of numbers before transmission.
- The transmitter sends the total along with the numbers.
- The receiver works out the total and compares it to the transmitted total.
- The two totals should match. If the two totals do not match then there has been an error. The data must be sent again.

You can use a checksum even if the sum value does not represent a real total. For example, you can use a checksum when sending a group of phone numbers. A number of this kind – which is not a real total – is called a hash total.

Test yourself

1. A check digit is calculated twice, once each by two different computers. Explain why.

2. What is 32 mod 10?

3. Why is any value mod 10 always a single-digit number?

4. What is the limitation with using a simple sum and mod 10 check digit?

5. When do we call a control sum a hash total?

Learning activity

1. Write down your phone number. Calculate a simple check digit for your phone number, using mod 10.

2. Collect the phone numbers of five friends. Calculate a checksum for this list of numbers.

3. Find a book with a 10-digit ISBN code. Using the first 9 digits, work out the check digit. Check this against the example you see on the real book. It should match.

Use of check digits

A credit card number includes a check digit. Since 1960, the Luhn method has been used to calculate check digits on credit cards.

Every book published is given a code number called the International Standard Book Number (ISBN). These numbers can be either 10 or 13 digits long (ISBN-10 or ISBN-13). Both formats include check digits.

Syllabus reference

1.2.3 Internet principles of operation

Learners should be able to show understanding of the role of an Internet service provider (ISP).

See also:

2.3 Safety online

2.2 The Internet

What is the Internet?

Introduction

You have learned about data transmission. Data transmission allows computers to send and share data. A group of computers linked together in this way is called a network. The Internet is the biggest network in the world. In this section you will learn about the Internet.

The Internet

Connected computers can share data through data transmission links. The Internet is a system of computer connections that covers the whole world. To be connected to the Internet a computer must have:

- a data transmission connection (wired or wireless)
- Internet software
- shared protocols.

Any computer can be connected to the Internet if it has these. There were very few computers with an Internet connection 20 or 30 years ago. Now there are literally billions of computers and other devices connected to the Internet. The Internet grows bigger every day. About half the people on Earth have used the Internet.

Nobody is in charge of the Internet. The Internet is the system of links that people can use to share data. Nobody checks that the data is correct. Nobody can control what is on the Internet.

The Internet can be very useful and helpful, but it can also have risks and problems. Learn more about risks and how to keep safe in *2.3 Safety online*.

↑ An illustration of the connections that make the Internet

Internet service provider (ISP)

You can buy a computer that can connect to the Internet. What does it connect to, though?

Most people are connected to the Internet by an Internet Service Provider (ISP). An ISP is an organisation that enables people to use the Internet. Many ISPs are commercial companies that offer Internet services for a connection fee.

The services that might be offered by an ISP include:

- sending signals between the Internet and your computer
- providing email services
- hosting a web page for you.

Different ISPs use different ways of connecting computers to the Internet. Some use the public phone lines; some use wireless, or cables.

Internet software

"Software" means the instructions that let your computer carry out actions. Several different types of software can be used to connect to the Internet. This software reads the signals that come via the Internet connection. It turns these signals into a form that you can see and use on your computer. It also converts the signals from your computer into a suitable form. For example, if you type a message, the software converts your text into a form that can be sent over the Internet and be understood by other computers.

The most common Internet software is a web browser. You will find out more about web browsers on page 47.

Shared protocols

Protocols are communication standards. They are standard rules about how data is turned into signals. If two computers share data, they must use the same protocols. All computers that connect to the Internet use the same protocols.

Key protocols of the Internet are TCP and IP (see pages 52–53).

Test yourself

1. Many ISPs are commercial companies. How do these companies make money?

2. As well as giving you an Internet connection, what other services might an ISP provide?

3. Who makes sure that there are no mistakes on the Internet?

4. As well as a wired or wireless connection, what else do you need to use the Internet?

Learning activity

Use online research to find out how many computers are connected to the Internet. If you find the answer on a website, or in a book, check the date that it was published. The answer is changing all the time.

Not the World Wide Web

The Internet is not the same as the World Wide Web. Find out the difference on page 46.

Syllabus reference

1.2.3 Internet principles of operation

Learners should be able to show understanding of the role of the browser.

What is the World Wide Web?

Introduction

You have learned that the Internet is a series of connections and standards. Many different services and features are available through Internet connections. The most popular is the World Wide Web. In this section you will learn what the World Wide Web is.

Website

The World Wide Web (also called the Web) is the collection of all the web pages in the world. The World Wide Web is the most popular service available through an Internet connection.

A web page is a multimedia document that you can read over the Internet. "Multimedia" means a document that can include many different types of data: text, images, sound and video. Web pages are created in a format called HTML. Find out more about HTML on pages 48–49. Web pages can be viewed by software called a web browser.

A website is a collection of web pages, stored on a web server. Anybody with an Internet connection can connect to the website and look at the web pages.

Some popular sites include:

- Google
- Amazon
- Twitter
- Facebook
- Wikipedia
- Youtube

↑ Wikipedia has been viewed by hundreds of millions of users

Web server

A web server is a computer that is permanently connected to the Internet. A web server hosts web pages, which means that the web server holds the content of the web page in its storage. A web server will send the contents of the web page along an Internet connection to another computer. The web page can be viewed by Internet users. Many ISPs offer web hosting as one of their services.

Web addresses

Every web server has its own numeric address, called an IP address, and a number of text-based names. Every website and web page hosted by the server has its own name, called a URL. The URL contains one of the web server's names. You will learn more about IP addresses and URLs on pages 52–53.

Web browser

A web browser is software that lets you look at web pages. To connect to a web page you type its URL into your web browser. The web browser will:

- get the web server's name from the URL, and use that to connect to the web server
- transfer a copy of the web page onto your computer
- display the web page so that you can interact with the content.

Web pages are written in a format called HTML. A web browser can read HTML. It will interpret the content and show it on your screen.

There are several popular web browsers, including:

- Internet Explorer
- Firefox
- Chrome.

Different browsers may display web pages slightly differently.

Web protocols

The use of web pages depends on shared protocols:

- HTTP is the protocol that allows web pages to be shared. Find out more about HTTP on pages 50–51.
- IP is the protocol that gives every web server an address. Find out more about IP on pages 52–53.

⬆ Google Chrome is one of the most widely used web browsers

Test yourself

1. What is the difference between a website and a web page?

2. What types of data can you find on a web page?

3. Many ISPs offer a web hosting service. What does that mean?

4. Describe the job of a web browser.

Learning activity

Choose one of the popular websites listed on the previous page.

Write a short report on the website you have chosen. What features does it have? Why is it so popular?

Download

When you download web content, you copy it from a web server onto your own computer. That means you can see and use the web content on your own computer.

Upload

When you upload web content, you copy it from your computer onto a web server. That means other computers can access it. You have made the content available to other people.

Syllabus reference

1.2.3 Internet principles of operation

Learners should be able to: show understanding of what is meant by HTML; distinguish between HTML structure and presentation.

HTML

Introduction

You have learned that the Web is made of all the web pages in the world. Web pages are made using HTML, which stands for "hypertext markup language". In this section you will learn about HTML.

Markup

HTML is a markup language. A markup language is used to add descriptions to pieces of text in a document. The descriptions are called tags. HTML tags tell a web browser how to display a document. When you make a web page you must enter the text, and also the HTML tags that tell the computer how to display the text.

Tags

Tags generally come in pairs. One tag turns a feature on, another tag turns it off. For example, the tag <h1> turns on the main heading style. The tag </h1> turns it off.

A web page may include the text "My Family". With HTML tags it may look like this:

```
<h1>My Family</h1>
```

When you open the web page in a browser you will not see those tags. The browser will display the words "My Family" as a large heading.

Example

Here is part of the HTML that defines the main (or home) web page of the OUP website: the publishers of the book you are reading.

As you can see, there are a lot of HTML tags. This is only a small part of the HTML that defines the page.

When your browser displays the same page it looks like this.

```
<title>Oxford University Press (OUP) - UK Home Page</title>

</td>
<td align="right" valign="top">
  <table cellpadding="0" cellspacing="0" width="100%" border="0">
    <tr valign="top" align="right">
      <td width="100%" class="noBorder"> 

      </td>

      <td nowrap="nowrap" class="topNavRow1Link">
        <a href="http://www.oup.com/uk/about/">About Us</a>
      </td>
      <td nowrap="nowrap" class="topNavRow1Link">
        <a href="http://www.oup.com/uk/contactus/">Contact Us</a>
      </td>
      <td nowrap="nowrap" class="topNavRow1Link">
        <a href="http://www.oup.com/uk/help/">Help</a>
      </td>
      <td nowrap="nowrap" class="topNavRow1Link">
        <a href="http://www.oup.com/uk/recruit/currvac/">Jobs</a>
      </td>
      <td nowrap="nowrap" class="topNavRow1Link">
        <a href="http://www.oup.com/uk/news">News</a>
      </td>
      <td nowrap="nowrap" class="topNavRow1Link">
        <a href="http://www.oup.com/uk/siteindex/">Site Index</a>
      </td>
      <td nowrap="nowrap" class="topNavRow1LinkLast">
        <a href="http://www.oup.com">OUP Worldwide</a>
```

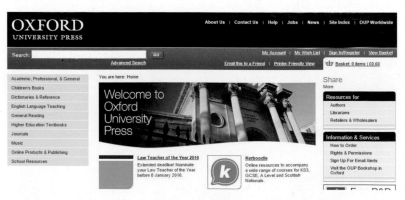

⬆ When the HTML is displayed by your browser it looks like this

⬆ This HTML defines the OUP home web page

Your web browser software reads the HTML, and displays this web page.

Structure and presentation

HTML tags tell the web browser how to display the web page. There are two main types of HTML tag. They have different effects:

- **Structure:** Some HTML tags control the layout of the web page. This includes adding a page title, headings, sections and paragraphs. For example, the tags `<h1></h1>` mark the start and end of a heading.

- **Presentation:** Some HTML tags change how the web page is displayed. For example the tags `<b></b>` mark the start and end of bold text.

You can also change presentation by adding "style" instructions to HTML. For example this command sets the colours for a whole web page:

```
<style>
body {background-color:yellow;}
h1   {color:red;}
p    {color:green;}
</style>
```

Can you work out what this page would look like? Do you think these are good colour choices?

You can store style commands in an external file called a "Cascading Style Sheet" (CSS). You can link lots of different web pages to the CSS file. All the web pages will have the same style. If you make a change to the CSS file, all the pages will change. This gives a consistent, professional feel to your work.

Hypertext

HTML means "hypertext markup language" – but what is hypertext?

Hypertext is text that makes a link to a new web page. Most web pages include hypertext. Hypertext links are often shown on the screen as blue, underlined text. When you click on a hypertext link your web browser will connect to the linked page. It will be displayed in your browser. In this way you can browse, moving from one website to another.

You have learned that HTML makes hypertext links. Links can be connected to images or areas of the screen as well as to text.

How to make a website

A web hosting service will help you to make a website. The pages of your site will be stored on their web server. That is called publishing your website. The pages can be seen by anyone with an Internet connection.

A web hosting service will provide software to help you make the web pages. The software makes it easy to design the web page. You do not need to type HTML tags. You choose features such as text colour and size from menus. The software turns your choices into HTML. It is similar to using a word processor to make an ordinary document.

Q **Learning activities**

1. Connect to a website with your browser. Right-click on the web page and pick "View page source" from the menu. You will see the HTML that made the page you are looking at.

2. Work in a group or as a whole class. Use a free online web hosting service. Create a web page about what you have learned so far in iGCSE Computer Science.

Q **Test yourself**

1. HTML stands for "hypertext markup language". Explain the meaning of "hypertext" and "markup".

2. HTML tags often come in pairs. Why?

3. A student made a website. She did not know HTML. How did she manage to make the site?

4. When you look at a website in your browser you do not see the HTML tags. Why?

Syllabus reference

1.2.3 Internet principles of operation

Learners should be able to: show understanding of what is meant by hypertext transfer protocol (HTTP and HTTPS); show understanding of what is meant by cookies.

See also:

6.2 Security protection

HTTP: Hypertext transfer protocol

Introduction

You have learned that hyperlinks are a key feature of web pages. Hypertext transfer protocol (shortened to "HTTP") is the protocol that makes hyperlinks work. In this section you will learn about HTTP.

Hyperlinks

A key feature of a web page is that it can include links (also called hyperlinks). A link is a piece of text on the page, or an image such as button. When you click on the link your browser connects to a new page and displays it in your browser. The hyperlink could take you to different part of the same website, or a new site.

Example

On the previous page you saw part of the HTML that defines the OUP website. The OUP website includes the following HTML. This HTML makes the text "News" into a hyperlink.

```
<td nowrap="nowrap" class="topNavRow1Link">
  <a href="http://www.oup.com/uk/news">News</a>
</td>
```

⬆ This HTML defines the word "News" as a hyperlink

⬆ The word "News" on this menu bar is a link

The HTML makes a hyperlink to the following web address:

http://www.oup.com/uk/news

The HTML displays the following link on the OUP page.

If you click on the word "News" on the OUP website, your web browser will connect to the web address shown above.

HTTP

HTTP is the protocol that makes hyperlinks work.

A protocol is a shared standard for communication. All web servers use the HTTP protocol. All web browsers use the HTTP protocol too. That is why links work on every web page, and with every browser. Without HTTP the World Wide Web would not work.

The address of every web page begins http:// or https:// That shows you that the page uses the HTTP protocol. Find out more about web addresses on pages 52–53.

HTTPS

HTTPS stands for "HTTP secure". HTTPS is an extended protocol. It has extra features: authentication and encryption. These are not part of the basic HTTP protocol.

Authentication

Some websites are fake. They look as if they are run by a well-known company, such as a bank, but they are not. Learn more about fake websites on page 55.

"Authentic" means not fake. Authenticating a website means checking that it is not fake. HTTPS authenticates a website. If a web page's URL begins with https, you can be sure it is not fake. Learn more about security protocols in *6.2 Security protection (Security protocols)*.

Encryption

When you are using a website you often type details such as your name and address. These details are sent to the website.

Encryption means putting data into a secret code. HTTPS encrypts everything you send to a website, so that nobody can see what you are sending there. This makes it safer to send data to the website. Learn more about encryption in *6.2 Security protection (Encryption)*.

Cookies

Websites often need data that relates specifically to you, for example your email account or bank account details. HTTP and HTTPS do not transmit user details, so when you go back to a website using HTTP protocol, it does not know who you are.

Websites get round this problem by using HTTP "cookies". When you use a website, it collects key data about what you do there. This data is packaged up as a small binary file called a cookie. The binary file is sent back to your computer. It is stored on your own computer, not on the website.

Next time you use the website, the cookie goes from your web browser to the site. The cookie tells the website key facts about you, for example what you bought last time.

Some people do not like cookies, because of privacy concerns. However, cookies are in very common use.

Test yourself

1. What key feature of every web page is supported by HTTP?

2. What is authentication? Explain how authentication makes it safer for you to use the Internet.

3. What is encryption? Explain how encryption makes it safer for you to use the Internet.

4. Explain what a cookie is. What are the advantages and disadvantages of cookies?

Learning activity

In the previous section your class created a web page. Expand the content by including a selection of links to useful websites.

Syllabus reference

1.2.3 Internet principles of operation

Learners should be able to: show understanding of the concepts of MAC address, Internet protocol (IP) address, uniform resource locator (URL).

See also:

6.2 Security protection (Security protocols)

TCP/IP

Introduction

You have learned that a protocol is a standard for communication. In this section you will learn about the main protocol system that allows the Internet to work.

Internet protocols

The main protocol system of the Internet is called TCP/IP:

- TCP stands for "Transmission Control Protocol". This protocol controls the way data packets are transmitted along Internet connections.

- IP stands for "Internet Protocol". This protocol makes sure the data packets go to the right place. Every location on the Internet has an IP address. IP sends the data to the right address.

IP address

An IP address is a number given to every device that is connected to the Internet. Every device has a different number. The IP address identifies the device. The IP address is used to find a route across the Internet to the device's local area network. This means data can be sent to the device down the route.

You have learned that numbers can be stored as binary digits (bits). The larger the number the more bits are needed. IP addresses are very large numbers: 128 bits are needed to store a modern IP address.

These numbers are stored by a service called the Domain Name System (DNS). DNS is an automated directory of all of the Internet servers in the world. You can use DNS to look up any server's name and find its IP address.

URL

URL stands for "uniform resource locator".

Every web browser has an address bar at the top of the screen. You enter the URL of a web page into this space. Then the browser will connect to the web server that hosts that page.

The URL is made up of these components, always in this order.

1. The name of the protocol that the page uses. It usually starts with http or https.

2. The domain name. This identifies the server (Internet computer) and website. You could use the web server's IP address here, but that would be more difficult to remember than a name. Also, when a web server hosts more than one website, it would not be able to tell which site you want.

3. The "path name". This identifies a web page on that server.

4. Sometimes extra details are added at the end.

Domain name

The domain name identifies the server that hosts the website. It also identifies the website itself, in case the server hosts more than one. A domain name typically begins with www. It ends with a short text code. This is the "top-level domain". It tells you the general category of the website.

The top-level domain code might tell you the type of business as follows:

- .com – a commercial organisation
- .gov – a US government organisation
- .edu – a US academic organisation such as a university.

Or it might tell you the country where the server is based. Here are some examples:

- .uk – United Kingdom
- .nz – New Zealand
- .ke – Kenya.

The official list of all top-level domains is maintained by the Internet Assigned Numbers Authority (IANA). There are over a thousand top-level domains.

Example

Here is a typical URL. It is for the website of the UK newspaper, *The Guardian*:

http://www.theguardian.com/world. The URL consists of these parts:

- The protocol is "http".
- The top-level domain is ".com". This tells you it is the domain name of a commercial organisation.
- The domain is "www.theguardian.com". This identifies the web server of *The Guardian* newspaper.
- The path name is "/world". This identifies the particular web page of *The Guardian* that summarises world news.

MAC address

MAC stands for "media access control". A MAC address is an identifying number, like an IP address. It identifies a single device such as a computer or printer. A device's IP address is used to route data across the Internet to its local area network, then its MAC address is used to switch the data across the local area network to the device itself. MAC addresses are often shown in hexadecimal form.

Test yourself

1. Why do people prefer to use a URL rather than an IP address?

2. An IP address is 128 bits. How many bytes is that?

3. An IP address identifies every domain on the Internet. What extra information is provided by the MAC address?

4. Here is a URL. Identify the protocol, the domain name and the page:

   https://www.amazon.com/gift-cards

Syllabus reference

1.2.2 Security aspects

Learners should be able to show understanding of the security aspects of using the Internet and understand what methods are available to help minimise the risks.

See also:

Chapter 6 Security

2.3 Safety online

Staying safe

Introduction

The Internet is a wonderful resource. We use it for work, for learning, and to make friendships. However, using the Internet has risks. In this section you will learn how to protect yourself online.

Passwords

Many websites store content that is personal to you, for example payment details or a personal profile. Nobody else should be able to access that content. Websites will protect your personal details with a password. By typing the password you confirm who you are. Unless you type the right password you cannot access the content that is personal to you.

You often have to choose a password when you are working online. Here are some rules about choosing a good password:

- Do not use obvious passwords such as "1234" or "password". Think of a password that is hard to guess.
- Make sure you can remember the password.
- Do not use the same password on every website.
- Never tell anyone else your password.

Real-life details

Most people using the Internet are friendly. However, there are people using the Internet with bad intentions. Young people are particularly at risk. Never give out your real-life details online. Do not give your full name, address, telephone number, etc. Do not arrange to meet a stranger.

Being careful online

The things you type when you are using the Internet could be stored forever. Your family and friends might see what you wrote. When have a job, your employer might see it. The police and other authorities can see it. It is important not to say cruel, offensive or criminal things. Never type words online that you would not want family, police and employers to see. Never share pictures that you might regret sharing.

Dealing with bullies

Some people make cruel and bullying comments for fun. Perhaps they don't stop and think. Perhaps they just don't care. They can make you feel very upset. It is normal to be upset. Bullying is not caused by anything you did. The bullies are the ones who are wrong.

The best way to deal with online bullying is to block the bully from contacting you. Do not read what the bully writes. You can tell a teacher or other responsible person.

Watch out for tricks

People try to steal money and personal details using online tricks. They set up fake websites. They send emails that pretend, for example, you have won the lottery. Someone might pretend to be a young woman online when he is really an old man. A good rule is to think twice. Only use websites you know. Do not believe every email you receive. Do not open files that a stranger sends you. If you are not sure, ask your teacher for advice.

Advice about staying safe online

There are many good websites offering detailed advice to young people about how to stay safe online. These are available in English and in other languages. Many are operated by charities or governments.

To find websites of this kind, type "staying safe online" into a search engine such as Google. Follow the links to read helpful advice.

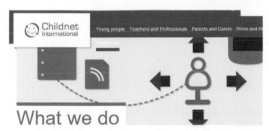

 www.childnet.com is an international website that gives advice about how to stay safe online

Protective software

You can install software on your computer that protects it against online risks. Learn more about protective software on pages 58–59.

Test yourself

1. Why are you advised not to use the same password on every website?

2. Why is "1234" a poor choice for a password?

3. A schoolboy said "I am going to rob a bank" in an online comment. Why was this a bad idea?

4. A stranger sends you an email asking to meet you. What should you do?

Learning activity

Create a poster for your computer room to remind students how to keep safe online.

Syllabus reference

1.2.2 Security aspects

1.2.3 Internet principles of operation

Learners should be able to show understanding of the Internet risks associated with malware, including viruses, spyware and hacking.

1.5 Ethical issues

Learners should be able to show understanding of ethical issues including hacking.

See also:

6.1 Security threats

Malware and hacking

Introduction

You have learned that there are risks when you use the Internet. Some risks are caused by software that can harm your computer. The general word for this is "malware". Malware is short for "malicious software". It is software made on purpose to harm your computer. In this section you will learn about malware.

Computer viruses

The most common type of malware is a computer virus. A virus is not a complete computer file, it is a set of computer commands. It attaches to a file that is already on your computer. Now the file has extra computer commands, which you didn't intend to be there. The virus copies itself into other files. If any of these is passed to another computer, that computer's files can end up with the virus too. The virus commands are attached to an existing file, so the virus is hidden and you may not know it is there.

Most computer viruses cause significant problems. A virus can:

- delete files or wipe the entire storage
- alter your computer settings
- make your computer carry out actions (such as sending emails).

How does a virus get onto your computer? It might be hidden in a file you download from the Internet. It might be hidden in a file attached to an email. It might be on a storage drive. You should always be careful when you open a file from an unknown source.

Why do people make viruses?

Some people make a virus as a joke or prank. Some people make a virus to make a political protest, to cause trouble, or to harm their enemies. Others make a virus to steal money. Once a virus is made it can spread right around the world. Copies can be passed along Internet connections.

Spyware

Spyware is a special kind of malware. Like a virus, spyware cannot be seen on your computer. Spyware records everything you do with your computer. The person who made the spyware can look at the record of your computer use. That might tell them every website you looked at, and what you typed on your computer.

Spyware can be used by companies and governments to monitor people's behaviour. Spyware is used by criminals to find out your password and personal details.

Types of malware

Often people use the word "virus" to mean any type of malware. In fact, there are many types of malware that are not viruses.

All malware needs to stay hidden from view. Otherwise people would just take it off their computers. The different types of malware use different ways to stay hidden, as follows:

- Virus: this is malware that hides itself inside another file.
- Worm: this is malware in its own file, which copies itself to other computers across the network.
- Trojan: this is malware disguised as a good file, such as a computer game or an image.
- Rootkit: this is malware that changes your operating system (see *5.1 Systems software*) so you cannot spot it.
- Backdoor: this is malware that switches off security software to let other malware onto your computer.

Hacking

You have seen that there are data links between computers. Some people use these data links without permission. They might look at the data on another computer. They might make changes to the data on a computer. This is called hacking.

For example, a hacker might change the data on a bank computer. The hacker might increase the money in his or her account. This is a form of stealing. A hacker might look at government secrets.

Hacking is against the law in most countries. You can go to jail for hacking.

Test yourself

1. What makes a virus different from other types of malware?
2. A student got an email from a person the student did not know. It had a file attachment. Explain why the student should not open the file.
3. A hacker used spyware to find out someone's secret password. Explain what that means.
4. Identify three possible effects of malware.

Learning activity

Write an article for a school magazine, explaining what malware is. Describe the different types of malware.

Syllabus reference

1.2.2 Security aspects

Learners should be able to explain how anti-virus and other protection software helps to protect the user from security risks.

See also:

6.2 Security protection

Protective software

Introduction

You have learned about malware and other Internet risks. Sensible actions can help prevent those risks. There is software that will help protect you. In this section you will learn about protective software.

Anti-virus software

Remember that malware is hidden. It cannot be seen and removed with ordinary computer usage. Anti-virus software is made specially to stop malware. Anti-virus software will:

- check all new files and emails for malware
- scan your computer to find hidden malware
- delete malware from your computer
- warn you about possible dangers, such as risky websites.

New viruses are being made all the time. Each new virus has special tricks to avoid anti-virus software. Anti-virus software must be updated regularly to keep up with these changes. The update will tell the software about the new viruses that have been invented. Then it can find and delete them all.

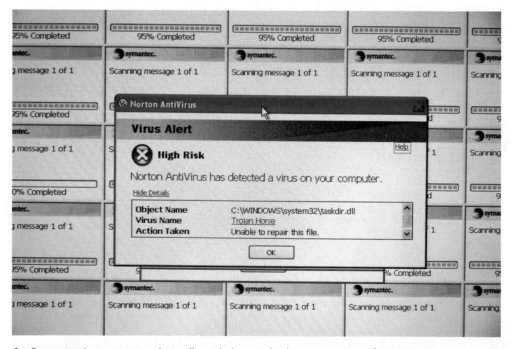

⬆ Symantec is a company that sells anti-virus and other protective software

Spam

Anti-virus software will detect and remove malware. It also has helpful features to protect your computer system from problems other than malware. For example, anti-virus filters will block spam emails.

Spam is a general term for bulk unwanted email. It is sent using automated email systems. A company might send a million spam emails in one go. Spam may contain adverts or fake offers. Often spam emails try to trick you into giving out personal details.

Internet filtering

An Internet filter blocks unsuitable content. An Internet filter is sometimes called a net nanny or parental control software. A filter like this is often set up by parents in a home computer system. The person in charge of the computer system can decide what to block, perhaps based on family rules. An Internet filter could block sites that are unsuitable for children. It could stop users from spending money on the Internet.

Schools and colleges often limit the sites that students can access. Businesses may have similar rules for their employees. This is generally to make sure people use the computer for work purposes, not for social networking or playing games.

Firewall

A firewall is software designed to screen all data that comes from the Internet. The firewall traps every packet of data. It checks the data using programmed rules. It will only pass on data that keeps to the rules. A firewall can prevent many Internet dangers:

- It will stop malware.
- It can prevent hackers getting onto the computer system.
- It can block unsuitable content.

Almost every Internet connection uses some kind of firewall. Business connections may concentrate on preventing access by hackers. Home connections may concentrate on filtering unsuitable content.

Test yourself

1. Why would you use anti-virus software instead of just deleting a virus yourself?

2. My anti-virus software scanned my computer. Why did it do that?

3. I bought anti-virus software two years ago. Why do I need to update it?

4. Why is a firewall a useful feature of a business network?

Learning activities

1. Write a letter to a business owner explaining why he or she should buy firewall software.

2. As a group or a class, find time to talk with the person in charge of the computer system in your school or college. Ask the person about virus protection and any other software that is installed to protect you against risks.

3. What rules should there be about use of the Internet in your school or college? Write a class list titled "Internet policy".

Review

Key terms

Download	When you download web content, you copy it from a web server onto your own computer.
Duplex	A two-way communication link. The signal can go both ways. Both participants act as sender and receiver.
Encryption	A method of protecting data by using a secret coding system.
Internet	The huge network of computer connections that covers the whole world. It uses a set of common protocols so all the connected computers can share data with each other.
Malware	Software designed to harm any computer on which it is held. Malware is usually disguised so you cannot see it on your system or easily remove it.
Parallel transmission	The eight bits which make up a byte of data are sent at the same time along eight different wires.
Peripherals	Hardware devices such as screen, keyboard and mouse that are attached to the processor of a computer.
Protocol	Protocols are communication standards. If two computers share data, they must use the same protocols.
Serial transmission	The eight bits which make up a byte travel along the same transmission medium, one after the other, in a series.
Simplex	A one-way communication link. The signal can only go in one direction from the sender to the receiver.
Transcription error	An error made in copying data, for example when typing it in.
Transposition error	An error where two letters or numbers are in the wrong order.
Upload	When you upload web content, you copy it from your computer onto a web server. That means other computers can access it.
World Wide Web	The collection of all the web pages in the world. Also called "The Web". It is not the same as the Internet.

Project work

One of the extension activities in this chapter was to create a simple web site. If you have not yet done so, find out about a web service which offers free web hosting. As an alternative find out how to create web pages which are hosted by your school's computer system.

As a class, select and upload a range of materials reflecting the work you have done on this course. This can include digital, audio and video materials, as well as items you have found online.

To conclude the project, write a short report on the experience of making a web site or web page. Discuss the software you used and how you decided what items to put on the site.

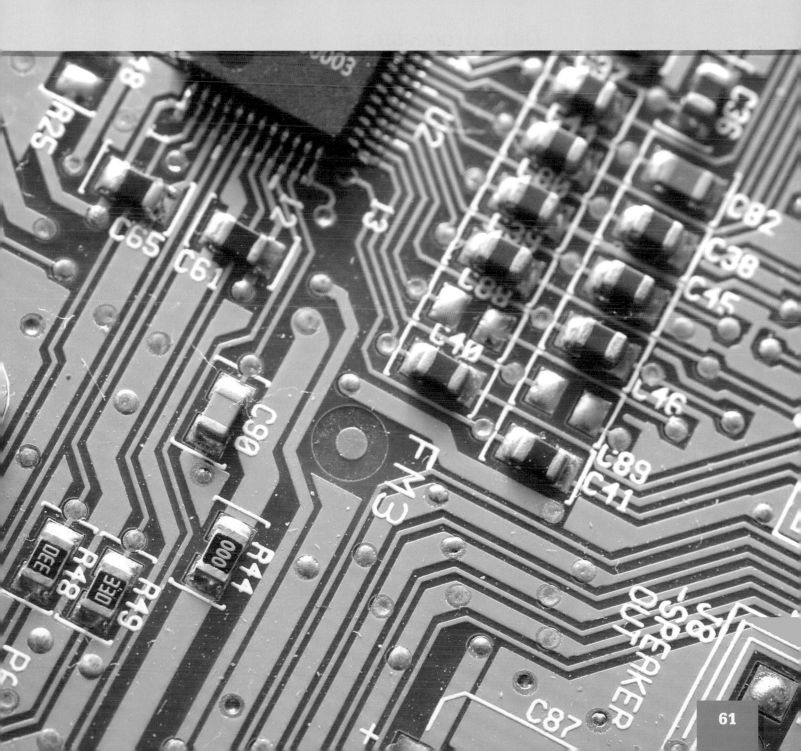

3 The processor

Syllabus reference

1.3.1 Logic gates

Learners should be able to use logic gates to create electronic circuits.

See also:

Chapter 1 Data representation
3.2 Logical processing (Solve a problem)

3.1 Logic gates

Electronic processing

Introduction

You have learned that data is stored in electrical form inside the computer. The computer does not only store the data. It also changes the data. This is called processing. In the next few sections you will learn about how the computer processes data.

Data processing

You have learned that a computer processes data to make information. The data is held inside the computer in the form of electronic signals. The data is processed by changing the electronic signals.

This happens inside a part of the computer called the processor. The processor is at the centre of the computer system. It is an electronic device. It transforms data into information by changing the electronic signals in regular and organised ways. In this chapter you will learn how the processor works.

Electronic devices

Many devices are electrical (they put electrical energy to work), for example an electric heater or a washing machine. Some devices are electronic. This means electrical energy in one circuit directly controls the flow of electricity in another circuit.

A digital electronic device has on/off switches inside it. When on, electricity can flow through a switch; when off, it cannot. An electronic switch is itself controlled by electricity. Electricity flowing in a switch's control (input) circuit may switch off its controlled (output) circuit, or the other way round. The output of one switch can control the input of any number of other switches. This means switches can be interconnected to vary the electrical flow in a complex way. That is how digital devices such as computers carry out their work.

On/off switches

When we describe the operations of the processor, we need to talk about on/off switches, and their effect on an electric circuit. We can use the terms:

- on and off, meaning the switch allows or does not allow current to flow in an electric circuit
- high and low, meaning the switch connects a point in an electric circuit to a relatively high potential (e.g. 3 volts) and low potential (e.g. 0 volts)
- 1 and 0
- True and False.

These are all ways of describing the state of the on/off switches inside a computer. When a switch is on, a current can flow through it; when off, no current can flow. A circuit can detect the difference, and use it to denote 1 versus 0, or True versus False.

Logic gates

On/off switches are combined to make electrical circuits. These circuits are called logic gates. Electrical signals pass into logic gates, and electrical signals pass out. Every logic gate has input and output:

- The input to a logic gate is the electrical signal that goes into the gate. For example, a potential of 3 volts might mean 1 or True, while 0 volts means 0 or False. Some logic gates have one input, some have two inputs.

- The output from a logic gate is the electrical signal that comes out of the gate.

Each input to a logic gate can be 1 or 0 (True or False). Each output is also 1 or 0 (or True or False). There are no other states for input or output. This means that a logic gate's inputs and output are binary digital values: each has only two possible states.

A logic gate uses the electrical signals at its inputs to decide whether its switch should be on or off. The switch setting determines what the output signal will be, 1 or 0 (or True or False). There are different types of logic gate. Each type decides its switch setting in a different way.

Logic circuits

Logic gates can be connected together into a logic circuit. The output of a gate can be connected to the input of other gates. Each gate transforms the signal in some useful way. Logic gates can be joined together in different ways to create many different circuits. Each circuit will transform its binary input signals in a different way.

You will learn more about logic circuits in *3.2 Logical processing (Solve a problem)*.

A logic circuit can have more than two inputs.

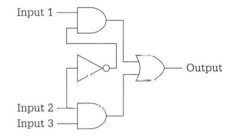

⬆ This logic circuit has three inputs and one output

Test yourself

1. What determines the output of a logic gate?

2. What does a logic gate do to an electrical signal?

3. The output from a logic gate can be in two different states. What are these two states?

4. Explain the differences between a logic gate and a logic circuit.

Learning activity

Do an online image search for diagrams of logic circuits. Copy one of the diagrams into a document and save it. Don't worry if you don't understand it yet. You will do more work with this image later.

Syllabus reference

1.3.1 Logic gates

Learners should be able to:
understand and define the
function of the NOT gate; draw
truth tables and recognise a logic
gate from its truth table; recognise
and use standard symbols used to
represent logic gates.

The NOT gate

Introduction

You have learned that logic gates are circuits that change a binary signal.
In this section you will learn about a logic gate called the NOT gate.

The NOT gate

The NOT gate is a simple logic gate. It changes every binary signal into its
opposite. If the signal is 1, it makes it 0. If the signal is 0, it makes it 1. In
logical terms, it changes True into False.

This gate works like the word "not" in everyday speech. If we put "not" into a
sentence it changes the meaning to the opposite. For example, "I am not tired"
means the opposite of "I am tired".

The word "not" reverses the meaning of a sentence. The NOT gate inverts a
binary signal.

Symbol

Each type of logic gate has a different symbol. This is the symbol for a NOT
gate.

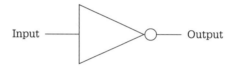

⬆ The symbol for a NOT gate

The line coming into the gate from the left is the input. The line coming out
on the right is the output. A NOT gate has one input and one output.

Input and output

Logic gates are predictable and logical. If we know the input to a gate, we
know what the output will be.

Only one signal goes into a NOT gate. This signal can be 1 or 0:

● If the signal going in is 1, then the signal coming out is 0.

● If the signal going in is 0, then the signal coming out is 1.

Possible states

The NOT gate can be in two possible states. They are shown in these
diagrams.

Input is 1 ————▷○— Output is 0   Input is 0 ————▷○— Output is 1

⬆ State 1: Input signal is 1, output   ⬆ State 2: Input signal is 0, output
   signal is 0   signal is 1

There are no other possible states for the NOT gate.

Truth table

A truth table is a way of showing all the possible states of a logic gate. Each state is shown on a different row of the table. The truth table for the NOT gate is very simple. It only has two rows.

Input	Output
0	1
1	0

The first row shows input 0, output 1. The second row shows input 1, output 0. Those are the only possibilities.

Test yourself

1. If the input to a NOT gate is 1, what is the output?

2. The NOT gate can be in two states. Describe the two states in words. Include a description of both input and output.

3. Discuss how the NOT gate has a similar effect to the word "not" in common everyday speech.

4. Why is it correct to say that the output of a NOT gate is "predicable and logical"?

Learning activity

1. Create a page on the computer or in your notebook where you will record information about the NOT gate. Include a description of the gate and draw its symbol and truth table.

2. Copy the diagram of a logic circuit on page 63. Identify any NOT gates in this logic circuit. Mark them on your copy with the word "NOT". Keep this copy of the diagram – you will need it for several activities you will be doing later.

Syllabus reference

1.3.1 Logic gates

Learners should be able to: understand and define the function of the AND gate; draw truth tables and recognise a logic gate from its truth table; recognise and use standard symbols used to represent logic gates.

The AND gate

Introduction

You have learned that logic gates transform binary signals. In this section you will learn about the AND gate. This gate transforms two inputs into a single output.

The AND gate

The AND gate is a circuit that takes two binary signals and turns them into one signal. The inputs can be 1 or 0:

- If both inputs are 1, the output is 1.
- In all other cases, the output is 0.

We can express this using True and False:

- If both inputs are True, the output is True.
- In all other cases, the output is False.

The AND gate is like the word "and" in a sentence. We use "and" to say that two things are both true. For example, "I like sport AND books", or "I am tired AND hungry". The sentence is only true if both parts are true. The AND gate works like this. The output is only True if both inputs are True.

Symbol

The symbol for the AND gate looks like this.

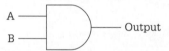

↑ The symbol for the AND gate

There are two inputs to the AND gate. We can label the two inputs as A and B. A and B are independent of each other: they don't affect each other.

Possible states

You learned that the NOT gate can be in two possible states (input 1 or 0, independent of the other). The AND gate is more complicated because it has two inputs, and each input can be 1 or 0. That gives four possible states altogether:

- A is 0, B is 0
- A is 0, B is 1
- A is 1, B is 0
- A is 1, B is 1.

The AND gate will only output 1 if both the inputs are 1.

Truth table

We use truth tables to set out all possible states for a logic gate. The four possible states are shown like this.

0	0
0	1
1	0
1	1

Did you spot that this is the same as the first four binary numbers? If you need a reminder, go back to *Chapter 1 Data representation*.

We can put those four inputs into a truth table. Each input is shown on a different row of the table.

A	B	Output
0	0	
0	1	
1	0	
1	1	

Now the output is filled in for each case.

A	B	Output
0	0	0
0	1	0
1	0	0
1	1	1

The output is always 0, except on the bottom row of the table. When both A and B are 1, the output is 1.

Test yourself

1. What are the four possible states of an AND gate? Describe them in words.

2. A and B are independent of each other. What does that mean?

3. Draw the symbol of the AND gate. Label the inputs A and B, and label the output.

4. If A and B both have value 1, this makes the binary number 11. What denary number does this represent?

Learning activity

1. Create a page about the AND gate on the computer or in your notebook. Include a description of the gate, its symbol and its truth table.

2. Look at your copy of diagram of a logic circuit from page 63. Identify any AND gates in this logic circuit. Mark them on your copy with the word "AND".

Syllabus reference

1.3.1 Logic gates

Learners should be able to:
understand and define the function
of the OR and XOR gates; draw
truth tables and recognise a logic
gate from its truth table; recognise
and use standard symbols used to
represent logic gates.

See also:

Chapter 1 Data representation

The OR and XOR gates

Introduction

You have learned about the AND gate and the NOT gate. In this section you will learn about two more logic gates: the OR gate and the XOR gate.

The OR gate

The OR gate takes two binary input signals and turns them into one output signal. Each input can be 1 or 0, True or False. The OR gate will output 1 if at least one of the inputs is 1. It works like this:

- If both inputs are 1, the output is 1.
- If one input is 1, and one is 0, the output is 1.
- If both inputs are 0, the output is 0.

The OR gate works like the word "or" in a sentence. We use "or" to say that at least one thing is true, for example "I will eat some cake or bread". The sentence is true if either part is true, or if both parts are true.

The OR gate works in the same way. The output is on if at least one of the inputs is on.

Symbol

The symbol for the OR gate looks like this.

⬆ The symbol for the OR gate

There are two inputs to the OR gate. In this diagram we have labelled the inputs A and B. Like the AND gates, these inputs are independent of each other.

Truth table

The truth table for the OR gate shows the four possible states of the OR gate. It shows the output in each state.

Columns A and B are the same as the truth table for the AND gate. The final column, which shows the output, is different. This is because the OR gate has a different effect.

A	B	Output
0	0	0
0	1	1
1	0	1
1	1	1

The output of the OR gate is 1 in every row except the first row.

The XOR gate

XOR stands for "Exclusive OR". It can be pronounced "ex-or" or "zor". This gate is sometimes called EOR. That is pronounced "ee-or". XOR and EOR mean the same thing.

The XOR gate only outputs 1 if one of the inputs is 1 and the other is 0. These rules apply:

- If both inputs are 1, the output is 0.
- If only one input is 1, the output is 1.
- If both inputs are 0, the output is 0.

In a sentence, the word "or" is sometimes used with this meaning. For example, the sentence "I can go to a party or go to sleep" means that I can do just one of those things, not both.

Symbol

The symbol for the XOR gate is like an OR gate, with a curved line in front of it.

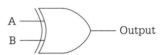

↑ The symbol for the XOR gate

Truth table

The truth table for the XOR gate is given below. The A and B columns are the same as the other truth tables we have looked at. Any logic gate with two inputs has the same logic table. The only difference is the final ("Output") column.

A	B	Output
0	0	0
0	1	1
1	0	1
1	1	0

The XOR gate has a different effect from the other gates you have learned about, so the content of the "Output" column is different.

Test yourself

1. Explain why the word "or" in everyday speech works in a similar way to the OR gate.

2. When is the output of the OR gate 0?

3. When is the output of the XOR gate 0?

4. Explain in your own words the difference between OR and XOR.

Learning activity

1. Create two pages on the computer or in your notebook where you will record information about the OR gate and the XOR gate. Use one page for each gate and draw the symbol for the gate, describe the gate, and draw the truth table.

2. Look at your copy of the diagram of a logic circuit from page 63. Identify any OR or XOR gates in this logic circuit. Mark them on your copy with the appropriate word.

Syllabus reference

1.3.1 Logic gates

Learners should be able to:
understand and define the function
of the NAND and NOR gates; draw
truth tables and recognise a logic
gate from its truth table; recognise
and use standard symbols used to
represent logic gates.

The NAND and NOR gates

Introduction

In this section you will learn about two final logic gates. They are called the NAND and NOR gates.

The NAND gate

The NAND gate is a logic gate. NAND stands for "NOT" plus "AND". The NAND gate works the same as a NOT and an AND gate joined together. The symbol is an AND gate with a small circle attached to it.

⬆ The symbol for the NAND gate

The NAND gate always outputs 1, unless both inputs are 1. It works like this:

- If both inputs are 0, the output is 1.
- If one input is 0, and one input is 1, the output is 1.
- If both inputs are 1, the output is 0.

The NAND gate is the opposite of an AND gate. Here is the truth table for the NAND gate.

A	B	Output
0	0	1
0	1	1
1	0	1
1	1	0

NOR gate

The NOR gate is a logic gate. NOR stands for "NOT" plus "OR". The NOR gate works the same as a NOT and an OR gate joined together. The symbol is an OR gate with a small circle attached to it.

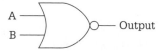

⬆ The symbol for the NOR gate

The NOR gate outputs 0 unless both inputs are 0. This is how it works:

- If both inputs are 0, the output is 1.
- If one or both inputs are 1, the output is 0.

The NOR gate is the opposite of the OR gate. Here is the truth table for this gate.

A	B	Output
0	0	1
0	1	0
1	0	0
1	1	0

Test yourself

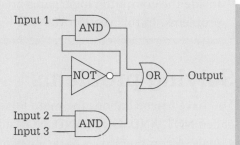

Here is the logic circuit from page 63, but with the gates labelled.

1. Produce a drawing of this circuit, but replace the AND gates with NAND gates.

2. Replace the OR gate with a NOR gate.

⬆ An example logic circuit with the gates labelled

Learning activity

1. Create notes for the NAND and NOR logic gates. For each one give:

- its name
- a description
- the symbol
- the truth table.

2. Mark up the logic circuit image you have been working on, identifying additional gates (if any) that are not yet labelled.

Class activities

Try to do these activities without looking at the answers in this book.

1. Choose any of the six logic gates you have learned about. Draw the symbol on a piece of paper. Do not label it. Pass the paper to another student.

2. You should receive a picture of a logic gate from another student. Write the name of the logic gate on the sheet. Pass it back for checking.

3. Choose any of the six logic gates you have learned about. Draw the truth table for this logic gate. Do not label it. Pass the truth table to another student.

4. You should receive a truth table from another student. Write the name of the matching logic gate on the sheet. Pass it back for checking.

You can repeat these activities with other logic gates to extend the test.

Syllabus reference

1.3.1 Logic circuits

Learners should be able to produce a logic circuit to implement a given written logic statement.

See also:

3.1 Logic gates (The AND gate)
3.2 Inside the CPU

3.2 Logical processing

Logic statements

> ### Introduction
>
> You have learned about logic gates. Logic gates transform binary signals. Inside the computer, logic gates are used to work out the answer to real problems. In this section you will learn how logic is applied to problems.

Solving problems

You have learned about the main logic gates inside the processor. They are called NOT, AND, OR, NAND, NOR and XOR. Each gate changes binary signals. A computer uses logic gates to solve real-world problems. This involves matching up the logic gates with real-world statements.

Logical statements

A logical statement is a sentence. It states a fact. It has the value True or False. Here are some sentences that are statements:

- It is your birthday today.
- London is the capital of Sweden.
- A triangle has three sides.

Which of these statements have the value True, and which False?

Composite statements

We can use logical terms to join statements together. Joining two statements together makes a new statement. It is called a composite statement.

Examples of logical terms we have learned are:

- AND
- OR
- NOT.

By adding these logical terms to statements we make composite statements.

"And" is used to join two statements together. A sentence with "and" in it is true if both parts of the sentence are true. For example here are two logical statements:

> A: I have a car.
>
> B: I am old enough to drive.

We can join the two statements with "and" to make this composite statement:

> A and B: I have a car AND I am old enough to drive.

The whole statement is true if the two parts are true.

Logical deduction

Logic is a method of working out whether conclusions are true. You start out with some known facts, and you work out the logical conclusions. If you follow the rules of logic you can be certain that your conclusions are true. The process is as follows:

- The statements you begin with are called premises. You know at the start whether the premises are true.

- The statements you end up with are called conclusions. Logic helps you work out whether the conclusions are true.

Here is an example. We might be given the rule:

> C: IF you have a car AND you are old enough THEN you can drive a car.

We know what AND means. It means the composite statement is true if both parts are true. Logic tells us whether someone can drive a car.

The process of working out conclusions is called deduction. In this book, we will look at some simple logical deductions. Computers can do very complicated logical deductions. Logical deduction is one of the main jobs of the computer processor. Learn more about the processor in *3.3 Inside the CPU*.

Truth table

As you saw on page 67, the truth table for the AND gate looks like this.

A	B	Output
0	0	0
0	1	0
1	0	0
1	1	1

The truth table for the "and" statement looks just the same.

I have a car	I am old enough	I can drive a car
No	No	No
No	Yes	No
Yes	No	No
Yes	Yes	Yes

The logic is the same in both cases.

Test yourself

This statement uses the word "or":

> IF it is sunny OR I have an umbrella THEN I will stay dry.

1. What are the premises? What is the conclusion?

2. Make a logic table that shows all the different possibilities for this statement.

3. Using the truth table work out what premises make the conclusion false.

4. Explain in words why a logic statement using "or" is like the OR gate.

Syllabus reference

1.3.1 Logic circuits

Learners should be able to produce a logic circuit to implement a given written logic statement.

See also:

3.1 Logic gates (The NOT, AND, OR, XOR, NAND and OR gates)

Simplify statements

Introduction

You have looked at logical statements written as English sentences.
In this section you will learn a simpler way of writing logical statements.
This uses letters to stand for the factual statements.

Simplifying logical statements

In the previous section we looked at logical statements. Logical statements are sentences that can be true or false. We used examples that made sense in the real world, for example "It is not raining." and "I have a car.".

The laws of logic are the same whether you are talking about cars, or the weather, or any other subject. Logic is universal. For this reason, we sometimes simplify logical statements. Instead of writing out statements in full we can use letters. We often use A and B. The letters can stand for any statement. This lets us concentrate on logic, and not worry too much about what the statements say.

For example, instead of writing out statements in full, we can say:

NOT A

A AND B

A OR B.

The connectors

We have learned about six different logic gates. These gates match the six different connectors that we can use to create logical statements.

Logical connector	Explanation	Matching logic gate
NOT A	Reverses the truth value of A	NOT gate
A AND B	True only if A and B are both True	AND gate
A OR B	True unless both A and B are False	OR gate
A NAND B	True unless both A and B are True	NAND gate
A NOR B	True if both A and B are False	NOR gate
A XOR B	True if A and B have different truth values (Short for "eXclusive OR")	XOR gate

Truth tables

You have learned the truth tables that go with the logic gates. These truth tables match the truth tables for the logical statements.

The truth table for **A AND B** looks like this.

A	B	A AND B
False	False	False
False	True	False
True	False	False
True	True	True

The truth table for the AND gate looks like this.

A	B	Output
0	0	0
0	1	0
1	0	0
1	1	1

The tables are exactly the same. This match means we can use logic gates to stand for logical statements. This is how a computer works. It uses a binary electrical signal, such as a high or low voltage, to stand for True and False.

Match to real-world statements

Remember that the logical structures can be matched up to real world statements. For example, here is a statement:

> To log in you must type your username AND password.

This has the logical structure **A AND B**. Here is the truth table for this statement.

Type the username	Type the password	Login
False	False	False
False	True	False
True	False	False
True	True	True

The table for this statement is the same as for the AND gate. It is not a coincidence that logic gates and logic statements match up like this. This is how computers work. This is why we can use computers to solve real-world problems.

Q

Test yourself

On this page there is a truth table for A AND B. It matches the truth table for the AND gate.

Create similar truth tables for the other logical connectors.

Syllabus reference

1.3.1 Logic gates; logic circuits

Learners should be able to: use logic gates to create electronic circuits; produce a logic circuit to implement a given written logic statement.

Logic circuits

Introduction

You have learned about logic gates. Logic gates can be wired together to make a logic circuit. In this section you will learn about simple logic circuits.

What is a logic circuit?

Logic gates take in binary signals and transform them. You can fit logic gates together. In real life that can mean literally wiring together electronic logic gates. Each gate's output flows as an electrical signal to the input of any gates wired to it.

A set of logic gates, wired together so that a logical signal can flow through, is called a logic circuit.

Drawing logic circuits

In real life you can make a logic circuit by wiring gates together. But you can also make a drawing of a logic circuit.

You have learned the symbols for six different logic gates. You can draw a logic circuit using the symbols for the logic gates. You draw the symbols next to each other. Then draw a line to show the wire that takes the signal from one gate to another. Here is an example.

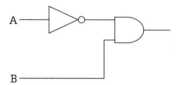

⬆ A simple logic circuit made from the NOT and AND gates

You can use special software to make neat diagrams of logic circuits. However, you should practise drawing them by hand, so that you can always draw a logic circuit if you are asked to.

Making circuits to match logic statements

You have learned to match up logic statements and logic gates. A short logic statement will match a single logic gate. A longer statement might need several logic gates joined together. In other words it will form a logic circuit.

Here is an example in words:

> You must enter your user identity AND password
>
> OR
>
> Press your thumb against the keypad.

Here is the same logical structure, shown in a simplified form:

> (A AND B) OR C

This statement consists of two parts. In the first example the two parts are shown on separate lines. In the simplified version the two parts are separated by brackets.

If you are making or drawing a logic circuit to match a statement, a good rule is to begin with the section in brackets. The section in brackets says "A AND B". Therefore, we begin the logic circuit by drawing the AND gate. A and B are the two inputs.

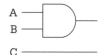

C is just a simple input. It does not have a logic gate. It is just shown as a line.

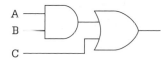

Now we can complete the logic circuit. These two parts are joined together by OR. We take the two outputs and join them with an OR gate. It looks like this.

The circuit is completed.

Test yourself

1. Draw a logic circuit to match this statement:

Take the temperature OR take the blood pressure AND

write up the case notes.

2. Draw logic circuits that match these three statements:

(A NOR B) AND C

(A AND B) XOR (C OR D)

(A NOR B) AND (NOT C).

Syllabus reference

1.3.1 Logic circuits

Learners should be able to produce truth tables for given logic circuits.

Truth tables and circuits

Introduction

In the previous section you learned to make logic circuits to match written logic statements. In this section you will learn to draw truth tables to match the circuits.

Example with two inputs

To make a truth table from a logic circuit you follow these steps.

1. Label all inputs and outputs.

2. Draw a truth table with a column for every input and output.

3. Fill in the inputs.

4. Fill in the outputs.

Below is a picture of a simple logic circuit. It has two logic gates that are wired together. In this section you will make a truth table to match the logic circuit.

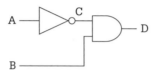

⬆ A simple logic circuit with outputs

Label all inputs and outputs

The truth table shown in this image has two logic gates. The first step is to label the input and output of each gate.

Here is how the circuit is labelled:

- The two inputs to the circuit are labelled A and B.

- The output of the NOT gate is labelled C.

- The output of the AND gate is labelled D.

D is the final output of the whole circuit.

Draw a truth table

Now we can make the truth table. There should be a column for every input and output in the circuit.

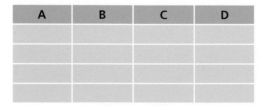

A	B	C	D

Show the inputs

First we fill in the initial outputs. You know how to count up in binary. Columns A and B are filled in using the first four binary numbers.

A	B	C	D
0	0		
0	1		
1	0		
1	1		

Work out the outputs

Now we fill in the value of C. C is the output of a NOT gate. A is the input to the NOT gate. This means C is the inverse of A.

A	B	C	D
0	0	1	
0	1	1	
1	0	0	
1	1	0	

Next we fill in the value of D. D is the output of the AND gate. B and C are the inputs to the AND gate. The output of an AND gate is 0 unless both inputs have the value 1. Now we can fill in the final column.

A	B	C	D
0	0	1	0
0	1	1	1
1	0	0	0
1	1	0	0

The truth table is now complete. We can use the truth table to find out what values of A and B produce a TRUE output.

A	B	C	D
0	0	1	0
0	1	1	1
1	0	0	0
1	1	0	0

If A is 0 and B is 1, the output of the circuit is 1. In all other cases the output is 0.

Test yourself

Here is a simple logic circuit.

1. Draw your own copy of this logic circuit. One of the outputs is not labelled. Add a label in the right place.
2. Describe this logic circuit in words.
3. Make a truth table for this logic circuit.
4. There is a single logic gate that has the same output as this logic circuit. What is it?

⬆ An example logic circuit with OR and NOT

Syllabus reference

1.3.1 Logic circuits

Learners should be able to produce truth tables for given logic circuits.

Truth tables (continued)

Introduction

In the previous section you learned to draw a truth table to match a logic circuit. In this section you will look at a more complex example.

Example with three inputs

This example circuit has three inputs.

We can use the methods we learned in the previous section to create a truth table.

1. Label inputs and outputs and draw the truth table.

2. Show the inputs.

3. Calculate the outputs.

1. Label inputs and outputs and draw the truth table

The first step is to label all inputs and outputs.

Then draw a truth table with a column for every input and output.

A	B	C	D	E

2. Show the inputs

Then we fill in all the initial outputs. There are three inputs. To fill in all the possible inputs, use the first eight binary numbers.

A	B	C	D	E
0	0	0		
0	0	1		
0	1	0		
0	1	1		
1	0	0		
1	0	1		
1	1	0		
1	1	1		

3. Calculate the outputs

D is the output of the AND gate. A and B are the inputs to this gate. D is 1 if A and B are 1.

A	B	C	D	E
0	0	0	0	
0	0	1	0	
0	1	0	0	
0	1	1	0	
1	0	0	0	
1	0	1	0	
1	1	0	1	
1	1	1	1	

E is the final output of the circuit. It is the output of the OR gate. C and D are the inputs to the OR gate. E is 1 if either C or D is 1.

A	B	C	D	E
0	0	0	0	0
0	0	1	0	1
0	1	0	0	0
0	1	1	0	1
1	0	0	0	0
1	0	1	0	1
1	1	0	1	1
1	1	1	1	1

Using this truth table we can see what inputs produce an output of 1.

A	B	C	D	E
0	0	0	0	0
0	0	1	0	1
0	1	0	0	0
0	1	1	0	1
1	0	0	0	0
1	0	1	0	1
1	1	0	1	1
1	1	1	1	1

There are five combinations of input that produce the output 1.

Test yourself

1. On this page you used a truth table to analyse a logic circuit. List all the values of A, B and C that produce an output of 1.

2. How would the table change if the final gate was an XOR gate instead of an OR gate? Draw this circuit and the truth table that goes with it.

3. Look at the four logic circuits you made in answer to questions 1 and 2 on page 77. Draw a truth table to match each of these logic circuits.

Syllabus reference

1.3.1 Logic circuits

Learners should be able to produce a logic circuit to solve a given problem.

Solve a problem

Introduction

You have learned how to make a logic circuit to match a complex logical statement. You have learned how to make a truth table from the logic circuit. In this section you will put these skills together to solve logical problems.

Logical deduction

A logical deduction starts with premises. Premises are statements that can be true or false. From the premises we can work out conclusions. The laws of logic will tell us whether the conclusions are true or false.

A truth table will help us to work out whether conclusions are true or false. Remember that 0 means False and 1 means True. The truth table will show us what inputs lead to True outputs. This will help us to work out the solution to logical problems and puzzles.

Example 1

This is the logic circuit from page 78.

The inputs are A and B. The output is D. Here is the truth table that goes with the logic circuit.

A	B	C	D
0	0	1	0
0	1	1	1
1	0	0	0
1	1	0	0

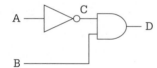

Using this table we can see that D is only True if A is False and B is True. That is the solution to the logic circuit.

Example 2

On page 80 you looked at this logic circuit.

The inputs are A, B and C. We made a logic table from the circuit.

Using this logic table we can answer the question: If A is True, and B and C are False, what is the value of E? The row that answers the question is highlighted.

A	B	C	D	E
0	0	0	0	0
0	0	1	0	1
0	1	0	0	0
0	1	1	0	1
1	0	0	0	0
1	0	1	0	1
1	1	0	1	1
1	1	1	1	1

By looking at the truth table we can see that when A is True and B and C are False, the final output is False (0).

Now use the table to answer these questions.

1. Is the value of E always the same as the value of C?

2. There are eight possible inputs to this logic circuit. How many result in a False output?

3. If A and B are False, and C is True, what is the value of the output?

Summary

To use a logic circuit to solve a problem, you must follow these steps.

1. Turn the logic statement into a logic circuit.

2. Make a truth table that matches the logic circuit.

3. Look at the truth table to see what inputs will produce the output you want.

Test yourself

Use this logic statement to answer the questions that follow:

(A XOR B) AND (NOT C)

1. Draw a logic circuit to match this statement.

2. Create a truth table that matches this logic circuit.

3. By looking at the truth table, say what inputs will produce a True output from the logic circuit.

Learning activity

Write a logic statement. Challenge another student in your class to draw a logic circuit and a truth table to match the statement you have written.

Syllabus reference

1.3.1 Logic circuits

Learners should be able to produce a logic circuit to solve a given problem.

Repeat inputs

Introduction

You have used logic circuits and truth tables to solve logical problems. In this section you will look at a final example. You will see how all the methods you have learned come together to solve a problem.

Input used twice

In some logic problems the same input is used in more than one logic gate. We will look at an example on this page.

Method

We will use the following method.

1. Draw a logic circuit to match the statement.

2. Label all inputs and outputs.

3. Create a truth table showing all inputs and outputs.

4. Fill in the inputs.

5. Fill in the outputs.

6. Use the truth table to answer a question.

Logic problem

We will start with this logic statement:

    (A OR B) AND (NOT B)

The question we have to answer is: What inputs produce a true output?

1. Draw a logic circuit

Look at the statements in brackets first. The first statement is (A OR B), so we show A and B as the inputs to an OR gate (see image 1).

The second statement is (NOT B), so we take the input B and send it to a NOT gate. It is like putting an extra wire into the circuit (see image 2).

Finally, the two statements are joined by AND, so we send the inputs to an AND gate (see image 3). This is the complete circuit to match the statement we started with.

2. Label all inputs and outputs

Now we need to add labels so that every input and output has a letter. The finished circuit, with all labels, is shown in image 4.

3. Create a truth table

We create a truth table with a column for every input and output.

↑ Image 1

↑ Image 2

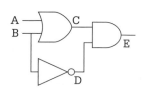

↑ Image 3

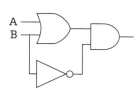

↑ Image 4

4. Fill in the inputs

A and B are the inputs. As there are just two inputs we fill in the table with the first four binary numbers.

A	B	C	D	E
0	0			
0	1			
1	0			
1	1			

5. Fill in the outputs

First we fill in the C column. C is the output of an OR gate. The inputs to the OR gate are A and B. That means C is True in every case, unless A and B are both False.

A	B	C	D	E
0	0	0		
0	1	1		
1	0	1		
1	1	1		

Next we fill in the D column. D is the output of a NOT gate. B is the input to the NOT gate, so we reverse the truth value of B.

A	B	C	D	E
0	0	0	1	
0	1	1	0	
1	0	1	1	
1	1	1	0	

Finally we fill in the E column. E is the output of the AND gate. The inputs to the AND gate are C and D. That means E is True if both C and D are True. In all other cases it is False.

A	B	C	D	E
0	0	0	1	0
0	1	1	0	0
1	0	1	1	1
1	1	1	0	0

The truth table is now complete.

6. Use the truth table to answer a question

The question was: What inputs produce a True output?

If we look at the truth table, we can see there is only one line where E is True. In this line:

- A is True
- B is False.

That is the answer to the question.

Test yourself

Using the method shown on this page, find out what inputs produce a true output from this logic statement:

> (A XOR B) NOR A

Learning activity

Create a logic statement that uses the same input twice. Challenge another student to solve the logic statement using the methods shown on this page.

Syllabus reference

1.3.2 Computer architecture

Learners should be able to show understanding of the basic von Neumann model for a computer system.

See also:

Chapter 1 Data representation
3.2 Logical processing (Logic circuits)

3.3 Inside the CPU

The central processing unit (CPU)

Introduction

You have learned that the computer is an electronic device. Electronic logic circuits process data inside the computer. The part of the computer that carries out the processing is known as the central processing unit (CPU). In this section you will learn about the work and structure of the CPU.

The computer system

The processor is at the centre of the computer system.

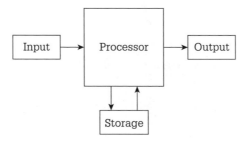

⬆ The structure of a computer system

The arrows in this diagram show the flow of data. Input devices send data into the processor. Storage devices hold data that the processor can use. Output devices display data from the processor.

You will learn about input, output and storage devices in *Chapter 4 Hardware*. Together, these devices are known as "peripherals".

The processor

The processor has two main components:

- the central processing unit (CPU)
- main memory.

These components share data through fast connections called buses.

The CPU

The CPU has two main components:

- the arithmetic and logic unit (ALU)
- the control unit.

Main memory

Main memory is also sometimes called main store, primary memory, primary store, random access memory (RAM) or immediate access store (IAS).

Main memory consists of a large number of memory locations. Each has an address: a number that identifies exactly that location. Each memory location can hold the value of one item of data, in the form of a binary number.

The instructions that tell the processor how to process the data are themselves numbers. Like any other numbers, they can be stored in main memory.

The CPU can only work on data that is stored in the main memory. Similarly, it can only follow instructions that are stored in the main memory.

The ALU

All processing happens in the ALU. In the ALU the binary electrical signals that represent data are passed through logic circuits. The logic circuits transform the data. The ALU does arithmetic processing and logical processing:

- Arithmetic processing means finding the numerical answer to mathematical problems.
- Logical processing means finding the true/false answer to logical deductions.

You will learn more about both types of processing in *Chapter 8 Programming*.

The control unit

The control unit controls the other parts of the processor. Its signals tell the ALU to read data from main memory, process it, and write the results back to main memory. It also tells peripherals to transfer data to and from the main memory.

The control unit has a timer to send control signals in the right order, giving each action time to finish before it sends the next signal.

Test yourself

1. What are the main components of the CPU?

2. What are the three types of peripheral?

3. What two types of work does the ALU carry out?

4. What happens to the new data that the ALU makes?

Learning activity

Use a graphics application to create a diagram of the components of a computer system including the parts of the CPU.

John von Neumann

The basic structure of the computer shown in this section is called the von Neumann model or von Neumann architecture. It is named after the US scientist John von Neumann who first proposed this model. Von Neumann based his work on the ideas of the computer pioneer Alan Turing. For more information see:

http://www.turing.org.uk/sources/vonneumann.html

Syllabus reference

1.3.2 Computer architecture and the fetch-execute cycle

Learners should be able to describe the stages of the fetch-execute cycle and the stored program concept.

See also:

Chapter 1 Data representation

The fetch-execute cycle

Introduction

You have learned that the processor is at the centre of the computer system. Processing is carried out in the CPU. Processing is done in a regular order called the fetch-execute cycle. In this section you will learn about this cycle.

The operation of the CPU

All the time that the computer is switched on, the CPU repeats a set of actions called the fetch-execute cycle.

1. The control unit **fetches** an instruction from main memory. The instructions are coded as binary numbers.

2. The control unit **decodes** the instruction so it knows what action to carry out.

3. The ALU carries out the action. That is called **executing** the instruction.

This three-part cycle of fetch–decode–execute is carried out over and over again while the computer is working. The computer carries out millions of cycles every second.

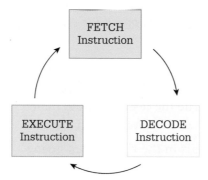

⬆ The fetch-execute cycle is repeated millions of times a second

Fetch

Before a piece of software is run, all its instructions will be loaded into main memory. This is because it is much slower to read individual instructions from external storage than from main memory.

The first step of the fetch-execute cycle is fetching the instruction from main memory.

The instruction, a binary number, is copied into a small storage space inside the CPU called the instruction register. The register holds only one instruction at a time.

Decode

Every CPU has a specific set of instructions it is able to follow. This is called the CPU's instruction set. CPUs from different companies may have different instruction sets.

Each instruction in the set is represented by a different range of binary numbers. A logic circuit in the control unit, the instruction decoder, analyses the number in the instruction register to work out which instruction it represents.

The control unit then selects the appropriate list of actions needed to make that instruction happen.

Execute

"Execute" in this context means to carry out an instruction.

After decoding the instruction, the control unit sends a series of signals to the ALU to tell it what to do. The ALU carries out each action. It will either solve an arithmetic problem (a numerical calculation) or make a logical deduction (a True/False comparison).

Some instructions send signals to a peripheral device instead of the ALU. These control the peripheral, for example telling it to transfer data to or from the main memory.

Stored program model

The early developers of the computer realised that both data and instructions could be stored as binary numbers in the computer's main memory. The control unit fetches instructions from memory and sends data to the ALU for processing. All computers follow this basic model. It is called the stored program model.

A slightly more complex computer model, called the Harvard model, sets aside different sections of memory for instructions and data. Instructions and data are accessed separately by the control unit. This is a more realistic model of the working of a modern computer. However, the basic idea of the fetch-execute cycle remains the same.

Test yourself

1. Draw a diagram of the fetch-execute cycle.

2. Explain how the instruction register is used in the fetch stage of the fetch-execute cycle.

3. How does the control unit decode the instruction in the decode stage of the fetch-execute cycle?

4. Where is the execute stage of the fetch-execute cycle carried out?

Learning activity

Carry out Internet research to find diagrams of the fetch-execute cycle. Find several examples. Some are more complex than others.

Syllabus reference

1.3.2 Computer architecture and the fetch-execute cycle

Learners should be able to describe the stages of the fetch-execute cycle, including the use of registers and buses.

1.1.2 Reasons for choosing hexadecimal notation to represent numbers

Learners should be able to represent numbers stored in registers and main memory as hexadecimal.

See also:

Chapter 1 Data representation
Chapter 2 Communications and the Internet

Registers and buses

Introduction

You have learned that a small area of storage called the instruction register is used in the fetch-execute cycle. In this section you will learn about how a range of registers are used in the complete cycle.

Registers

Registers are small areas of fast memory inside the CPU:

- Some registers hold addresses for locations in the main memory. Addresses are binary numbers.

- Some registers hold instructions telling the CPU to carry out an action such as adding or subtracting. Instructions are binary numbers too.

- Some registers hold data. Again, this is held in the form of a binary number.

A register holds only one binary number at a time. As the computer runs, the numbers in its registers constantly change.

Different registers

Some registers are just used as fast memory, to hold partial results during a calculation. These are called general registers, or accumulators. Others have a special role in the fetch-execute cycle:

- The program counter (PC) holds the address of the next instruction to fetch.

- The memory address register (MAR) holds an address to read from or write to.

- The instruction register (IR) holds the instruction currently being executed.

- The memory data register (MDR) holds data just read from memory, or about to be written to memory.

The program counter (PC)

The PC holds the address of the next instruction to fetch:

- After each fetch, 1 is added to the PC, so the next fetch reads the next location in memory.

- Some instructions change the PC, to make the next fetch jump to a new location in memory.

- Peripherals can send signals which change the PC to interrupt the CPU. Learn about interrupts in *5.1 Systems software (Functions of an operating system)*.

- When the computer halts, the PC stops counting up through memory.

The memory address register (MAR)

The MAR holds an address in main memory to be read from or written to:

- During fetch, the control unit copies the address from the PC into the MAR. If the contents of that location is an instruction, it ends up in a register called the IR (see the next page).

- Sometimes the location holds data. Main memory reads the data into a register called the MDR (see below).
- When the processor has finished a task, and has a result to send back to memory, the MAR holds the address to use.

The instruction register (IR)

The IR holds the instruction currently being executed. The control unit decodes the instruction in the IR to work out which sequence of signals to send to the ALU. This controls the execute part of the fetch-execute cycle.

The memory data register (MDR)

The MDR holds one item of data being copied between the CPU and main memory. The MDR is used for reading and writing. For example:

- the MDR receives the data arriving from memory.
- the MDR holds the data to be sent to memory, for example the results of a calculation the ALU has just performed.

Buses

The different registers and components in the processor are connected by short wire connections called buses. There are three types:

- An address bus transmits addresses
- A data bus transmits data
- A control bus transmits control signals, telling the receiver to do something.

The MAR and MDR are the CPU's link to the main memory's address bus and data bus. The bits in each register correspond to wires on the bus.

Use of hexadecimal

Data is held in registers and in main memory in the form of binary numbers. Sometimes computer professionals need to refer to the contents of an individual register, or a memory location. In this case they would typically use hexadecimal numbers, rather than writing a binary number using only 1s and 0s.

Test yourself

1. How does the program counter set the next memory address?

2. What does the MAR do during the fetch-execute cycle?

3. The control unit decodes the instruction in the instruction register. What does it do with that information?

4. Describe two functions of the MDR.

5. What is a bus, and how are buses used in the fetch-execute cycle?

Learning activity

Describe the three stages of the fetch-execute cycle. At each stage describe what registers are in use, and what each register does.

Review

Key terms

ALU	Arithmetic and Logic Unit. It is part of the CPU. It passes data through logic circuits. The circuits change the data using the rules of logic and arithmetic.
Bus	A short communication link which joins up two parts of the processor.
Control Unit	The Control Unit controls the flow of data through the processor, and from the processor to peripherals.
CPU	The Central Processing Unit of the computer. This is where data from main memory is processed. It is made of two parts: the ALU and the Control Unit.
Fetch-execute cycle	The cycle that goes on inside the processor. First the CPU takes data and instructions from memory (this is called "Fetch"). Then the data is changed according to the instructions (this is called "Execute").
Logical deduction	Logic is a method of working out whether conclusions are true. You start out with some known facts, and you work out the logical conclusions.
Logic gate	The on/off switches inside the processor are combined to make electrical circuits. These circuits are called logic gates. Electrical signals pass into logic gates, and electrical signals pass out. Every logic gate has input and output
Logical statement	A logical statement is a sentence. It states a fact. It has the value True or False.
Main Memory	The Main Memory is where data and instructions are stored inside the Processor. They are stored in electronic digital form.
Processor	The centre of the computer system. It processes data. The processor is made of the CPU plus Main Memory.
Register	A small area of memory that typically stores one address, one item of data, or one instruction.

Project work

In this chapter you have created a range of diagrams and images. This includes the structure of the processor, the fetch-execute cycle. You have hand-drawn many different logic gates and logic circuits.

Now use suitable computer software to produce high-quality images of at least some of these items.

You may have access to specialist software which is designed to help you draw logic circuits. You may use free digital graphics software such as Microsoft Paint or Open Office Draw. Or you may use specialist graphics software such as Visio.

You may wish to upload examples of well-produced graphics to the class web site (see Chapter 2) or print them out and display them in your classroom.

4 Hardware

Syllabus reference

1.3.3 Input devices

Learners should be able to: describe the principles of operation (how each device works) of these input devices: keyboards, mice; describe how these principles are applied to real-life scenarios.

See also:

1.3 Data storage

4.1 Input devices

Keyboard and mouse

Introduction

This chapter is about hardware. Hardware means the physical devices that make up a computer system. The first topic is input devices. They are used to input data to the computer. Two of the most common input devices are the keyboard and the mouse. In this section you will learn how they work, and how they are used.

What is an input device?

An input device converts data into digital signals that can be processed by the computer. There are many different types of data that can be input to the computer. In this section you will learn about:

- input of text data using the keyboard
- input of positional data using the mouse.

The keyboard

Keyboards are used to input text characters (such as letters and punctuation). The computer uses a different binary number code to represent each text character. A keyboard has a range of buttons or keys. Keys for text characters are labelled with their character. Each key has an electrical connection underneath it. When you press the key, that closes the connection so that electricity can pass. A binary code is sent down the wire, or by a wireless connection, to the processor. Inside the processor, ASCII code or Unicode is used to represent every text character as a binary number.

The layout of a computer keyboard is based on the old typewriter keyboard. People are used to that keyboard layout. It may not be the most efficient design, but it is unlikely to change.

⬆ A keyboard

Keyboards do not only send text. They have additional keys that let you control what the computer does. Keys can be pressed alone or in combination. An example is Control and Alt and Delete: pressing these together restarts the computer. Control keys work by sending control signals to the processor.

The mouse

A mouse is used to input positional data. A mouse controls the position of the pointer on the computer screen. You roll the mouse on a flat surface. The pointer on the screen makes the same movements. The mouse also has one or more buttons that you can click when the pointer is in the right position.

Early mouse designs had a rolling ball underneath. As you moved the mouse on a flat surface, electrical sensors inside the mouse detected the movement of the ball. A modern optical mouse uses a light sensor to detect movement. A 3D mouse uses motion detectors to sense movement through the air, not just on a flat surface.

↑ An optical mouse

Other positional devices

Other devices such as a trackball, a laptop touchpad or a game console may be used to send positional data to the processor:

● A trackball is used by people who find a mouse uncomfortable to use. The ball is moved by the fingers and the device stays still.

● A touchpad is used when you don't want to plug any other devices into the laptop.

● A game console gives you 3D control over a computer game.

↑ Some people find using a trackball more comfortable than using a mouse

Advantages and disadvantages

The mouse and keyboard are manual devices. That means data is entered by hand. They have many advantages. They are easy and convenient to use for most people. They are included free with a typical computer. They can be used for a wide range of tasks.

However, there are disadvantages. Manual devices are slow to input data compared to automatic input devices. A human user can easily make mistakes using a manual device, such as typing errors. They can be tiring or stressful to use.

↑ A touchpad sends positional data

Q Test yourself

1. What code is used to represent text characters in the computer system?

2. Name three keys on the keyboard that are not used to send text characters, and explain what they are used for.

3. What type of data is sent to the computer from a mouse?

4. Identify two advantages and two disadvantages of entering data into the computer with a keyboard.

Syllabus reference

1.3.3 Input devices

Learners should be able to:
describe the principles of operation
(how each device works) of these
input devices: touch screen,
interactive whiteboard; describe
how these principles are applied
to real-life scenarios for example
touch screens on mobile devices.

See also:

4.2 Output devices

Touch screens

Introduction

Most desktop and laptop computers have a keyboard and a mouse. Hand-held devices such as smartphones and tablets are more likely to have a touch screen. In this section you will learn how a touch screen works and how it is used.

Touch screens

A touch screen has a double function:

- It is an output device that displays information for the user.
- It is an input device that lets the user make selections from the display, including selecting characters to enter.

⬆ A touch screen works as an input and an output device

To use a touch screen you literally touch the screen at the spot that shows your choice. The screen detects the presence of your finger. It sends a positional signal to the processor.

There are three main types of touch screen:

- A resistive screen has two layers that conduct electricity. When you touch the screen you push the two layers together, allowing electricity to pass through them. This is the least expensive option, but this type of screen can be quite easily damaged.

- A capacitive screen uses conductive strips either side of a transparent sheet, at right angles so the strips make a grid. An electric charge on the screen changes when you touch it. The screen checks which strip on either side has the changed charge: your finger is at the place where the two strips cross. A capacitive screen is stronger than a resistive screen, and makes a brighter image.

- An infra-red screen has two sets of invisible beams projected at right angles across the screen, making a grid. A finger or other item, such as a pen or pointer, will break the beams. This is how the computer detects the position. It does not have to be used with something (like a finger) that lifts electricity.

Touching the screen

Resistive and infra-red touch screens detect anything that contacts the screen surface, including a stick, a pen or a gloved hand.

Capacitive touch screens only work with something that will change the electrical charge on the screen, such as a bare finger.

Mobile devices

Modern mobile devices use touch screens. This means you don't need to plug extras, such as a keyboard, into the device. The device is light and portable. One feature – the screen – allows all input and output.

A mobile device lets you input text as if you are using a keyboard. A keyboard is shown on the screen. You choose a character by touching the display. Many people find this more difficult than using a physical keyboard. A touch screen keyboard is not suitable for entering large amounts of text.

The screen of a mobile device typically includes a lot of small images called icons. The icons stand for different applications (apps). You touch the icon to start the app. Once the app is running, you can touch options on the screen to control how the app works.

⬆ The small images on the screen are called icons

Interactive whiteboards

An interactive whiteboard is a large touch screen. It is used in schools and meetings, for example. The screen displays content for everyone in the room to see. The person leading the discussion can touch the board and change the display.

You can write directly onto the screen with a special pen. You can also type text at the computer keyboard and it will appear on the screen. When you have finished you can save the work you have done.

⬆ An interactive whiteboard is a touch screen device

Test yourself

1. Explain how the three types of touch screen work.

2. Why are touch screens so useful with mobile devices?

3. Why is it harder to use an onscreen keyboard than a physical keyboard?

4. What advantage does an interactive whiteboard have for a teacher, compared to an ordinary projector display?

Learning activity

Use a device with a touch screen. It could be a smartphone, tablet or whiteboard. Make a sketch of the screen, marking the key features. Write a short user guide, explaining how to use the touchscreen to input content and control the device.

Syllabus reference

1.3.3 Input devices

Learners should be able to: describe the principles of operation (how each device works) of these input devices: digital cameras, microphones; describe how these principles are applied to real-life scenarios.

See also:

1.3 Data storage (Digital graphics; Digital sound and video)

Introduction

You have learned that images and sounds can be held inside the computer. They are held as a set of binary numbers. Representing something as numbers is called a digital form of that thing. Digital cameras and digital microphones convert real-life images and sounds into digital form. In this section you will learn how cameras and microphones work.

Digital camera

A digital camera has an aperture (a hole) at the front. The aperture contains a lens. A lens is a curved slice of transparent material that focuses light. "Focus" means the light is concentrated into a small area. Light from the scene in front of the camera is focused by the lens. The light is focused onto a sensitive electronic surface. It is made of a grid of tiny sensors. The electronic sensors on the surface react to light. They turn the pattern of light and darkness into electrical signals. Turn back to *1.3 Data storage* for information about how images are held as electronic signals.

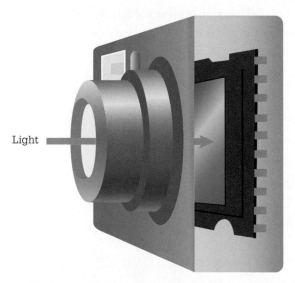

⬆ The sensors inside the camera turn light into electrical signals

The electrical signals from the camera can be sent directly into a processor. For example, the camera in a mobile phone is connected to the processor of the phone. Alternatively, the signals from the camera can be saved on secondary storage. Learn about digital storage in *4.3 Memory and storage*.

Microphone

Sound is movement of the air. The air moves in a wave pattern called sound waves. Our ears can detect those sound waves. A microphone does the same thing.

It has a component that vibrates when hit by sound waves. Some microphones have a diaphragm, a sheet that is stretched tight, with a coil of wire around a magnet to generate electricity when the diaphragm vibrates. Some have a metal foil ribbon with a magnet around it.

Whatever the component is, its electrical output is converted to a digital signal. The signal can be processed by the computer or stored for later.

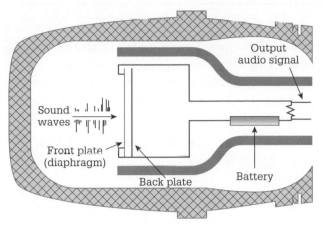

↑ The microphone converts sound waves into an electrical signal

You learned in Chapter 1 that audio data can be held in the processor in digital form. There are several audio formats. The microphone converts sound waves into a digital audio format.

Use in everyday life

Modern smartphones have microphones and digital cameras included in a single hand-held device. It is common for people to use their phone to make and share recordings of their day-to-day life. Although this is a very convenient way of making a recording, the result is often not of very high quality.

Test yourself

1. Explain why a digital camera must have a lens as well as an aperture.

2. The sensors in a black-and-white digital camera detect light and darkness. What other property of light is detected by a modern digital camera?

3. The signals from a camera or microphone may be sent directly to the processor. What is the alternative to this?

4. Research one of the types of electronic microphone. Describe how its components detect sound waves in the air.

Learning activity

Work with a partner. Using a digital camera or smartphone, take a photograph of an input device. Record a short talk describing how that device works.

Syllabus reference

1.3.3 Input devices

Learners should be able to: describe the principles of operation (how each device works) of these input devices: barcode readers, quick response (QR) code readers; describe how these principles are applied to real-life scenarios, for example barcode readers at supermarket checkouts.

Barcode readers

Introduction

In this section you will learn about automated input device. These devices make it quicker to input data by using codes the computer can read.

Barcode

A barcode is a way of holding a code number. The number is turned into a pattern of vertical bars. The bars are of different widths. Patterns of wider and narrower bars represent different digits.

Barcodes are printed on the wrappers and labels of products. Each product has a different code. When you buy the product the barcode is scanned. The code number is input to the computer.

Other information about the product, such as its name and price, will be stored on computer. Using the barcode, the computer can look up the details of that product. For example, it will find the price of the product and add it to your bill.

Barcode reader

A barcode reader flashes light at the barcode, or scans light across the code. The light bounces back to the reader. The reader is like a very simple digital camera. Sensors in the reader can detect the pattern of light and dark from the barcode. That means the reader can tell what number the barcode represents.

↑ Barcode reader in action

Advantages

A barcode reader has advantages over other types of input:

- The code could be typed in by hand, but this would take much longer and there is more chance of an error.
- The code could be input using other methods such as magnetism or electricity, but preparing these formats needs special equipment.
- A barcode can be printed by an ordinary black and white printer.

Disadvantages

A barcode reader also has some disadvantages:

- It can only do one task – read barcodes – unlike a keyboard, which can be used for many different tasks.
- A barcode reader is not part of an ordinary computer: it must be bought separately.

QR code

QR code, a trade mark standing for "quick response code", is like a two-dimensional barcode. QR codes are printed on wrappers, labels, and posters. Like barcodes, QR codes can be printed by ordinary printers. They are more complex than barcodes and can store more data. QR codes can be used, for example, by companies to track products in warehouses and factories.

QR codes can be read by special devices, but can also be read using a smartphone app. The camera in the phone takes a picture of the code. Special software in the phone examines the image to convert it to a code that the processor can understand. This code might tell the phone to open a web page, allowing the QR code to be used for special offers and advertising.

 A QR code can be read by a mobile phone

EPOS terminal

EPOS stands for "electronic point of sale". An EPOS terminal is used at the checkout of many shops. An EPOS terminal includes a barcode scanner to record purchases. It will work out the cost of the shopping. It can take payment using cash or cards.

 An EPOS terminal uses many different input and output devices

Q

Test yourself

1. At the bottom of a barcode the code number is shown as human-readable numbers. Why is this?

2. A poster advertising a concert has a QR code at the bottom. Explain why the band might have included this code on their poster.

3. Write an email to a shopkeeper, explaining the reasons for and against installing a barcode reader in his shop.

4. Describe three input devices used with the EPOS terminal.

Q

Learning activity

Find examples of QR codes and barcodes. If you have access to a mobile phone that can read QR codes, see what happens when you scan the code. Write a report on what you have found.

Syllabus reference

1.3.3 Input devices

Learners should be able to: describe the principles of operation (how each device works) of these input devices: 2D and 3D scanners; describe how these principles are applied to real-life scenarios, for example scanning of passports at airports.

Scanners

Introduction

You have learned how input devices can be used to put data into the computer. In this section you will learn about scanners that take a complete image of a document or object.

1D, 2D, 3D

"D" stands for "dimension". Dimension means a direction of measurement:

- A line is one-dimensional (1D).
- A flat surface is two-dimensional (2D).
- A solid object is three-dimensional (3D).

A barcode is 1D. The information is read in only one direction: the width of each line. A QR code is 2D: the pattern has both width and length.

Document scanner

A document scanner works in two dimensions. It scans a flat surface such as a piece of paper. It takes a picture of the document. There are many types of document scanner:

- Flat-bed scanners have a glass surface. You put the document face down on the surface and close the lid.
- A roller scanner feeds the document through.
- A hand-held scanner can be moved or rolled across a document.

The simplest scanner will just record the image of the document. This is like taking a digital photograph of it.

OMR

OMR stands for "optical mark recognition". An OMR scanner detects the presence of marks on a sheet of paper or card. Data is passed to the processor that says whether a mark is present or not at each position. OMR readers are used to mark multiple choice exams, surveys and votes in elections. A form, clearly showing the options participants can choose from, must be printed in advance. People mark their choices, usually with a pencil.

OMR scanning can only be used to read simple choices, not complex data.

↑ A sheet must be prepared for people to mark

OCR

OCR stands for "optical character recognition". An OCR reader will scan text. Software linked to the scanner can interpret the shape of letters. A simple document scanner will make a digital photograph of the document. An OCR reader will make a text file.

OCR scanning is much quicker than typing, but it can only read text that already exists. You cannot use it to write a new document.

3D scanner

A 3D scanner records the shape of a solid object. It does not just take a picture, which shows only a flat (2D) image of the object looking from a single direction. Instead it records the whole 3D shape, no matter which direction you look at it. All the information about the shape of the object is sent to the processor. 3D scanners use many different methods to measure an object, including shining a light and physical contact. They can scan single objects, buildings, or large areas of ground.

3D scanners have many uses:

- industrial: to scan an object so a copy of it can be made
- medical: to scan a part of the patient's body to find damage or disease
- research and archaeology: to scan a location to find out more about it
- cultural and entertainment: to record works of art, or to make realistic video games.

The processor can use the 3D information to create a physical model of the object, or an image that can be rotated to view all sides.

Test yourself

1. What is the difference between 2D and 3D?

2. Compare the advantages and disadvantages of typing and OCR as ways to input text into the computer.

3. A teacher wants to use OMR to mark a class test. What preparations must she make?

4. A historian wants to make a record of a famous battlefield. What is the advantage of using a 3D scanner instead of a digital camera?

Case study

Uganda's historic Kasubi Tombs are a UNESCO World Heritage Site. They are the ancient tombs of kings of this region. In 2009 a 3D scanning project was done. It produced detailed architectural models of the tombs. A fire in 2010 burned down most of the structure. Information from the 3D scan makes it possible to reconstruct the site.

⬆ The Kasubi Tombs in Kampala, Uganda

Syllabus reference

1.3.3 Input devices

Learners should be able to:
describe how a range of sensors
can be used to input data into a
computer system, including light,
temperature, magnetic field, gas,
pressure, moisture, humidity, pH
and motion.

Sensors

Introduction

You have learned about manual input devices. You have learned about devices that record images and sounds. In this section you will learn about devices that measure other features of the world, and input the measurements as digital signals.

Sensors

Sensors are automatic input devices. A sensor is designed to measure one feature of the environment. The environment is defined as any area outside the computer. The measurement is converted to a digital value and input to the processor.

Sensors work automatically – without a human user. For example, it is possible for a human to read a thermometer, and then type the temperature into a computer. A sensor will detect the temperature and send the data into the processor, without needing to involve a person.

Types of sensor

It is possible to develop an electronic device to sense almost any feature of the environment. In each case, the measurement is converted to a digital electronic signal:

- Light – a digital camera or scanner uses light to make an image. A light sensor is simpler. It simply detects how much light there is. For example, a light sensor could be used to turn on street lights when it gets dark.

- Temperature – temperature sensors can detect the temperature of a room, or record the weather. Other sensors are designed to work at very high or low temperatures. These may have industrial or scientific uses. For example, some foods must be cooked at a particular temperature to be safe to eat. Temperature of the food and the oven may be monitored by computer systems.

- Pressure – a pressure detector measures touch. Any computer-controlled device that moves around independently must have a way of detecting collision. A pressure detector can tell the computer if it touches an obstacle.

- Magnetism – a compass system uses the Earth's magnetic field to find where North is. Magnetic sensors are an alternative to pressure sensors in control technology. They avoid contact or wear and tear, but only work with metal objects. They can help a moving device avoid collision, without touch.

- Moisture and humidity – some sensors can detect water, or water vapour in the air. They can be used for weather prediction or warning of water damage. A greenhouse may have an environmental monitoring system including measurement of temperature and humidity. Keeping heat and moisture at the right level ensures that plants grow well.

⬆ Pressure detectors tell a robotic vacuum cleaner when it has run into an object

- Acidity (pH) – pH is the measure of acidity. Acidity measurement is important in science and in medicine. The pH of blood will increase in some medical conditions, including oxygen starvation. Breweries and water treatment works require accurate measurement of water acidity.

- Motion – a sensor can be used to detect motion in a room. For example a burglar alarm may use a beam of infra-red light. If the beam is broken a camera may switch on or an alarm might sound. Some computer games use a camera or light system to detect the movement of a person playing the game. Another kind of motion detector will record the movement of a single object. For example a games controller can be moved around in the air. Motion detectors inside the controller will measure the its movement in three dimensions.

 Sensors inside the hand-held controller detect its movement in all directions

 This computer can detect the motion of the game player

Test yourself

1. What are the advantages of a temperature sensor, compared to a person reading a thermometer and typing the temperature into a computer?

2. A restaurant needs to store food in strictly controlled conditions. Explain how sensors can help with this.

3. Explain why an object that moves about on its own needs to include a pressure sensor.

4. If you were to set up a weather station what sensors would you include and why?

Learning activity

Pictures on this page show different type of motion and pressure sensors used in common devices:

- to clean a floor
- to read human body movement
- to play sports.

Investigate one of the devices shown, or a similar device, and write a report on the technology in use.

Syllabus reference

1.3.3 Input devices

Learners should be able to describe how sensors are used in real-life scenarios, for example: street lights, security devices, pollution control, games, and household and industrial applications.

See also:

4.2 Output devices (Actuators; Manufacturing objects)

Control systems

Introduction

You have learned that sensors detect environmental conditions and convert them into digital data. Sensors operate automatically. Computers fitted with automated sensors can be used to control physical processes. You will learn about control systems in this section.

Feedback

You have learned that a computer processes input and produces output. In a control system, the computer:

- monitors an environmental condition (this is the input)
- controls a physical process that changes the environmental condition (this is the output).

The computer measures the effect of its output. It takes this measurement as an input, to decide how to adjust its output. This is called feedback.

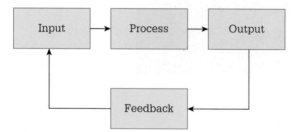

↟ The computer output "feeds back" to input

For example, a computer may control a bread oven. The computer measures the temperature of the oven (input). The computer turns the heat on and off (output).

If the oven is too warm, the computer turns the heat off. If the oven is too cool, the computer turns the heat on. This cycle of input and output continues without any need for a human operator. The computer adjust its output, and measures the effect. Using this method of input, output and feedback a computer can control a wide range of physical processes in the real world.

Why control systems are useful

Systems that use sensors to measure and control processes are very common. They can run continuously without a human user working the controls. Computer-controlled processes have many advantages:

- A computer can monitor a process constantly without getting tired or bored.

- With the right sensors, computers can measure a wide range of conditions very accurately.

- Computers can go to places where it is hard for humans to go, such as under the sea or inside an industrial process.

- Computers can react very quickly in an emergency situation.

There are some disadvantages. Computer systems can only carry out predefined responses. In extreme or unforeseen conditions, the computer response could be wrong. In that case, a human operator will step in to make repairs or adjustments.

Examples of systems that use sensors

- Manufacture – computers fitted with sensors can control machines, for example in factories. Computer-controlled machines can make things very quickly and accurately. For example, cars are built using computer-controlled systems. Learn more about computer-aided manufacture on pages 114–119.

- Warnings – a computer can monitor a process or environment and raise an alarm if it goes outside safe limits. Examples include fire or flood warning systems. Security systems can be monitored by computers.

- Research – a computer can take readings and measurements and record them for research. The computer provides continuous accurate measurements day and night. Another advantage is that a computer can take measurements in places a scientist could not go. An example is the Mars Rover project.

- Household uses – computers can control household processes and devices such as washing machines or central heating.

- Transport – computers can control aeroplanes and ships. The autopilot takes measurements such as speed and altitude and adjusts the controls. In recent times, self-driving cars are being developed.

⬆ A computer in the car monitors the environment and controls the car's motion

Test yourself

1. Why are sensors needed for a control system?

2. What is feedback?

3. What are the advantages of using a computer to control an industrial process?

4. What are the advantages of using a computer to monitor a patient in hospital?

Learning activity

Research the development of the self-driving car. Do you think these cars will be common one day?

Syllabus reference

1.3.4 Output devices

Learners should be able to: describe the principles of operation of the following output devices: flat-panel display screens, such as liquid crystal display (LCD) and light-emitting diode (LED) display; LCD projectors and digital light projectors (DLP).

See also:

4.1 Input devices (Touch screens)

4.2 Output devices

Monitors and display

Introduction

This chapter is about hardware. This topic is about output devices. Output devices convert the information inside the processor into a useful form outside the computer. In this section you will learn about monitors or screens, which display information in a form human users can read and understand.

Key features of monitors

A monitor is the screen attached to a computer. The monitor is an output device. It displays text, images and video. A monitor display is known as "soft copy" of data.

A monitor gives instant results. As you work at the computer you see the screen display respond immediately to your actions (such as typing). A key disadvantage of a monitor, however, is that as the display changes you lose the previous information. You have to save or print your work if you want to keep it.

How monitors work

At one time all computer and TV screens used cathode ray tube (CRT) technology. These screens were not flat. They were large and heavy. You would not have been able to use them with portable devices or laptops. Nowadays flat-screen technology is used. There are two main types of flat screen: LCD and LED.

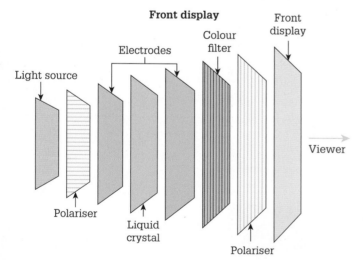

↑ LCD cross-section

Liquid crystal display (LCD)

Some computer monitors contain a layer of liquid crystal held between transparent sheets. In an electric field, the structure of the crystal alters to line up its molecules. This then affects light passing through. An originally opaque display will become transparent, letting light through.

Sending different electrical signals to the display makes a pattern of opaque and transparent spots. A microscopic colour filter over each position changes the colour of each spot.

The LCD itself does not emit light. A backlight shines through the display to make coloured patterns as it shines through the surface.

Light-emitting diode (LED)

A light-emitting diode (LED) is an electronic device that makes coloured light when an electric current flows through it. An LED is like a small light bulb.

It uses less power and emits less heat than an ordinary light bulb, but it is much more expensive to buy. Small LEDs can be joined together to make indicators and warning signs. In large numbers, controlled by a computer, they can make large display screens for pictures without much detail.

Millions of tiny organic LEDs (OLEDs) arranged in a grid are used to make bright, clear high-resolution displays for smartphones and tablet computers. OLED displays for larger TVs are far more expensive than LCDs.

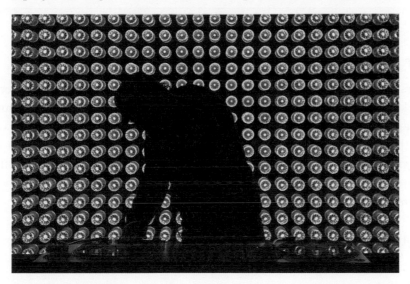

⬆ LEDs produce light

Projectors

Projectors are used to display computer images for a large group of people to look at. There are two common types:

- An LCD projector where a beam of light passes through the LCD and onto a wall screen, and you look at the screen.
- A digital light projector (DLP) works by shining a light onto a grid of thousands of tiny mirrors that can move. As the mirrors tilt, some shine light towards the wall screen, and some deflect the light away. This makes the shapes and colours of the image. DLP is used in many cinemas. This is called digital cinema.

Q

Test yourself

1. Contrast the light source of an LCD and an LED display.
2. LED bulbs use less electricity than ordinary light bulbs. Why don't houses use LEDs for all their lighting?
3. To see the display from a projector you need another item. What is it?
4. What are the advantages of an LCD display compared to an LED display?

Q

Learning activity

Research the advantages of digital cinema over other ways of distributing and showing films in cinemas.

Syllabus reference

1.3.4 Output devices

Learners should be able to describe the principles of operation of the following output devices: inkjet and laser printers.

See also:

4.2 Output devices (Manufacturing objects – 3D printers)

Printers

Introduction

A printer is an output device that converts the digital data inside a computer into a permanent paper form. This is called hard copy. In this section you will learn about printer technology.

Key features of printers

Printers take longer than monitors to produce output from the computer. It may take a few minutes for information inside the computer to be output onto paper. Paper copy takes up a lot of space compared to digital data stored inside the computer. However, the big advantage of printing data is that you have a permanent copy of the data. Hard copy can be taken away from the computer. Hard copy is still available when the computer is turned off or being used for other work.

How printers work

The most common types of printer are inkjet and laser printers.

Inkjet

The most common type of printer is an inkjet printer. Small inkjet printers are the least expensive form of printer. Inkjet printers spray ink from nozzles onto paper. The ink is sprayed in lines across the page. Different nozzles spray different colours. The spray from each jet is turned on and off by an electrical signal. By changing the signal the computer can change what is printed out.

⬆ A small inkjet printer

Inkjet printers can produce a wide range of high quality colour printing. They are a good choice for a small classroom or a family printer. They are not very fast. The main disadvantage is the price of the ink. Refilling the ink when it runs out can be almost as expensive as buying a new printer.

Laser

A laser printer does not use ink. Instead it uses a fine black or coloured dust called toner. The laser printer contains a drum (a cylinder). The drum is coated with static electricity. The pattern of static electricity is altered by a laser beam shining on the drum.

The static electricity picks up the toner and makes it stick to the outside of the drum. It picks up toner in the shape of a complete page of printing. A piece of paper rolls past the drum and the toner drops off the drum onto the page. This transfers the image onto the paper.

Laser printers are typically larger and more expensive to buy than inkjet printers. They work much faster. The fastest prints 200 pages a minute. They are good for organisations that need to produce a lot of printed material. A laser printer might be shared by everyone in a large office.

Many laser printers can print in black and white only, but colour printers are available.

Choosing a printer

To choose the right printer, you have to consider:

- how much money you have to spend
- how fast the printer needs to be
- what quality of output you want
- whether you will most be printing in black and white, or colour.

There is no hard and fast rule about which type is best. You have to compare quality, price and speed of particular printers, having decided which factors are most important for your needs.

The highest quality realistic colour images are produced by "photograph quality" inkjet printers.

⬆ A large laser printer

Test yourself

1. A friend asks you what printer he should buy. Explain what factors he should consider when choosing a printer.

2. Continuing to answer your friend, compare the advantages and disadvantages of an inkjet printer and a laser printer.

3. Some printer manufacturers sell printers at a loss – they charge less to buy the printer than it costs them to make it. How do these companies manage to make a profit?

4. Explain how the two types of printer work. You may carry out additional Internet research to help with your answer.

Learning activity

Research the best printer for your classroom. Take all the factors into account. Write a report explaining your choice.

Syllabus reference

1.3.4 Output devices

Learners should be able to: describe the principles of operation of the following output devices: speakers and headphones; describe how these principles are applied to real-life scenarios.

See also:

4.1 Input devices (Camera and microphone)

Sound

Introduction

Sound is formed by vibrations in the air. Computers can output data that makes sound. In this section you will learn about sound output.

Key features of sound output

Sound output is temporary. It fades and changes immediately, leaving no record. However, sound output can attract your attention or give you information when you are busy with other activities. Warning sounds and instructions from the computer use sound output. Sound is a way of getting information from a computer when you cannot stop to look at a screen display. Sound output such as music is valued in its own right.

How sound output is made

All sound output depends on turning electronic signals from the computer into vibrations in the air.

Speakers

A speaker, also called a loudspeaker, makes a sound that can fill a room. Most speakers contain a plastic or metal cone. The bottom of the cone is fixed to a coil of wire that surrounds a magnet. Electrical signals make the magnet attract and repel the coil. The coil moves backwards and forward, pulling and pushing the speaker cone. The moving cone pumps sounds out into the air.

Other types of speaker are available to convert digital signals into sound waves.

Most types of speaker can be plugged into a computer. The speaker will produce sounds from the electrical signals it receives from the computer.

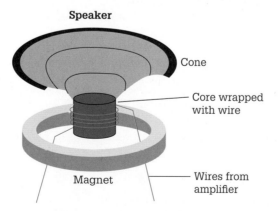

Speaker

Cone

Core wrapped with wire

Magnet

Wires from amplifier

⬆ A speaker turns electrical signals into sounds

Headphones

Headphones allow people to listen to music, or hear information from a computer, without disturbing anyone else.

Headphones have two earpieces. They fit into the listener's ears, or outside each ear. Each earpiece has a very small speaker in it. It works in just the same way as a large speaker. As the speaker is inside or close to the ears, the sound can be quiet, but the listener will still hear it very clearly.

Choice of sound output

Most computers have built-in speakers. The quality of the sound is usually not very good. People who want better quality sound can buy better speakers and plug them into the computer. Very expensive speakers are available. They make high-quality sound, even at loud volume. This is a good choice for people who are very serious about music. However, loud music can harm your hearing, and annoy other people, so use speakers sensibly and with consideration for others.

People who want to listen to sound privately, for example in a shared office or classroom, will use headphones. When you plug in headphones, the main speakers stop working. The sound only comes through the headphones. There are concerns that using headphones with the sound too loud can harm your hearing.

 Ear buds are tiny speakers that fit inside the ear

When you are choosing a sound output device, think about your own needs, and the needs of the people who are sharing space with you.

Test yourself

1. In this section you learned about one of the most common types of speaker. Explain how it turns digital signals into sound waves.

2. A tablet computer has a built-in speaker, or you can plug in headphones. Explain a situation where you would choose to use the built-in speaker and a situation where you would use the headphones.

3. What are ear buds and how are they used in headphones?

4. List the factors you should take into account when choosing a sound output device.

Learning activity

Research four different headphones that are for sale. Compare their features. Which one do you like best?

Syllabus reference

1.3.4 Output devices

Learners should be able to: describe the principles of operation of the following output devices: actuators; describe how these principles are applied to real-life scenarios.

See also:

4.1 Input devices (Control systems)

Actuators

Introduction

We often think of computer output as visual or printed display of information. However, computers are also used to control machines and this is a form of output. In this section you will learn about how computers control movement. This is the technology that makes robots work.

Control as output

The data inside a computer is in binary electronic form. It cannot be understood by a human user. Output devices are used to turn this data into a form people can understand. This is what we often think of as computer output.

Another type of output is where the computer controls a process. Instead of showing you the data, the computer uses the data to do something useful.

Use of actuators

An actuator is any motor that moves objects about. In the modern world most actuators are electrical. The motion of an electrical actuator can be controlled by a computer.

In *4.1 Input devices (Control systems)* you learned about control systems. A computer controls a process. The computer uses feedback to monitor the process. Many control systems use actuators.

Automation

Automation uses the principles of feedback to control a process. Automation needs input devices and output devices. Actuators and sensors are used as follows:

- Actuators are used as output devices. The computer controls the movement of a machine.
- Sensors are used as input devices. They measure the effect of the actuator. They feed this data back to the computer.

The computer adjusts its control of the actuator, based on the feedback from the sensors. Instructions inside the computer tell it how to respond to different inputs. For example, if an engine gets too hot, the computer can shut it down to cool off.

The key fact about automation is that this process runs on its own. Automated processes can take place without a human user.

Servomechanism

A servomechanism is a machine that uses feedback to regulate motion. Instructions tell the computer where an object is supposed to be. The computer measures where the object actually is. It moves the object to bring it to the right place.

In real life this can be quite a complex process. For example, a computer can be used to keep a aircraft at a constant altitude, measuring changes in air pressure to detect that altitude has changed.

↑ A robot uses actuators and sensors

Robotics

A robot is a machine controlled by a computer that can move around on its own. The computer, the sensors and the actuator might all be held in the same case. One of the tasks of the robot is to control its own motion. It uses the servomechanism method.

A robot is usually designed to do useful tasks. It will have actuators that let it do this work. For example, the Mars Rover moves about the surface of Mars where a person cannot go. It takes measurements and readings and sends the data back to Earth.

 Each Mars Rover moves without direct human control

In stories, robots often look like metal people, with faces and arms and legs. In real life, robots do not need faces with eyes and nose, because they have input sensors. They do not need human-shaped arms and legs; they have mechanisms to do particular tasks.

Q Test yourself

1. An actuator is often paired with a sensor to make an automated process. Explain why automation requires sensors as well as actuators.

2. "Not all output devices display data for humans to read." Explain this statement.

3. Why does a robot need a servomechanism?

4. What are the advantages of using a computerised system to take measurements on the surface of Mars, instead of a person doing this?

Q Learning activity

Create a sketched design for a robot that could pick fruit from a tree. Indicate the sensors and actuators that would be needed.

Syllabus reference

1.3.4 Output devices

Learners should be able to: describe the principles of operation of the following output devices: 2D and 3D cutters, 3D printers; describe how these principles are applied to real-life scenarios.

Manufacturing objects

Introduction

You have learned that computers can control the movement of machines. Computers can control machines that make solid objects. In this section you will learn about some of the ways computers can create objects.

Making objects

Computers can control machines that make objects. This is computerised manufacture.

There are many advantages to using computers in manufacturing processes. Computers can work with great accuracy. They can carry out the same action in exactly the same way over and over again. They do not get tired. Often the objects are produced more cheaply than those made by human hands.

There are some disadvantages. The equipment can be expensive. Computers cannot invent new objects, or work creatively. Many people like the variation and uniqueness of hand-made objects.

Computerised manufacture is used when objects need to be made quickly and very accurately, for example car parts.

There are two main ways that computers make objects:

- They start with a solid block of material, and cut some away of this to leave the required shape (cutters)

- They start with nothing and add layers of material until the required shape has been formed (3D printers).

Cutters

Cutters use various methods to cut matter away. One example is a laser beam controlled by a computer.

What is a laser?

Ordinary white light radiates energy from its source as electromagnetic waves moving in all directions and with a lot of different wavelengths. A laser generates its light in such a way that the waves reinforce each other, moving in the same direction and with the same wavelength. This makes the laser's beam much more effective at transferring energy to a small area.

A powerful enough laser focused on a small spot transfers enough energy to heat up and melt steel.

2D cutter

A focused laser beam is directed at a block of material. The material might be metal, plastic, silicon, fabric or even diamond. The laser melts, burns or vaporises the material. It cuts very precisely and leaves a high-quality surface. The laser beam can also be used to engrave a pattern.

Remember that 2D means a flat surface. A 2D cuts a flat shape or design, normally cutting from above as it moves in two dimensions over the workpiece.

↑ A 2D cutter in action

3D cutter

A 3D cutter uses cutting technology to remove material just as a 2D cutter does. It works from a variety of angles, cutting the material into a solid shape. With a 3D cutter almost any shape can be carved out of a solid block of material.

Cutters use high temperature and can produce dust, shards, or gas as the material is cut away. This makes them dangerous to use.

3D printer

3D printers make a 3D shape out of material such as plastic. A print head moves over a table, melting and sticking tiny dots of the material where it is needed. The joined-together dots solidify into a flat layer of material. The first layer is laid directly on the table; then the print head moves up slightly and lays the next layer on the first. It continues until it has built enough layers of dots in the right places to make the entire shape.

3D printers need not be expensive to buy or to use. It depends on the type of material used to form the shape.

Test yourself

1. What are the advantages of computerised manufacture compared to making things by hand?

2. Explain the difference between a 2D and a 3D cutter.

3. Contrast the way a cutter and a 3D printer create objects.

4. A museum wants to make an exact replica of a dinosaur skull. What input and output devices might they use?

Learning activity

Look at cutters and 3D printers in action, and make notes. If you cannot see them in real life, look at demonstration videos on YouTube.

⬆ A 3D printer in action

Syllabus reference

1.3.4 Output devices

Learners should be able to: describe how output devices are applied to real-life scenarios for example use of small screens on mobile devices; printing single items on demand or in large volumes.

Output in real life

Introduction

In this section you have learned about some of the output devices that are available. Output devices turn the digital signals inside the computer into a useful form. Some output devices make digital content understandable. Data could be displayed, or printed as hard copy, or made into sound. Other output devices use the digital signals inside the computer to control a device or make an object. In this section you will review some of the real life uses of output devices.

Screens: mobile devices

Mobile devices are very compact. The touchscreen of a mobile phone or tablet works as both an input and an output device. The screen is small. Although people want a clear image, they also want a very small device. The design of an app for a mobile device must take the screen size into account.

⬆ The screen of a mobile phone is the main input and output device

Changes in technology that have made mobile devices possible include:

- smaller and cheaper components
- flat screens
- screens that can be used as input and output devices.

Printers: hard copy

Printers vary a great deal. Some are inexpensive and handle limited printing. Others are very expensive and can handle a large print run. Quality also varies. The highest quality is photographic quality.

In ordinary personal computer use, the monitor is the main form of output. A permanent record is not needed. A typical individual user will print out a small number of pages a day, for example a letter to send or homework to hand in. The printer may sit unused for most of the time.

A large commercial organisation may produce hundreds of pages of printing a day – or even more. Large amounts of important data may be output as lists and tables of figures. Each sheet has different data. Printing is used because a permanent record of the data is needed.

Commercial printers use digital printing technology to produce multiple copies of the same item, for example magazines, advertising leaflets or food wrappers. In this case every item of printing is produced using the same data. It is a manufacturing process.

Manufacture: CAD/CAM

3D printers are usually used in a system called CAD/CAM, which stands for "computer aided design/computer aided manufacture". Objects are designed on the computer screen. Special design software lets you create a 3D image. You can rotate it on the screen to see the shape from all sides.

There are advantages to designing using the computer. It enables you to:

- try out different designs without having to make them all
- run tests on the strengths and stresses of an object
- see how well different objects fit together
- work out what materials are needed and what the cost will be.

When the design is ready, it can be sent to a 3D printer that makes the shape.

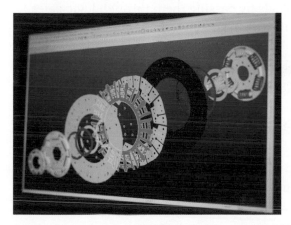

⬆ An object can be designed on screen using CAD/CAM

Test yourself

1. What are the advantages and disadvantages of using a mobile tablet compared to a laptop?

2. Imagine you have been put in charge of printing a school or college magazine. Discuss the features you would want from the printer.

3. A city wanted a new bridge. An architect created a new bridge using CAD. What information could he get from the on-screen design?

4. The screen is an important input and output device of a mobile phone. What other input and output devices might a mobile phone have?

Learning activity

In the future, examinations may be taken on mobile devices instead of written on paper. Design the screen for a mobile app a student could use to take an examination in your favourite subject. Remember to consider input and output options.

Syllabus reference

1.3.5 Memory, storage devices and media

Learners should be able to show understanding of the difference between: primary, secondary and off-line storage; read-only memory (ROM), and random access memory (RAM).

See also:

1.3 Data storage
3.3 Inside the CPU

4.3 Memory and storage

Primary storage

> ### Introduction
>
> You have learned that computers process data in digital form. Storage devices hold digital data when it is not in use by the processor. In this section you will learn about primary storage. This is storage that is attached directly to the CPU.

Inside the CPU

In Chapter 3 you learned about the CPU, which transforms digital data. The data is held in memory as electric charges and passes down buses as electrical signals. The CPU changes those signals by passing them through logic gates and returns them to memory. In this way the computer changes data into information.

Inside the processor, data and instructions are held in registers. A register can hold only one item at a time, and there is no room in the CPU for more than a few registers. However, as they are inside the CPU, they are very fast: the CPU can read and use their contents with almost no delay. There is no need to wait for a signal to arrive from outside the CPU.

The speed of a computer is limited by how quickly the computer can access its data; that is, how quickly it can fetch data and put it into the registers.

Main memory

Main memory holds data as electrical charges. Main memory holds the instructions and data the CPU needs for its current task. Data passes from main memory to the CPU along fast connections called buses.

Main memory is made using a memory system called RAM.

Random access memory (RAM)

RAM is the active electronic memory of the computer. It holds all the data and instructions the CPU needs for whatever task it is currently doing. The CPU can access the data in RAM very quickly. A computer with a lot of RAM is a fast computer. If a computer does not have enough RAM, then it will be slower.

RAM works by storing electrical charges. The charge (or lack of charge) at a single location represents a 1 (or 0) bit in a binary number. When the electricity is switched off, the charges dissipate, so all the data disappears. Memory that forgets its contents when the electricity is turned off is called volatile memory. To summarise:

- The advantages of RAM are that it holds lots of data and instructions, and it is quick for the CPU to access.

- The disadvantage of RAM is that it is volatile: it loses all its data when the computer is switched off.

When you first turn on a computer, its RAM is empty. That means RAM cannot be used to store the start-up instructions for the computer.

Read-only memory (ROM)

ROM is a small area of non-volatile memory. As ROM is read-only, the computer can read data or instructions stored there, but cannot write to ROM. This means it cannot store completed work or new instructions. The contents of the ROM are set up in the factory when the computer is made. To summarise:

- The advantage of ROM is that its contents are not lost when the computer is switched off.
- The disadvantage of ROM is that its contents cannot be changed, so it cannot be used to store new data.

ROM is used to store the instructions that make the computer start up. These instructions are read by the CPU when you switch on the computer.

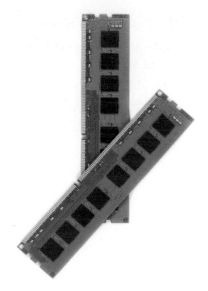

⬆ By adding extra RAM to a computer you can make it work faster

Test yourself

1. What does "volatile" mean?

2. Why does a computer speed up when you install more RAM?

3. What does "read-only" mean?

4. Why is the RAM completely empty when you turn on a computer?

Learning activities

1. Complete the following table to set out the advantages and disadvantages of each type of memory.

Type of memory	Advantage	Disadvantage
Registers		
RAM		
ROM		

2. The instructions held in ROM are called the BIOS. Research what BIOS means and why it is needed when the computer is switched on.

Syllabus reference

1.3.5 Memory, storage devices and media

Learners should be able to calculate the storage requirement of a file.

See also:

1.3 Data storage

Measuring storage

Introduction

You have learned about digital storage. In this section you will learn how file size is measured in bits and bytes.

Bits and bytes

In Chapter 1 you saw that all binary data is stored as a pattern of 1s and 0s. A single binary digit – a 1 or a 0 – is called a bit. "Bit" is short for binary digit. Bytes are grouped into kilobytes, megabytes and gigabytes. Look back to *1.1 Binary systems (Bits and bytes)* to remind yourself how many bytes there are in each of these.

You learned that primary storage is RAM. A modern computer might have 8 gigabytes of RAM.

Secondary storage

Secondary storage, sometimes called permanent storage or permanent memory, is storage outside main memory. The data in secondary storage is not lost when the computer is switched off. However, access to secondary storage is much slower than access to primary storage.

Most secondary storage uses magnetic or optical media, or semiconductor flash memory. You will learn more about these different types of secondary storage in the rest of this chapter.

Files

Data in secondary storage is organised into files. A file is a collection of data or instructions which all belong together. Here are some examples:

- If you make a document or image it is stored as a file.
- The instructions in a program to run software such as a game or a word processor are stored as a file.

Files are contained in folders. When you open a folder you can look at the files that are stored there. The files may be shown as small pictures called icons.

⬆ This folder holds several different files

File size

Different files can be of very different sizes. Look back at *1.3 Data storage* to see how data is stored. Some data formats use a lot of space.

File size is measured in different units:

- A page of text may be 5 kilobytes (5KB).
- A picture may be 3 megabytes (3MB).
- A movie may be 4 gigabytes (4GB).

You can change the display from the operating system of your computer to show file sizes as well as their names.

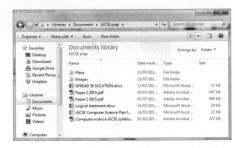

⬆ These file sizes are shown in kilobytes

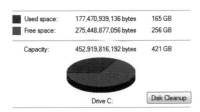

⬆ This hard disk has a total capacity of 421GB and 256GB is available

Storage requirements

Different types of storage have different capacities. Videos and high-quality sound use a lot of storage.

Like file size, storage capacity is measured in kilobytes, megabytes and gigabytes. Typically, some of the storage capacity will have been used, and some will be empty. You can use the empty space to store another file, provided that the storage space is bigger than the size of the file. You should try not to fill storage to maximum capacity, as this slows the computer.

Not all the empty storage space is available: you will probably be unable to fill the store exactly.

Test yourself

1. A file is 0.5MB. How many kilobytes is that?
2. In the picture on this page the hard disk has a capacity of 421GB. How much of it is already in use?
3. I want to store a movie with a file size of 15GB. Is there space on this hard disk?
4. I have 1GB of available storage. How many photographs that each have a file size of 10MB could I store?

Learning activity

Investigate the storage area you use in your school or college to save your work. What is the capacity of this storage? How much of it is currently in use and how much is free?

Syllabus reference

1.1.3 Data storage

Learners should be able to show understanding that sound, pictures etc. are stored in different formats.

1.3.5 Memory, storage devices and media

Learners should be able to calculate the storage requirement of a file.

See also:

1.3 Data storage

Introduction

You have learned that file size is measured in bits and bytes. In this section you will learn how to estimate the size of a data file from the amount and type of data that it contains.

Why file size matters

File size is related to data quality. A high quality sound or image makes a larger file. Large data files take up more storage space. A large file takes more time to transmit through a communication link. It is important to:

- Estimate file size when making choices about file formats.
- Check file size before transmitting or saving to storage media.

File sizes are expressed in bytes. A byte is 8 bits.

Text files

A text file consists of a series of characters. ASCII code uses one byte to store one character. So the file size of a text file is the same as the number of characters (including spaces). However, there are exceptions:

- Unicode has codes for more characters so it uses more bytes: up to 4 bytes per character
- A document includes extra bytes which store data about formatting, such as font and page size.

See page 22 for more information on text storage.

Example

To estimate the size of an ASCII text file, assume one byte per character. A file with 50 000 characters uses about 50 kilobytes of storage.

Image files

An image is made of individual dots called pixels. A bitmap image file stores information about each pixel. The number of bytes used depends on:

- How many pixels there are in the image: a large image or a high resolution image will have more pixels
- How many bits are used to store each pixel: images with more complex colour choices use more bits for each pixel.

See pages 24–25 for more information on image storage.

Example

To estimate the size of an image file, multiply the number of pixels by the number of bits per pixel. Then divide by 8 to give the number of bytes.

A small image is 40 rows of 150 pixels. Each pixel uses 256 bits.

> Number of pixels: 40 * 150 = 6000
>
> Number of bits: 6000 * 256 = 1 536 000 bits
>
> Number of bytes: 1 536 000 / 8 = 192 000

How many of these images could you store in one megabyte?

Sound and video files

The number of bits needed to store one second of sound or video is called "bit rate". To calculate the size of a sound or video file you multiply the bit rate by the number of seconds of recording. Bit rate is affected by bit depth, sample rate and number of channels. See pages 26–27 for more information about bit rate.

Example

One second of audio-quality sound uses 176 400 bytes. Multiply this by the number of seconds in the recording:

> 30 seconds = 30 * 176 400 bytes = 5 292 000

So, speaking roughly, we need just over 5 MB for a 30-second recording of high quality sound.

Other factors

Almost all files include additional information as well as the data content. This information helps the computer to use the file. This extra information uses extra storage space. The amount of extra information varies a great deal. When you estimate file size, remember the real file will be bigger because of this extra information.

Test yourself

1. A plain ASCII text file has 20 000 words. Each word has an average of 7 characters. Estimate the number of bytes in the file.

2. A bitmap image has 500 rows of 800 pixels. It uses the 256-colour format. How many bytes in this file?

3. If the same image was stored in monochrome, how many bytes in the file?

4. Roughly how many seconds of high quality sound could you store in 1GB of storage?

Learning activity

Find examples of audio and video clips that are stored as files. Divide the file size by the number of seconds in the clip to estimate the bitrate of the recording.

Watch or listen to the clips to see if you can spot a difference in quality. Is quality strongly linked to bitrate?

Syllabus reference

1.3.5 Memory, storage devices and media

Learners should be able to: describe the principles of operation of a range of types of storage device and media including magnetic; secondary storage (hard disk drive – HDD), off-line storage (removable HDD).

Magnetic storage

Introduction

You have learned that secondary storage is a non-volatile store for data accessed through a peripheral device. "Non-volatile" means the data is not lost when the computer is switched off. One way that data is held is using magnetic storage. In this section you will learn about the different types of magnetic storage.

Magnetic storage

Some materials such as iron oxide are easy to magnetise by bringing a magnet near them. The magnetised spot of material is itself a magnet, with a north pole and a south pole. The direction the magnetised spot faces (NS or SN) can be used to represent one bit of binary data: one direction means 1 and the other means 0.

A magnetic storage device converts data from the computer into spots of magnetism. The device uses an electric current in a coil of wire. Current flowing in one direction writes a 1 and in the other it writes a 0.

The spot stays magnetised after the electric current is taken away. That means the data remains even after electricity is switched off. If you delete a file, the spots can be remagnetised, so they can be used for new files.

Hard disk drive (HDD)

Secondary storage is storage outside main memory. It takes longer for the processor to access data in secondary storage than in main memory, but the data in secondary storage is not lost when the computer is switched off.

The main type of secondary storage is a hard disk drive (HDD). This is a stack of rigid discs spinning in a metal case. The discs are magnetised and used to store data. There is a direct wired connection between the HDD and the processor.

⬆ If you open the computer case you will see the hard disk drive (HDD)

Storage on the HDD has advantages and disadvantages:

- As it is wired directly to the processor, access to the HDD is quite fast.
- An internal hard drive is fixed inside a single computer, so you cannot easily take it away to use on another computer.

Off-line storage

Off-line storage is like secondary storage but it is outside the computer. The storage must be plugged into the computer through a port. Access to off-line storage is slower than secondary storage.

Portable hard disk

A portable (or removable) hard disk works in the same way as a normal HDD. The only difference is that it is outside the case of the computer. It is connected through a cable that plugs into the computer case. When using a portable hard disk:

- access may be slower than an internal hard drive because the portable hard disk is outside the computer
- you can unplug the drive and move it to another computer, so you can take the data with you.

⬆ A removable HDD can be moved between computers

Magnetic tape

Magnetic tape is a long reel of plastic tape. It can be magnetised to store data. Tape is inexpensive and it can store a lot of data. However, it is very slow to get the data off the tape. That is because you have to wind through the whole reel of tape to get to the data you want. Tape is used to make backups.

Advantages and disadvantages

Type of magnetic storage	Advantage	Disadvantage
Internal hard disk	This allows quick access to high capacity storage	Data can only be accessed from one computer or its local network
Portable hard disk	Portable – you can take the data between different computers	Access to stored data can be slower than with an internal disk
Magnetic tape	This has very high capacity and is not too expensive	Access to stored data is very slow

⬆ Magnetic tape

Test yourself

1. What is the advantage of magnetic storage compared to electronic storage in RAM?

2. Why is it quicker for the computer to access data from an internal hard drive than from a portable hard drive?

3. If I want to access my stored data quickly I would not use magnetic tape. Why not?

4. What is the advantage of an external hard drive?

Syllabus reference

1.3.5 Secondary storage – optical

Learners should be able to describe the principles of operation of a range of types of storage device and media including optical, off-line: compact disc (CD), digital versatile disc (DVD), Blu-ray disc.

Optical storage

Introduction

You have learned about digital storage. In this section you will learn about optical storage, which is storing digital data in a form that can be read by a laser beam.

Optical storage

All digital data is in the form of 1s and 0s. On an optical disc, the 1s and 0s are represented by microscopic pits or marks made in a spiral pattern on a thin reflective layer.

To read the data, an optical drive spins the disc and focuses a laser's light onto its surface. When the light hits a pit or mark, its reflection from the disc is dimmer than from the unmarked background. A light sensor on the drive detects this. The difference in light represents the 1s and 0s of digital data.

The laser that reads the pits can focus on a very small spot, so the pits can be made very small and close together. A CD pit is less than one micrometre across. A micrometre is one millionth of a metre. Millions of pits can fit on the disc surface, so it can hold a lot of data.

⬆ A CD uses optical storage

Storage media

Storage media means the material that is used to store data, for example magnetic tape or CD. Optical media can be used for any data, but the most typical use is to store sound and video:

- CD – a standard CD will hold about 80 minutes of music.
- DVD (digital versatile disc) – the pits on a DVD are read with a narrower laser spot than is used for a CD. The pits on DVD are smaller than those on a CD so a DVD can store more data. A DVD can hold several hours of video.
- Blu-ray – a Blu-ray disc has even smaller pits and can hold high-resolution video. Blu-ray systems use blue laser light to read the disc.

Read and write access

Data on a standard CD cannot be changed. The pits have been moulded into the surface so the data is fixed. Different types of optical media offer different types of access.

Read-only

You can buy a CD with music on it, or a film on DVD. This storage is "read only". Your computer or DVD player will be able to read the data, but you cannot make changes to it. it. It is manufactured by stamping the pattern of pits all at once into the molten plastic disc as it is moulded.

Write-once

You can also buy blank discs called CD-R and DVD-R. A computer's DVD writer works by focusing a laser onto the disc's reflective layer to burn marks into it. Its less powerful reading laser can detect these marks the same way it detects the pits from a stamped CD or DVD. You can store extra files at the end of the disc, but once it is full you cannot clear it for new data.

Rewritable

The data on a standard CD or DVD cannot be altered or deleted. A different type of disc has a special surface that can be melted, so its marks disappear. The data is erased and the disk can be used for new data. This type of disk is called CD-RW, DVD-RW or DVD+RW (RW stands for "rewritable").

Advantages and disadvantages

CDs and other optical media are a cheap form of storage. CDs are portable, light and don't take up much space. A disadvantage is that standard CDs cannot be erased to hold new data. CDs can be broken or scratched.

Test yourself

1. What is the difference between a read-only, a write-once and a rewriteable CD?

2. Explain why a DVD can hold more data than a CD.

3. What is the advantage of using a CD for storage compared to using an internal HDD?

4. What is the disadvantage of optical storage compared to magnetic storage?

Syllabus reference

1.3.5 Solid state drive, USB flash memory

Learners should be able to show understanding of currently available storage solutions; solid state drive (SSD), USB flash memory.

See also:

2.1 Data transmission (Data bus – USB)

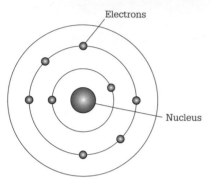

↑ Electrons are one of the basic particles of matter

Solid state (flash) storage

Introduction

The most recently invented type of storage is called "solid state storage" or "flash memory". Use of this type of storage is widespread because it has many advantages. Learn about solid state in this section.

Solid state storage

All atoms are composed of electrons in motion around a nucleus. Electrons are very small particles. An electric current is a flow of electrons. A material that doesn't normally let electrons flow is called an insulator.

Flash memory works by trapping electrons. A "flash" of electricity forces electrons through an insulator. When the electricity is removed, the electrons are stuck there. The memory device can detect the stuck electrons, so they represent data: a location with stuck electrons represents a 0 bit, and if it has none, it represents a 1.

Once the electrons have been put in place, they stay there even when the computer is switched off. A flash of electricity in the reverse direction will drain any trapped electrons and erase the data. This means flash memory is readable, writable and erasable storage.

This type of storage is called solid state because the storage happens inside the solid structure of matter. It is called flash because of the flash of electricity that sets the electrons in place.

Storage media

Flash memory is built into an integrated circuit (IC). It can be packaged in many different ways.

USB flash drive

You have learned that USB stands for "universal serial bus". USB is a type of connector that allows all types of peripherals to be plugged into a computer. A USB flash drive is a flash memory IC in a USB plug. It can be plugged into any modern computer. This is a very convenient type of storage. It holds a lot of data for its size.

Using a USB drive for storage is very popular. There are several other names for a USB drive, such as a thumb drive, flash memory or data stick.

Solid state drive (SSD)

Flash memory can be used in place of a computer's built-in hard disk drive (HDD), which you learned about on page 126. A solid state drive (SSD) uses the same case and connections as an HDD but contains a number of flash memory ICs. It is sometimes called a solid state disk, but it does not contain magnetic discs or any other moving parts.

Compared to a magnetic hard drive, flash memory is reliable and has high storage for its size. The disadvantage is that it is more expensive, adding to the cost of the device.

↑ A USB drive

⬆ A solid state drive

Mobile devices

Many mobile devices such as smartphones and tablets use solid state storage. This means they can hold a lot of data, and they are light and portable.

Advantages and concerns

Solid state storage has many important advantages compared to other types of storage. It is small, light, stores a lot of data, and is erasable and rewriteable. For this reason, flash memory is a very popular choice, and has replaced other types of storage in everyday use.

Flash memory is slightly more expensive than magnetic memory. However, its price is coming down.

Some people are concerned about the long-term reliability of flash memory. Flash memory is guaranteed for a certain number of read or write actions. This number is very high – hundreds of thousands of actions. However, when this number is exceeded the storage may start to lose data. Flash memory was invented fairly recently, so nobody can be certain whether it will retain data in the long term.

Test yourself

1. Explain what happens at the atomic level when solid state storage is used to read, write and erase data.

2. Why has the development of solid state storage been so important for the mobile phone industry?

3. What are the advantages and disadvantages of a solid state drive compared to an HDD?

4. What are the advantages of a USB flash drive compared to a CD?

Syllabus reference

1.3.5 Storage solutions

Learners should be able to describe the principles of operation of a range of types of storage devices and media and how these principles are applied to currently available storage solutions.

Use and choice of storage

Introduction

You have learned about the different types of storage. In this section you will look at some of the ways that storage is used. You will review how people choose the right storage for their needs.

Making backups

It is important to make regular backups of stored data. A backup is a copy of all the data. If your storage media breaks or fails you could lose all your data, unless you have made a backup.

A backup should be stored in a safe place. Normally it will not be used. However, if your main data is lost, you can use the backup to restore your lost data.

Storage media for backup should be reliable and inexpensive. It must have high capacity. Fast access to the data is not needed. Often magnetic tape is used.

Cloud storage

Many people use cloud storage. This means the data is sent along an Internet connection. The data is stored by an Internet company on its computers. The Internet companies have large magnetic or solid state drives. These drives store the data for millions of users. Examples include Google Drive and Dropbox, but there are many others.

Advantages of cloud storage include the following:

- You don't need to buy your own storage devices and media.
- You can access your data from any device with an Internet connection.
- The company backs up the data so it is not at risk of being lost.
- Cloud storage doesn't take up any space on your own device, so it is very popular for use with smartphones and tablets.

These are two of the disadvantages:

- There will be concerns about the privacy and security of your data, because it is held by someone else.
- You cannot access the data if your Internet connection fails.

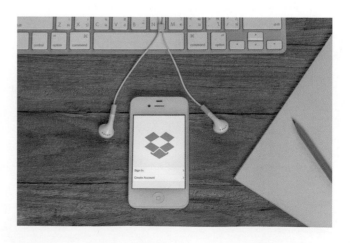

Choice of storage

When choosing storage you must consider a range of factors:

- Capacity: How much data do you need to store?

- Portability: Do you need to move your data between computers?

- Costs: How do the options compare?

- Speed of access: Hard drives wired into the computer are the fastest, tape is the slowest

- Reliability and durability: How likely is it that the data will be lost or spoiled?

Different storage choices suit different needs. Flash drives and cloud storage are good choices for small mobile devices. Devices with solid state drives tend to be more expensive than those that use magnetic storage.

Test yourself

1. Explain the advantages and disadvantages of making a weekly backup of your data.

2. Explain why magnetic tape is suitable for making a backup, but not for most other storage uses.

3. A business woman asks you if she should use cloud storage for her financial records. Explain what cloud storage is, and the advantages and disadvantages of this type of storage.

4. Evaluate flash memory in terms of capacity, portability, reliability, cost and speed.

Learning activity

You are going to set up an imaginary mail-order business selling storage solutions.

1. Investigate what items you might sell in your business. Find real examples, for example of USB drives.

2. Make a web page or a document that advertises the different types of storage you will offer for sale. For each type include an image, a description and a price guide. You can find out prices and specifications from online research. Include enough information for your customers to be able to choose which type of storage is right for them.

Review

Key terms

Actuator
: A motor that moves objects about. In the modern world most actuators are electrical. The motion of an electrical actuator can be controlled by a computer.

Control system
: A control system uses feedback to control a physical process. A control system can run without a user, at least for some time.

Feedback
: Feedback is when the computer measures the effect of a process that it controls. Input sensors "feed back" the result of the computer's actions to the processor.

Input device
: An input device converts data into digital signals that can be processed by the computer.

Primary storage
: Storage inside the processor. It consists of RAM and ROM.

Output device
: An output device converts the information inside the processor into a useful form outside the computer.

RAM
: Random Access Memory. This is read-write storage inside the CPU. RAM is volatile.

Read-only
: The processor can take data and instructions from read-only storage (this is called reading from storage). It cannot be used to store new data.

Read-write storage
: The processor can take data from read-write storage, and it can store new data or instructions (this is called writing to storage).

ROM
: Read-Only Memory. There is ROM inside the CPU. It is non-volatile. It is used to store the start-up instructions for the computer.

Storage device
: A storage device retains data and instructions in digital form.

Secondary storage
: Storage outside the processor. It is non-volatile.

Volatile
: Volatile storage uses electricity. When the electricity is off the data is lost.

Project work

Your task is to find out more about a wide range of input and output devices and control systems. This should include 3D printers or cutters and CAD-CAM systems.

Here are some approaches you can use:

- If there are devices like these in use in your school, for example in the engineering or design areas, visit the location and take extensive notes.
- Go on a class trip to an industrial or scientific location (such as a University) where these devices are used.
- Look at videos on Youtube of these devices in action.
- Write to a manufacturer and ask for information about the devices they make: they may be able to send you brochures or other information.
- Invite a guest speaker to your class, who works with control systems, for example in a factory.

Write up your findings as a report on control and manufacturing systems.

5 Software

Syllabus reference

1.3.6 Purpose and function of an operating system

Learners should be able to describe the purpose and function of an operating system and why it is needed.

See also:

3.3 Inside the CPU

5.1 Systems software

What is software?

Introduction

In Chapter 4 you learned about hardware. In this chapter you will learn about software – the instructions that tell the computer what actions to carry out.

Software

You have learned that in the fetch-execute cycle, the CPU fetches instructions from memory and executes them (carries them out). The instructions are held as binary code numbers. Each CPU has an instruction set. The instruction set is a list of all the instruction codes, and the action that goes with each one.

Where do the instructions come from? From software – every software file is a collection of instruction codes. To use software you must load it and run it.

- When you start software, all the instruction codes in the software file are copied from secondary storage into main memory (RAM). This is called loading the software.

- Now the instructions are in RAM. The CPU fetches the instructions one at a time and carries them out. This is called running the software.

There are two types of software:

- application software
- system software.

Application software

Application software is any software that carries out useful work for us. Most of the software you might buy or use with a computer is application software. For example:

- a word processor on your school computer
- the email software on your laptop at home
- a game on a games console
- a social media application (app) on a tablet or smartphone.

A modern computer typically shows the available applications (apps) as icons. Those are small images. Each image stands for a different file of instruction codes.

When you click on an icon the software is loaded and starts to run. Usually a screen display will appear showing you a menu or other choices. What happens next depends on the software, and the choices you make.

⬆ These icons represent different apps

System software

As well as application software, every computer needs system software. This is the software that enables the computer to work properly. The instructions in system software help the CPU to run the whole computer system, for example to:

- start up the computer
- load and run applications
- control the flow of data from the input devices and to the output devices
- organise memory and storage.

Learn more about system software on pages 138–141.

How software is made

Software is created by programmers. A programmer would very rarely write the binary instruction codes the CPU needs. Instead a programmer writes a computer program. The program is written in a programming language. When the program has been written, it can be converted into binary instruction codes that the CPU can understand. You can learn more about:

- computer languages on pages 142–145
- how to write computer programs in *Chapter 8 Programming*.

Test yourself

1. What happens when you load software? Why does software have to be loaded before you can use it?

2. What happens when you run software? Which part of the computer runs software?

3. What is an icon, and what happens when you click on an icon with the mouse, or touch an icon on the screen of a mobile device?

4. The instructions in software are held using a binary number code. What do these binary numbers stand for?

Learning activity

Investigate any computer system that you have access to. It might be your computer at school or at home, or a tablet or smartphone you use.

1. Make a list of the applications that are available on the computer. If there are a lot, list the first ten you can find. Explain what each one does and why you think it would be valued by the people who use the computer.

2. If you can, take a screen shot or image of the screen that shows the icons of the available applications. Explain what each one is for.

Syllabus reference

1.3.6 Purpose and function of operating systems

Learners should be able to describe the purpose and function of an operating system and why it is needed.

See also:

4.3 Memory and storage (Primary storage; Measuring storage)

Operating systems

Introduction

In the previous section you learned that software is a set of instructions the CPU can carry out. System software is software that controls the operation of the computer. In this section you will learn more about system software.

Operating systems

In modern computers, most of the system software that the CPU needs is collected together into one big software file. This is called the operating system. When the computer is turned on, the first action of the CPU is to load the operating system into RAM. The operating system stays in RAM all the time the computer is switched on. It operates in the background to make the computer work properly.

Learn about the work an operating system does on pages 140–141.

Booting up

When you switch the computer on, the first action is to load the operating system from storage into RAM. Now the computer is ready to use. This is called booting up or starting up.

ROM BIOS

The first instructions that the computer needs are stored in read-only memory (ROM). ROM is non-volatile so these instructions are retained when the electricity is off. They are available as soon as the electricity comes back on. On a PC, these start-up instructions are called the BIOS, which stands for "basic input/output system". The BIOS instructions get copied to main memory and executed. They start to control the computer's peripherals, and look in secondary storage for the operating system.

Loading the operating system

The operating system is stored in secondary storage. This storage must be accessed as soon as the computer starts up. The operating system is typically stored on the hard disk of the computer. This is because the internal hard disk is not removable, so it is a reliable storage location. Once the operating system is in place the computer can start to work.

Learn more about what functions the operating system carries out on pages 140–141.

Different operating systems

Different companies make different operating systems. Here are some examples:

- Microsoft Windows is the most widely used operating system in the world. There are several different versions of Windows. The different versions are numbered (for example Windows 10). Most laptop and desktop computers use Windows.

- Apple Mac OS X is the operating system used with Apple computers. Software designed for Apple computers cannot run on other computers.

- Linux is a free operating system. It can be more technically complicated to use than Windows or Mac OS. It is favoured by many computer experts.

- Android is an operating system used on many mobile devices such as tablets and smartphones. It is not the only mobile operating system. Apps written for Android devices will not run on devices that use a different operating system.

⬆ There are many different operating systems made by different companies

You will see from these descriptions that the choice of operating system affects all of the other software choices you make. When you buy software you need to know it is compatible with your operating system (that is, it was designed to run on that system).

Test yourself

1. The BIOS is stored in ROM not in RAM. In your own words explain why ROM is used to store this software.

2. When you buy a software application you need to know what your operating system is. Explain why.

3. Explain why you would store the operating system on your hard disk and not on a USB drive.

4. Until the operating system is loaded you cannot use any applications. Why not?

Syllabus reference

1.3.6 Purpose and function of an operating system

Learners should be able to: describe the purpose and function of an operating system and why it is needed; show understanding of the need for interrupts.

See also:

3.3 Inside the CPU (The fetch-execute cycle; Registers and buses)

Functions of an operating system

Introduction

Whenever the computer is on, the operating system is running. The operating system makes the computer work. In this section you will learn the different functions of the operating system.

What an operating system does

You have learned that the operating system is loaded into random-access memory (RAM) as soon as the computer is switched on. It stays in RAM, carrying out important functions until the computer is switched off. What does it do?

Control the hardware

The computer system is made up of many different items of hardware. You learned about these in *Chapter 4 Hardware*. The operating system lets the CPU communicate with the different items of hardware. The CPU can send digital data to and from the peripherals. It can control the operation of the devices. This lets the user work with the computer.

The user interface

The user interface is what you experience when you use the computer. For example, you will see a screen display. You may hear sounds. You can move a mouse pointer or touch the screen. These features, which allow you to use the computer, are called the user interface. The interface turns the digital data inside the computer into a form you can see and understand. Most computers have a graphical user interface (GUI) with icons and other graphical items.

Load and run applications

With the interface, you can select what application software you want to use. The operating system will load and run the applications.

Errors and problems

Things can go wrong when the computer is running. For example:

- an item of hardware might not work properly
- an application program might be poorly designed and contain some incorrect instructions
- the user might make a mistake.

It is the job of the operating system to cope with problems and breakages. It will typically identify the error, interrupt the current application, and display an error message on the screen. It might also use sound to alert you, for example a beep.

Interrupts

In *3.3 Inside the CPU (Registers and buses)* you learned about the program counter (PC). During the fetch-execute cycle the PC counts through the instructions in memory. Normally the PC counts through the addresses in the memory unit one by one. In each fetch-execute cycle the PC adds 1 to the previous address. Some instructions can change the address in the PC counter to a new value, so execution continues from a new place in memory. This is called a jump. Sometimes the program counter jumps back to a previous instruction. This means a group of instructions will be repeated. This is called a loop.

Sometimes the PC needs to change to a new address even without executing a jump instruction. This is called an interrupt. There are several reasons to interrupt the program:

- Hardware interrupts: when you use an item of hardware, for example when you click the mouse button, this can interrupt what the computer is doing. Your action can change the instructions the computer is using. A signal from the hardware interrupts the software sequence and swaps to a new set of instructions. An error signal from hardware is another type of interrupt, for example you might see a message saying your printer is out of paper.

- Software interrupts: software will also send interrupts to the CPU. These usually deal with problems, for example an interrupt saying that a web page is taking too long to load.

- Another use of interrupts is to let the CPU swap between two or more different programs. In this way the computer can carry out more than one task at the same time.

The operating system is constantly scanning the signals received from hardware and software. If an interrupt is received, the CPU interrupts the current program.

Test yourself

1. Describe one way that sound might improve a user interface.

2. What features of a user interface might reduce the number of user errors?

3. Explain why a games console must have an operating system.

4. Explain how system interrupts help the operating system to deal with software and hardware errors.

Syllabus reference

1.3.7 Low-level languages

Learners should be able to: show understanding of the need for both high-level and low-level languages; show understanding of the need for assemblers when translating programs written in assembly language.

See also:

3.3 Inside the CPU (The fetch-execute cycle)

5.1 Systems software (What is software?)

5.2 | Computer languages

Low-level languages

Introduction

You have learned that software is a set of instructions that can be carried out by the CPU. Computer programmers create software by writing programs. They write programs in programming languages. In this section you will learn about programming languages.

Machine code

Everything inside the computer is in digital form. All instructions are stored as binary number codes. The CPU fetches the binary code, interprets it and executes it. There is a binary number to match every action of the CPU. The set of all these codes is called the instruction set. Different types of computer may have different instruction sets.

The general term for the number code that matches numbers to instructions is "machine code". A computer file made of machine code is called an executable file. In Microsoft Windows it has the file extension .exe. When you run the file the instructions are carried out. Software applications are stored as executable files.

Writing software

If you want to develop a new software application you have to write the instructions.

You could just write the machine code. You would type in lots of hexadecimal numbers. They would stand for everything the software needs:

- instructions
- data
- memory addresses.

However, it is difficult to write software in machine code. The numbers are hard to read and it is easy to make a mistake. For these reasons, computer languages were invented.

Computer languages are easier for a human programmer to write, read and understand than machine code, so it is rare for programmers to write software in machine code.

When a complete set of instructions have been written in a computer language, they are converted into machine code. The computer can understand the machine code. It can carry out the instructions.

Machine code is occasionally used for fixing errors or for writing very short programs.

Assembly language

The first computer language to be invented was called assembly language. Assembly language uses short text words instead of binary number codes. That makes it easier for the human programmer to write it. For example, in machine code the instruction to add two values will be a binary or hexadecimal number. In assembly language it might be the word "ADD". A line of assembly language might also include some hexadecimal numbers. These represent data values and memory addresses.

A piece of software called an assembler is used to convert these code words into machine code that the computer can understand:

- The input to the assembler is a program written in assembly language.
- The output of the assembler is an executable file.

The process of turning a program into machine code is called translation.

Assembly language is quite similar to machine code. There is a very close match between the words of assembly language and the binary numbers used by machine code. In general, one line of assembly language turns into one instruction of machine code.

Low-level languages

A language that is similar to machine code is called a low-level language. Assembly language is a low-level language.

It is quite difficult to write a program in a low-level language. Low-level languages are not used by most programmers. Many low-level languages are based on a particular manufacturer's instruction set. A program written in that language may not work on any other make of computer.

However, there are some advantages. Low-level languages have a structure similar to the computer's own instruction set. That means assembly language programs let the programmer work directly with the instruction set. Low-level languages can give the programmer better control over the way the computer operates.

Assembly language is sometimes used to write system software. Device drivers are instructions that let the CPU communicate with peripherals. Assembly language is often used to create device drivers for new types of hardware. These programs are short and work quickly.

Test yourself

1. What type of data would you find inside an executable file?

2. What is the input to an assembler? What is the output?

3. An assembly language program includes code words. What do they represent?

4. Explain why assembly language is called a low-level language.

Syllabus reference

1.3.7 High-level languages

Learners should be able to: show understanding of the need for compilers when translating programs written in a high-level language; show understanding of the use of interpreters with high-level language programs.

High-level languages

Introduction

You have learned that a computer program is written in a programming language. Low-level languages are very similar to machine code. High-level languages are less similar to machine code. In this section you will learn about high-level languages.

Most programs are written in a high-level language. A program written in a high-level language is not very similar to machine code. Instead high-level languages are designed to make it easy to write the program.

High-level languages are not linked closely to a single instruction set, so they can be run on any computer once they have been translated into that computer's machine code.

Different languages are designed for different purposes. You would choose a language by considering what you want to do. Here are some examples:

- To build a program using visual building blocks you might use Scratch or App Inventor.
- To learn good programming methods you might use Python or Pascal.
- To work with logic you might use Lisp or Prolog.
- To make system software you might use C or C++.
- To create programs to run in a web page you might use JavaScript.

In this book you will learn Python programming. For more information see *Chapter 8 Programming*.

Translating into machine code

Programs written in high-level languages must be turned into machine code so the CPU can execute the code. This is called translating the program. There are two pieces of software that do this job: compilers and interpreters. They work in different ways.

Compilers

A compiler turns the program into machine code, and saves it as a file:

- The input to the compiler is a high-level language program.
- The output is an executable file.

The new executable file is placed in storage. The instructions in the file will not be executed until you decide to load and run the file.

Languages translated by compilers are called compiled languages.

Interpreters

An interpreter translates the program code and executes it as it translates. It reads enough of the code to work out the next action to take. Then it uses the instruction set to carry out this action. When the action is complete the interpreter moves on to translate and execute the next part of the program code.

Languages translated by interpreters are called interpreted languages. Python is an interpreted language.

Advantages of different translators

The advantage of using a compiler is that it creates an executable file. The executable file will run on its own like any application program. It can be sold, or shared with others. There is a disadvantage: if you make changes to the program, you need to create a new executable file. The old file is now out of date.

The advantage of using an interpreter is that it is easy to make changes. After making a change you can immediately run the program and see the effect. You only need the program code. There is no executable file. There is a disadvantage: the program will not run unless you have the interpreter on your computer.

	Compiler	**Interpreter**
Advantage	Makes an executable file. The executable file can be given to another person, or sold.	If you make a change you can test the effect immediately. You only need one file – the program code file.
Disadvantage	If you make a change the program must be compiled again.	No executable file. The program can only run if you have the interpreter on your computer.

Test yourself

1. Which type of translator leaves you with an executable file?

2. Describe all the advantages of having an executable file.

3. Why are there lots of different high-level languages? Wouldn't it be easier to just have one common language?

4. Python is a good language for learning programming. Why is an interpreted language particularly good for learners?

Learning activity

Choose three different high-level languages. Research their features on the Internet. Write a report on the three languages you have chosen. Explain whether the language is compiled or interpreted. What type of programming is the language used for? Find an example of program code written using each language.

Review

Key terms

Assembly language	Assembly language is a low-level language. A program written in assembly language is turned into executable code by a piece of software called an assembler.
Compiler	A piece of software which turns a program written in a high-level language into a file of executable code.
Executable code	A set of instructions in binary digital form which can be executed (carried out) by the processor.
High level language	High-level languages are designed to help human programmers create executable code. A program written in a high-level language can be converted to machine code using a compiler or an interpreter.
Interpreter	A piece of software which reads a program written in a high-level language. It sends the instructions from the program to the processor in executable form. It does not create a file of executable code.
Interrupt	The processor typically counts through the software instructions in memory, one at a time. Sometimes it needs to jump to new instruction in response to external events. This is called an interrupt.
Low level language	A language which is similar to the sequence of machine code instructions that is carried out by the processor.
Machine code	A code which stores instructions using a binary code. The processor can "decode" and execute machine code instructions.
Operating system	In modern computers, most of the system software that the CPU needs is collected together into one big software bundle called the operating system.
Software	Instructions which tell the computer what to do.
System software	Software that enables the computer to work properly. The instructions in system software help the CPU to run the whole computer system.

Project work

Computer programmers often introduce a programming language by writing a standard demonstration program called "Hello World!". This is a simple program that displays the message:

Hello World!

Carry out an Internet web quest to find examples of "Hello World!" in different programming languages. Collect as many samples of code as you can. Here is what you may find:

- There are many different high-level languages.

- They use a range of methods, even to produce such a simple output.

- Some program code is easy to understand, some is more difficult.

Write a short report on what you found. In this book you will learn how to code in Python. What other languages are you interested in learning?

6 Security

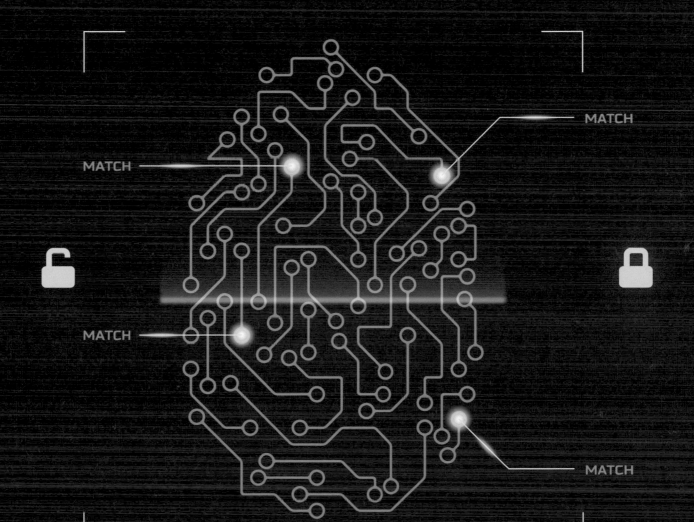

MATCH

MATCH

MATCH

MATCH

Syllabus reference

1.4.1 The need to keep data safe

Learners should be able to: show understanding of the need to keep data safe from accidental damage and malicious actions.

1.5 Computer ethics

Learners should be able to show understanding of the ethical issues, including hacking.

See also:

3.3 Inside the CPU

2.3 Safety online

6.1 Security threats

Data security

Introduction

You have learned that data means facts and figures. Computers are used to store and process data. Data is valuable, so it must be protected. The general term for protecting computer data is "data security". In this chapter you will learn about threats to data security and the methods that are available to protect data.

The value of data

In this section we will be talking mainly about data used in business. Data is valuable to a business for two reasons:

- The business will have had to invest time and money into collecting and processing data.

- Data can be used to create value for a business: data is a business asset.

Like any business asset, data must be protected from loss or damage.

What is data security?

Data security means protecting data from loss, corruption or unauthorised access.

Loss

Data loss means the data no longer exists in storage. For example, portable storage such as a USB flash drive could be mislaid, or a file could be deleted by mistake.

Data loss can severely affect businesses. A business may have compiled a list of its customers' bank details. If this data is lost, the business will not be able to get money from its customers.

Corruption

Data corruption means the data has been damaged or changed. Changes mean the data is no longer accurate, or has the wrong format. For example, if customer bank details are altered, money might be taken from the wrong bank account. Damage to storage media can corrupt data, for example a CD-R can be scratched.

If data corruption is severe, the data will no longer make sense and the computer will no longer be able to read it.

Unauthorised access

Some people have permission to see or alter data. Typically, they are people who work for the organisation that owns the data. Other people do not have permission. If they look at the data, copy it or make changes this is called unauthorised access.

Privacy

Privacy means data is only seen or copied by people who have permission. Unauthorised access is a term referring to a situation where someone who does not have permission has seen or copied the data. For example, a thief may take customers' bank details, enabling that person to steal money from people's accounts.

Integrity

Integrity means the data is protected from unauthorised changes. Someone who does not have permission might make changes to the data. This is sometimes called "hacking" and it is a threat to data integrity. For example, people might alter their bank details to increase the amount of money in their own accounts.

Test yourself

1. A company collects data about new ingredients for a soft drink. Give two reasons why this data is valuable to the company.

2. A company stores data about all their employees so they can be paid. Explain the need for data security.

3. A journalist looked at a film star's emails to her husband. What type of security problem is this?

4. A student went on his school's computer system and changed his test result. What type of security problem is this?

Learning activity

Investigate any current news stories involving data security. Working as a class, create a news sheet that gives details of data security issues currently in the news.

Syllabus reference

1.4.1 The need to keep data secure

Learners should be able to show understanding of the need to keep data safe from accidental damage, including corruption and human errors.

See also:

2.3 Safety online
3.3 Inside the CPU
Chapter 7 Ethics

Security threats

Introduction

You have learned that data security and privacy are important. In this section you will learn about issues that can threaten data security and privacy.

Internal threats

Internal threats to data security are issues within a company that can cause problems.

Hardware faults

Faults in storage devices and storage media can result in data loss. Sometimes a computer is not built correctly. Or it can be damaged by careless handling when it is being moved. A fire can destroy a computer system. The cables and the wireless signals used to transmit data can have faults or interference, meaning that the data received is incomplete.

One solution to hardware faults is to make a backup of all important data. Then lost or corrupted data can be restored. Handling equipment carefully and observing safety procedures can reduce the risk of hardware faults.

Software faults

Software is the instructions that control the computer. If the software has faults then the computer might do the wrong thing. For example, we often use a computer to carry out calculations. If the software does the calculations incorrectly, the data will be corrupted. In other cases, the software might accidentally delete data or send it to the wrong person.

Software faults can be prevented by thoroughly testing the software before it is used. Buy software from a company or a programmer that you trust.

Human error

The human users of a computer system can make mistakes. They might enter the wrong data or make mistakes when they are using the software. They might work in a way that risks damaging hardware. People may be careless with equipment, for example tipping a soft drink onto a laptop. They may be careless with storage media. For example, a civil servant left a USB flash drive with government secrets on a train.

Human errors can be reduced by training staff to use the computer properly. There should be clear guidelines about safe and sensible working practices. Trainees and learners should get help and support. Good software design will help to reduce human error. Software that is clear and easy to use helps staff to work safely at the computer.

⬆ Training will reduce human error

External threats

Every company is part of a community and a country. Issues within the community and the country will affect businesses. Events outside a company can have a bad effect on the company's computer systems. These events can include power cuts, floods, earthquakes and social unrest. Some companies have their own electricity generators to ensure no loss of power. All data should be backed up.

In this section we have considered external threats caused by accidents or faults. Threats can be caused on purpose, through deliberate human action. These threats include:

- crime and malpractice (see *6.1 Security threats* and pages 152–153 for more details)
- computer viruses and other malware (see *2.3 Safety online*)
- computer hackers (see *7.1 Ethics*).

Q Test yourself

Imagine you are running a company that makes computer games.

1. You have developed a new computer game. It is stored as a file on the main computer in your office. Explain what hardware and software faults might cause the loss of this important file.

2. What actions could you take to protect the file?

3. Everyone needs to eat and drink. What rules would you have for your employees about eating and drinking at work?

4. Thinking of your own country and city, what are the main external threats that might harm your computer system?

Q Learning activity

This activity is an extension of the questions you have just answered. It is based on you running a company that makes computer games. Write a computer policy for your business. It should set out rules for your employees to follow when they use the work computer system. You can be as strict or as lenient as you like. What are the advantages of different levels of control over your employees' actions?

Syllabus reference

1.4.1 The need to keep data safe

Learners should be able to show understanding of the need to keep data safe from malicious actions, including unauthorised viewing, deleting, copying and corruption.

1.4.4 Security examples

Learners should be able to: describe how the knowledge from 1.4.1 can be applied to real-life scenarios.

1.5 Ethical issues

Learners should be able to show understanding of ethical issues, including hacking.

See also:

2.3 Safety online (Malware and hacking)

7.1 Ethics (Hackers and crackers)

Malpractice and crime

Introduction

In the previous section you learned about issues that can accidentally harm data. In this section you will learn about deliberate actions that can harm security, privacy and data integrity.

Unauthorised access

If someone has unauthorised access to data it means that the person can see or alter data without permission. It could be someone inside the company or someone from outside who has gained access through a computer communication link.

Viewing or copying data

People sometimes look at the data on a computer system without permission. They might take a copy of it for themselves. It can be hard to tell that this has happened because the data is not changed. This type of action is a threat to personal privacy; for example, someone might learn how much money another person has in a bank account. It is also a threat to business profits; for example, someone might steal details of a new car design from a company. People sometimes make illegal copies of films, games and music.

Deleting or changing data

People sometimes gain access to computer data without permission. They delete or change the data. This is called "hacking". For example, someone might change the data on a bank computer to increase the amount in his or her own bank account. This is the same as stealing money.

Malpractice

Malpractice means not doing your work properly usually by mistake. Malpractice can be a threat to data security. Mistakes you might make when using the computer include:

- leaving the computer logged on when you go out of the room, so that someone else can access your files

- telling someone else your password, so that the computer system is no longer secure

- downloading software from the Internet or opening a damaging email, which can put malware onto the computer

- using work computers for personal business, which wastes work time and increases the risk of malware.

In general malpractice is not criminal activity. It is just careless. To prevent malpractice employees should be trained and supervised. Company policies should be written setting out the actions expected from employees in order to maintain data security.

Malpractice should not be confused with malware. Malware is software (see more information in *2.3 Safety online*). Malpractice is human activity.

Crime

Crimes are more serious than malpractice. Computer crime can cause a lot of damage and problems. Some examples are:

- taking a copy of music, games, movies, etc., without permission, sometimes called piracy

- hacking (gaining unauthorised access to ICT systems) – hackers find out passwords or bypass security systems

- creating and distributing malware

- identity theft, which is stealing someone else's personal details, and pretending to be that person, typically to take money out of the person's bank account

- deliberately damaging or stealing computer hardware and storage media.

Executable files

You have learned about malware. Malware files are executable files (or parts of a file). These files can get into your computer without you noticing, having been designed to load and run themselves. When the CPU executes the instructions in the malware file it causes damage to your computer.

Test yourself

1. Why shouldn't you tell anyone else your password?

2. Who is authorised to access your school computer system?

3. Explain the difference between crime and malpractice.

4. Why can downloading software from the Internet to your school computer cause a problem?

Learning activity

Extend the policy document you wrote in the previous section to cover the issues mentioned in this section.

Syllabus reference

1.4.3 The need to keep online systems safe

Learners should be able to show understanding of the need to keep online systems safe from attacks including denial of service attacks, phishing, pharming.

1.2.2 Security aspects

Learners should be able to show understanding of the security aspects of using the Internet.

1.4.4 The need to keep online systems safe

Learners should be able to describe how the knowledge from 1.4.3 can be applied to real-life scenarios.

Online attacks

Introduction

The Internet is a very useful business resource. It is a great source of data. Businesses use an Internet connection to buy and sell products. However, the Internet also creates new security challenges. Online attacks are threats to security that arise from use of data communications and the Internet. In this section you will learn about online attacks.

Denial of service

A denial of service (abbreviated to DoS) attack is a way of harming a company's computer services. It works by preventing the computer services from doing their job, for example by flooding the computer with many requests or messages. A DoS attack might make the computer go very slowly, or make it too busy to do its normal work. A DoS attack might make it impossible for customers to contact the company, because all the connections are busy.

Automatic software can be set up to send millions of messages to the computer from a single address. A more serious attack is called a Distribute Denial of Service (DDoS). The messages seem to be sent from hundreds of different addresses, so they cannot all be blocked. A DDoS attack will be set up by someone who wants to harm the company, for example a business rival. It might be done in protest against a company.

Identity theft

Identity theft happens when a criminal finds out your personal details. These might include your bank account, your passwords and your personal ID. The criminal can then use this information to pretend to be you online.

Opportunities for identity theft arise when people do their banking online and buy products online. A criminal pretending to be you can take money from your bank account. The criminal can buy things using your identity, so you have to pay for them.

Obtaining personal details

Identity theft can enable criminals to steal a lot of money. For this reason there are lots of tricks that people use to get your personal details. Two examples are called phishing and pharming.

Phishing

Phishing is typically done by sending a fake email or other message. It will look like an email from a respectable company, such as your bank, and it might ask you to confirm your password or ask you to send your bank details. However, it is a trick. Criminals have sent the email to try to get your details so they can commit identity theft.

Real companies should never ask you to send private details like this. Never reply to an email that asks for private details. If you are in doubt, telephone the company and check that they have contacted you. Do not use the phone number in the email though, because that might be a trick too. Find the phone number some other way.

Pharming

Pharming is typically done by making a fake website. It looks like the website of a real company such as a bank or a website that sells products. You might look at the website and think it is the real one. You might log on, or enter your name and bank details. Now the criminals know your details and they can use them to get money in your name.

Be extra careful that you have connected to the right website. Check for spelling mistakes and false URLs.

Test yourself

1. Why does a DoS attack slow down a computer system?

2. How can pharming be used for identity theft?

3. You get an email from your bank, asking you to phone a number to check your security settings. What is the risk?

4. The owner of a small business said "There are too many online risks so I will never use the Internet." Explain why this is not a sensible statement.

Learning activity

Write an article for your local newspaper explaining the dangers of identity theft.

Syllabus reference

1.4.2 Use of passwords and biometrics

Learners should be able to show understanding of how data are kept safe when stored and transmitted, including use of passwords, both entered at a keyboard and biometric.

See also:

2.3 Safety online

6.2 Security protection

Introduction

In the previous section you learned about security threats that can cause loss, damage or disclosure of data. In this section you will learn about methods that can be used to protect data from these threats.

Proof of identity

Proof of identity is important for data security:

* to control access to data
* to prevent identity theft.

The main methods used for proof of identity are passwords and biometrics.

Passwords

We all know what a password is. It is a string of characters such as letters and numbers. You think of a password for yourself. You keep the password secret. When you have to prove who you are, you enter the password. It can by typed into a computer using a keyboard, keypad or touchscreen. It can be transmitted to any Internet site.

Criminals will try to gain access to a system by guessing passwords. They have software that will try a million different passwords, until they find one that works. For this reason, you should use a complex password with a mix of different characters. This is called a strong password. The stronger the password, the harder it is for criminals to guess it. You should use different passwords for different computer systems.

Unfortunately, many people use weak passwords, such as the numbers 1234. Passwords like this are easy to guess. Another mistake people make is to tell their password to a friend. You should never do that.

⬆ A palm scan proves your identity

ID cards

An alternative to a password is an ID card or swipe card. It can be read by a special card reader. Sometimes a card is combined with a password. For example when you use a cash machine you swipe your bank card, which identifies you. You also enter a four-digit pass code. This confirms your identity. An ID card can be checked by a person, as well as read by a computer. The card often has your photograph on it for use as an additional check.

Biometric check

An alternative to a password or an ID card is a biometric check. Biometric means a record of a physical characteristic, used to confirm identity. Examples of physical features used for biometrics include:

* a finger print, thumb print or palm print
* the pattern of your iris (the coloured portion of your eye)
* features of your face such as the distance between your eyes.

⬆ The retina of your eye has a unique pattern

Checking physical features needs special equipment and software. For example:

- a palm reader
- an iris scanner
- a facial recognition system.

However, it is difficult for criminals to pretend they are someone else if a biometric check is used. You can find out someone's password or steal their ID card, but you can't borrow their physical features.

Nowadays some smart phones have a built-in fingerprint check so nobody else can use your phone.

Advantages and disadvantages

All of the methods to prove identity that we have looked at have advantages. Passwords are easy and cheap to use. A strong password with many different characters is hard to guess. The disadvantage is that unfortunately people sometimes forget their passwords and cannot access their data.

Biometric checks have many advantages. You do not need to carry anything or remember anything to use them. However, the equipment can be expensive to install.

⬆ A cash point uses both a card and a numerical pass code

	Passwords	Biometrics	ID card
Advantages	Easy to input on any device. Can be changed as often as you like.	You do not need to remember anything. Uses features that are unique to you.	Can be changed or taken away if permissions change. Can be checked by a person as well as a computer.
Disadvantages	Easy to forget. Some people choose weak passwords.	Reading biometric features needs special equipment. Biometric scanning is more expensive than the other options. Biometric features cannot be changed if the security system is compromised.	Scanning a card needs special equipment. Cards can be lost or stolen.

Stealing biometric features

Some people worry that criminals will use violence to get round biometric systems. For example they worry that someone might cut your finger off to get your finger print. Doing this would not work. The fingerprint scanner uses electrical sensitivity. It cannot read the print from a cut-off finger. The idea is a scary story, nothing more.

Test yourself

1. Give two reasons why you might want to prove your identity.
2. How can you make your password harder to guess?
3. Give two physical characteristics that might be used for biometric identity checks.
4. What are the advantages of biometric checks compared to the alternatives? Are there any disadvantages?

Learning activity

Design an ID card that could be used to access the school or college computer system.

Syllabus reference

1.4.2 Use of firewalls

Learners should be able to show understanding of: how data are kept safe when stored and transmitted; use of firewalls, both software and hardware, including proxy servers.

Firewalls

Introduction

In this section you will learn about a computer's local area network (LAN) and about firewalls. A LAN is a collection of computers joined by cables or a wireless connection. A firewall is used to protect the computers in the network from malware and other harmful data or signals.

Router

A local area network (LAN) connects all the computers in a single building. A LAN is extremely useful for a business. All the computers connected to the LAN can share data and software. Most businesses and many families have a LAN connecting their computers.

The device that joins the LAN to the Internet is called a router. Again, a router is very useful. It means all the computers in the business can get data from the Internet. They can use the connection for buying and selling and other business tasks. Almost every modern business has an Internet connection.

However, there is a risk. The Internet is a source of malware and other dangerous content. This content might get in through the router to the LAN. Then it could spread to all the computers in the network. It could cause a lot of damage.

Proxy servers and firewalls are put in place to reduce this risk.

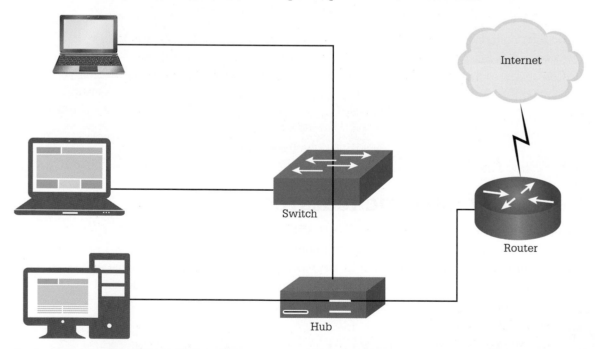

↑ A router connects a LAN to the Internet

Proxy server

A proxy server handles all the communications between two computers or two networks. A user will request data, such as a web page, from the Internet. The proxy server will take the data from the Internet. The user will get the data from the proxy server. This means that the user does not make a connection directly to the web page.

This has several advantages:

- It speeds up the connection. The proxy server connects to the website once and downloads the content. Now the content from the website is on the proxy server, close to local users. Any network users who want to look at the page can get it from the proxy server using a fast local connection.

- The people who run the proxy server can check what websites people look at.

- There is no direct connection between the user and the website. This gives the user privacy protection.

- It is safer. All content from the website can be checked before it is passed on to the user.

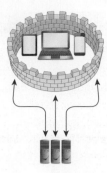

⬆ All data from the Internet must pass through the firewall

Firewall

A firewall is a barrier between the Internet and the local network. The firewall checks all the data that passes in or out of the local network. It will only pass on data if it passes all the checks.

A firewall consists of:

- Hardware – a firewall device is a piece of hardware. The wired or wireless link must pass its data through the firewall device to get in or out of the network. It contains a processor.

- Software – the firewall software is a set of instructions. They tell the processor what to do with the signals that pass through the firewall device. The firewall software will have rules that help it tell the difference between safe data and dangerous malware.

A modern company will have a firewall in place to protect the computers in the local network. Firewall technology is improving all the time. The software is getting better at telling the difference between good and bad data.

Test yourself

1. What is the job of a router?

2. What is the job of a proxy server?

3. What are the advantages of using a proxy server to connect to the Internet?

4. What are the two components of a firewall system?

5. How does a firewall improve data security?

Learning activity

Investigate firewall hardware and software systems that are for sale. What services do they offer?

Syllabus reference

1.4.2 Security protocols

Learners should be able to show understanding of how data are kept safe when stored and transmitted, including use of security protocols such as secure sockets layer (SSL) and transport layer security (TLS).

See also:

2.2 The Internet (TCP/IP)

Security protocols

Introduction

You have learned that a protocol is a standard for communication. Devices that use the same protocols can communicate with each other. Some protocols are designed to preserve data security. You will learn about security protocols in this section.

Open systems interconnection (OSI)

In this context, the word "standard" means a system used by everyone. A protocol is a standard for communication. These protocols can be described in terms of a model called open systems interconnection (OSI). OSI groups protocols into seven layers. For example, layer 1 has the protocols for physical hardware and layer 2 has the protocols for transmitting binary digits. The OSI model is an ideal system and it has never been fully implemented.

Transport layer

Layer 4 of the OSI model is called the transport layer. This layer has the protocols for how two devices at either end of a long communication link talk to each other. There might be many different cables and devices between the two. Transport protocols control the end-to-end communications, not the links in between. The TCP/IP protocol is part of the transport layer.

Transport layer security (TLS)

Transport layer protocols control communication between two distant devices. Transport layer security (TLS) is a way of making this communication private. No other device can read a message sent between the two devices and nobody can make changes to the message.

A message protected by TLS is safe, even though it has to pass through lots of connections to get to its end point. Remember that not all Internet communication is protected by TLS.

TLS has two parts:

- TLS record protocol – a standard method to break the communication down into parts called records
- TLS handshake protocol – see below.

Handshake

The TLS handshake protocol is a signal sent between the two devices at the start of communication. The handshake lets each device check that the other is genuine. A genuine website has a security certificate, issued by a recognised certificate authority (CA). During handshake the security certificate is checked. The TLS handshake establishes a private link between the two devices. During the handshake the two devices can exchange an encryption key. Learn more about encryption on pages 162–163.

Certification authority

Authentication is an important part of the handshake process. Authentication means checking the computer at the other end of the communication link is genuine. Is it what it claims to be? For example it is really your bank? Authentication uses a digital certificate. That is like an electronic ID card which proves the computer's identity.

Certificates are issued by a certification authority (CA). An example of a CA is Verisign. A CA is an organisation that everyone trusts. If a business requests a certificate from a CA it will check that the company is what it claims to be. Then it will issue a certificate. The CA will check each certificate regularly. If the company has been involved in Internet fraud the certificate will be revoked.

Your computer has a list of trusted CAs. When your computer receives the certificate, it will check that it was issued by CA from this list. If the CA is trusted, then the certificate is good. Now communication can proceed in safety.

Secure sockets layer (SSL)

Secure sockets layer (SS)L is the name of the protocol that was used before TLS. It has different methods of encryption and it is less secure. However, its overall purpose is the same. The two are grouped together as TLS/SSL. You would use one or the other, not both together.

Example: online shopping

If you buy a product online you need to provide your bank card details. If the connection was not secure, a criminal could take your details and take money from your bank account. The TLS protocol prevents this. First, it checks that the website you are using is real. Then it sends your bank information using encryption (secret code). Find out more about encryption on pages 162–163.

Test yourself

1. What are the two parts of the TLS protocol?

2. What protection is offered by TLS?

3. Explain how a handshake is used to establish a secure connection.

4. When I buy a book from Amazon my computer checks that I am connected to the real Amazon website. Why is that?

Syllabus reference

1.4.2 Use of encryption

Learners should be able to show understanding of how data are kept safe when stored and transmitted, including use of symmetric encryption (plain text, cypher text and use of a key), showing understanding that increasing the length of a key increases the strength of the encryption.

Encryption

Introduction

You have learned that encryption is used to put messages into a secret code. This protects them from being read or changed as they go through Internet links. In this section you will learn how encryption works.

Plain text and cypher text

Plain text is ordinary words and numbers. Plain text is not secure. Remember that an Internet message goes through lots of connections and devices on its way to its destination. The plain text could be read by anyone with access to those connections.

Cypher text is text that has been scrambled or changed using a secret formula. For example, the computer could swap each letter for the letter two places further along in the alphabet:

> Ecp aqw tgcf vjku oguucig?

The process of turning a message into cypher text is called encryption.

Encryption

Sometimes you will want a message you send to be private. For example if you log in to an online bank service using a password, you don't want anyone else to know your password. When a message needs to be secure it can be sent as cypher text. The process of turning plain text into cypher text is called encryption. Encryption is done by the computer before the message is sent. The sender doesn't have to work out the cypher and doesn't see the scrambled text.

There are two stages to encryption:

- Encrypt: when plain text is turned into cypher text.
- Decrypt: when cypher text is turned back into plain text.

Two computers are involved in encryption:

- The sender encrypts the message (and sends it).
- The receiver decrypts the message (when it receives it).

Encryption key

Encryption uses a key. The key can be a string of text characters or a number. The key tells the computer how to encrypt plain text. It also lets the computer decrypt the cypher text. Encryption and decryption are done using a mathematical formula. As with passwords, a long and complex key gives stronger protection.

Remember that as a computer user you do not have to know the key. For example, when you buy a product from Amazon your bank details are encrypted. You don't notice the encryption that is used. The computer encrypts and decrypts the messages before you see them.

Symmetric encryption

In symmetric encryption the key is kept secret. Only the sender and receiver know the key. The sender uses it to encrypt the message. The receiver uses the same key to decrypt it. The problem with the secret key is that it has to be sent over the Internet before encryption can begin. Anyone who finds out the secret key can decrypt the messages.

Asymmetric encryption

In asymmetric encryption there are two keys: a public key and a private key. The two are mathematically linked. A message encrypted with one key can only be decrypted with the other key. These are features of the two keys:

- The public key is shared with any computer that needs to send a message. Any computer can download the public key: it is not a secret. Computers that want to send messages to you can use the public key to encrypt the messages before sending them.

- The private key is kept secret on your computer. Your computer can use it to decrypt the messages that are sent to you. The private key is never transmitted.

This means that anyone can send you a secret message, but only you can decrypt the messages. You never need to see the public and private keys. The computer generates them automatically, stores them securely, and takes care of encryption and decryption. The messages you see are all plain text.

Asymmetric encryption is safer than symmetric encryption, but slower.

Test yourself

1. Why is cypher text more secure than plain text?

2. Explain why the use of cypher text requires a key.

3. What is the difference for a computer user between using a password and using an encryption key?

4. Why is asymmetric encryption safer than symmetric encryption?

Learning activity

1. You have seen an example of encryption where every letter in a message is replaced by the letter two further along in the alphabet. Working with a partner, develop a secret code. Use a similar method, but choose the letter three along, or four along, or any other number you like. Use your code to send messages to each other.

2. Challenge another pair of students to decode your secret messages.

3. Write a report about the code you used, with examples of encrypted messages. The code you used was an example of symmetric encryption. Explain why.

Syllabus reference

1.4.4 Security examples

Learners should be able to describe how the knowledge from 1.4.1, 1.4.2 and 1.4.3 can be applied to real-life scenarios including, for example, online banking and shopping.

Security examples

Introduction

So far in this chapter you have learned about security risks and the methods used to protect data. In this section you will see how these ideas are applied to real-life computer systems.

Banking

A bank account keeps your money safe. When you want to make a payment you instruct the bank to send money from your account. There are many ways to instruct the bank. The most common examples are cheque, debit card and direct transfer.

Online banking lets you do all your banking tasks on the Internet. For example, you may use your home computer. You can check your account to see how much money you have got. You can make payments to other people. You can transfer money between different bank accounts.

Every time you instruct the bank to make a payment you must be able to prove your identity. You do not want someone else to make payments with your money. Online banking uses passwords, encryption and security protocols to make sure nobody else can access your account.

E-commerce

E-commerce means buying and selling things over the Internet. Most large retail businesses use e-commerce. Sites such as Amazon, eBay and Etsy specialise in e-commerce.

To buy things over the Internet you must trust the retailer. You will send them your bank account details. They will only take the amount agreed. Customer safety and trust is vital for these businesses.

However, you must be sure you are sharing data with a company that has reliable security systems. You must make sure you are connected to the right website. You must make sure you use a safe and private communication link.

Security methods that you have learned about in previous sections will let you:

- prove your identity so nobody else buys things using your account
- encrypt your message so nobody finds out your bank details
- check it is the real site, not a pharming site.

Teleworking

Teleworking means that you work from home. You connect your home computer through an Internet link to a computer at the company you work for. These are some of the advantages and disadvantages of this way of working:

- Teleworking has many advantages. It saves travel time. You can work outside of normal office hours. Your employer can have smaller offices, so their premises are less expensive.

- Disadvantages of teleworking include the following. Not all types of work can be done using a computer link. It can be hard to supervise people who are not in the office.

For teleworking you need a safe and secure link from your home computer to your company's computer. Data that is sent between the two computers is encrypted.

Cloud services

You have learned that cloud storage lets you save your work over an Internet connection (see *4.3 Memory and storage – Use and choice of storage*). Internet companies offer other cloud services. Examples include email and document creation. You do not want anyone else to access your private online storage. For this reason, cloud services require passwords and often use encryption.

Your responsibility

Safe use of e-commerce, banking and teleworking requires technology, including software and protocols. Remember though that users must also play a part – they must behave in a sensible and cautious way.

Q Test yourself

Modern data security measures let us carry out many different activities online at low risk. Some people see a downside to increased use of online activities – they think this has harmful effects on society.

1. What are the advantages and disadvantages of online banking compared to visiting a bank in person to carry out your business?

2. What are the advantages and disadvantages of buying from a website instead of visiting a shop?

3. What are the advantages and disadvantages of teleworking instead of going in to work in your employer's workplace? How might teleworking change our society?

Q Learning activity

1. Go to a website where people can buy products online. Search the site to find out what policies and procedures the website has in place to protect customers' privacy and security. You may find an explanation in the online "Help" section.

2. Using the information you found about your chosen website, create a presentation that explains what security protection is in place for users of the website.

Review

Key terms

Asymmetric encryption	An encryption system where the encryption key is kept secret by one side of the communication.
Biometric check	A security check which relies on checking one or more of your physical features like your fingerprints.
Cypher text	Text which has been hidden using encryption. Cypher text can only be read by a computer which knows the "encryption key".
Decryption	Turning cypher text into plain text which anyone can read.
Denial of Service	An attack on a computer system by overloading it with messages and queries so it stops working.
Encryption key	A hidden number value which the computer can use to decrypt cypher text.
Firewall	A combination of software and hardware which screens the data flowing in and out of a network.
Identity theft	Pretending to be another person online, for example so that you can take their money.
Malpractice	Making mistakes when you use a computer system. This can cause loss of data or loss of privacy.
Pharming	Making a fake website – typically pretending to be a respectable organisation – to trick people into sending you their identity details.
Phishing	Sending out fake emails – typically pretending to be a respectable organisation – to trick people into sending you their identity details.
Symmetric Encryption	An encryption system where the encryption key is known by both sides of the communication.

Project work

A substitution cypher is a secret code where each letter of the alphabet is substituted for another.

A keyword cypher is a type of substitution cypher that uses an encryption key. The key is a word. Pick a word which has no repeated letters in it. You put the letters of the encryption key under the alphabet starting at A. In this example the encryption key is XRAY.

A	B	C	D	E	F	G	H	I	J	K	L	M	N	O	P	Q	R	S	T	U	V	W	X	Y	Z
X	R	A	Y																						

Then complete the table by adding the remaining letters of the alphabet, in order.

A	B	C	D	E	F	G	H	I	J	K	L	M	N	O	P	Q	R	S	T	U	V	W	X	Y	Z
X	R	A	Y	B	C	D	E	F	G	H	I	J	K	L	M	N	O	P	Q	S	T	U	V	W	Z

Can you decipher this message using the encryption key XRAY?

QEB MIXKP XOB RSOFBY SKYBO QEB PQXQSB

1. Working alone or in a small group, develop a keyword substitution cypher, and use it to encrypt and send a message to another group.

2. One group is the receiver of the message. Give them the encryption key and the message.

3. Another group is the interceptor of the message. Give them the message but NOT the encryption key.

4. Everyone work to decrypt the messages they have received or intercepted.

Write a report on what you did. If you have time discuss the limitations of a simple substitution code and suggest alternatives.

7 Ethics

7.1 Copyright

> ### Introduction
> Ethics means the study of right and wrong. In this chapter you will look at some of the issues relating to right and wrong ways of using computer systems. First, the chapter explores the issue of copying other people's work.

Ethics

Ethics is the study of right and wrong. People disagree about what behaviour is ethical. People's views about ethics are influenced by religion, tradition and family life. The Internet lets us interact with people all over the world. They may have different views from the ones we are used to. This means computers make us think hard about ethical issues.

Ethics is not the same as law. Some unethical actions are against the law, but some unethical actions are lawful. That does not make them right. Technology is always changing. Sometimes the law has not caught up with technology. New laws might be needed, and until that time, legal protection may be unclear. Sometimes computers make it easier for criminals to break laws.

For all of these reasons, the use of computers brings us ethical challenges and risks.

Easy copying

Computers make many tasks much easier than they used to be. An example is copying. Data on the computer is very easy to copy. This is very useful and so we make copies all the time. However, copying brings ethical challenges. Do we always have permission to copy other people's work? What are the rules about copying?

Intellectual property rights

Your intellectual property (IP) is anything you made with your own ideas and creativity. It could be music, a book, an invention or a design. You have intellectual property rights (IPR). That means nobody is allowed to copy your intellectual property without your permission. IPR is protected by international agreements.

Copyright

Copyright law tells us what we have the right to copy. Copyright law protects IPR. It includes all types of electronic data, for example:

- text in documents and books
- music
- movies and TV programs
- software including games.

You can only copy this material if you have permission. Generally, to obtain permission you have to pay for the content.

Why are there copyright laws? Why are we not allowed to make any copies of any material we want? Because people have spent time and hard work making digital content. For example, programmers work hard to make a computer game and the companies employing them will have made a huge financial investment. If you make a copy without paying, they do not get any reward.

Plagiarism

Some people make a copy of someone's work and then pretend the material is their own work. This is called plagiarism. Sometimes people copy a whole piece of work, but it is also plagiarism if you only copy part of some text.

For example, if you copy and paste someone else's material (such as text, tables, pictures or graphs) into your school or college work you must say where the material came from: you must give a reference to the original source. Teachers will fail students for plagiarism. However, it is often acceptable to use text if you reference its source correctly. Your teachers will explain how to give proper references in your work.

Fair use

Despite copyright law you are allowed to make some use of digital material. The laws vary between countries but the general term is "fair use". In general, using content made by someone else in your own work counts as fair use if:

- you only take a small part of the work
- you credit the original source.

The boundaries of what is fair are not always clear. For example a lot of modern music includes samples of older music tracks. There have been some legal battles about whether this is fair use.

Test yourself

1. Why has the spread of computers made IPR such an important issue?

2. A student wrote a review of a book for their school magazine. She included some extracts from the book in her review. Explain whether she broke any laws.

3. A student bought a computer game. He made five copies of the game and sold them to his friends. Explain whether he broke any laws.

Learning activity

Have a class discussion about copyright and fair use. How much copying do you think is fair? How much music is it fair to sample in a track?

Syllabus reference

1.5 Free software

Learners should be able to distinguish between free software, freeware and shareware.

See also:

Chapter 5 Software

Free software

Introduction

You have learned that software is covered by intellectual property rights (IPR). You cannot use software without permission from its maker. Often you have to pay to use software, but in some cases software is free. In this section you will learn that there are different types of free software.

Key terms

All software is covered by IPR, but some programmers have special arrangements that let you use the software they made without paying. This is legal and ethical, if you follow the rules. To understand the different types of free software that are available you must understand some key terms:

- free
- open source
- public domain.

The meaning of "free"

Free software can be free in different ways. In this context, "free" can mean you don't have to pay for the software or it can mean you can do anything you like with it. Be careful about the different meanings.

Open source

You have learned that programmers write programs in a computer language. This is called source code. Then they compile it to make an executable file (in machine code). Usually, when you buy software you only get the machine code. A person cannot read or edit it.

With open source software you can get the source code too. You don't have to do anything with it, but if you understand programming you can make changes to the code. You can make new versions of the software. You can share your new version. Sometimes thousands of programmers will work together to improve the source code. One example of an open source operating system is Linux.

Public domain

Software that is in the public domain has been made freely available for anyone to use. The people who made it have given up their IPR. Nobody has any legal ownership of the software.

Types of software

Using these key terms helps us to understand the different types of software:

- free software
- freeware
- shareware.

Free software

Free software is not always free of charge. As mentioned above, the term "free" can mean that you can do anything you like with the source code. Free software:

- is open source
- is sometimes in the public domain, but not always
- sometimes has to be paid for, but once you get it you can do what you like with it: you can make changes to the software; you can even sell it.

Freeware

Freeware is software that is available for no charge. In this case "free" means you do not pay. Freeware:

- is not open source
- is not in the public domain
- is free of charge, at least at first
- is available for you to use, but you are not allowed to sell it.

You cannot sell freeware because the IPR is still owned by the programmers. Freeware that you might know about includes:

- Adobe Acrobat Reader, which lets you read PDF files
- Skype, which lets you make phone calls through your Internet connection
- AVG anti-virus software.

Shareware

Shareware is similar to freeware. Shareware:

- is not in the public domain
- is free of charge
- is available for you to share with other people.

Shareware is different from freeware because there is an expectation that its users will pay for shareware at some point. Typically, free use of shareware will run out after a few months. Other limitations may have been placed on how you can use the software. Paying for the software will overcome these limitations or unlock new features. Shareware you might know includes Winzip, which is a file compression software.

Test yourself

1. "Linux is an open source operating system." Explain in full what this sentence means.
2. You have learned about free software and freeware. Explain what the word "free" means in each case.
3. A company made a computer game. It was shareware. Explain some different ways the company could make money from this computer game.
4. A virus check program is in the public domain. Who owns the IPR of that software? Explain your answer.

Learning activity

Investigate examples of freeware, shareware and free software. Make a directory of some of the most important examples. Which ones do you think you might use now, or in the future?

Syllabus reference

1.5 Ethical issues

Learners should be able to show understanding of the ethical issues raised by the spread of electronic communication and computer systems, including hacking, cracking and production of malware.

See also:

Chapter 6 Security
2.3 Safety online (Malware and hacking)

Hackers and crackers

Introduction

In Chapter 6 you learned about computer security. There are people with very high expertise in using computers. They can use their skills to overcome computer security measures. They are called hackers. In this section you will learn about hackers and what they do.

Hacker

The word "hacker" is used in different ways. Among people with good computer skills it is sometimes used to mean a person who likes to investigate and work with computer systems, to understand them better. More generally, "hacker" is used to mean a person who breaks into computer systems to steal data or make changes.

To make things clearer people sometimes divide hackers into different categories:

- Black hat hackers are hackers who break into computer systems. They are also called crackers. They will work in secret. If they find a problem with the security system they will exploit it to gain access. They might make changes to the data or make copies of the data. They might put the data into the public domain. They are usually breaking the law.

- White hat hackers are people who have permission to work with computer systems. Sometimes they are employed to test the security system. They will let the owners of the system know they are working with it. If they find a problem they will report it so it can be fixed.

- Grey hat hackers are the large number of hackers who do not fit into the two previous categories. They may work without permission. However, they may not do any damage. Like white hat hackers, they may let the owners know if they find a problem. Grey hat hackers are often breaking the law. However, the main priority of the police will probably be stopping the hackers who cause damage.

Some hackers cause a lot of damage to computer systems. In extreme cases this can lead to financial loss or even harm to people. Although it is not publicised, it may be that some governments use hackers to spy on other governments' computer systems.

Malware

Malware is software that can damage the computer system or delete data. For a reminder of the details, turn back to *2.3 Safety online (Malware and hacking)*. The most common example is a virus.

Malware is hidden. The user cannot see it on the computer. You need good programming skills to create malware.

Some people make malware for a prank or a joke. Others make malware to achieve particular goals. Malware can be used to break into security systems. For example, malware can be used to record every key you press during the day. The malware will send this information through a computer connection to the hacker. In this way the hacker will find out your passwords.

Test yourself

1. Explain the difference between a white hat hacker and a black hat hacker.

2. A hacker put hidden software on a computer to record keystrokes. How did this help the hacker to break computer security?

3. A hacker made a computer virus to harm a person he did not like. The virus did not only harm that person though. Explain why.

4. A student looked on her computer and did not see a virus. Does that mean her system is safe?

Learning activity

Your challenge is to read a book or watch a film about hackers and crackers. Here are some suggestions.

Films:

- Die Hard 4
- The Net
- Hackers
- Tron
- The Matrix
- War Games.

Books (fiction and non-fiction):

- *The Hacker Crackdown* by Bruce Sterling
- *Neuromancer* by William Gibson
- *We are anonymous* by Parmy Olsen
- *Little Brother* by Cory Doctorow
- *Coding Freedom: The Ethics and Aesthetics of Hacking* by Gabriella Coleman.

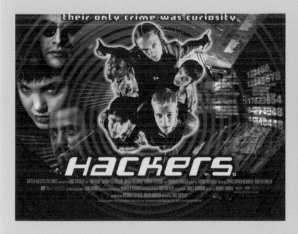

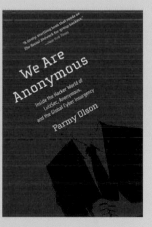

Review

Key terms

Copyright	The right to control who can copy an item, for example an intellectual or creative product. Computers have made it easier to take copies without permission.
Hacker	This term has more than one meaning. In normal use it means a person who gains access to a computer system without permission.
Intellectual property	Anything you have made using your own ideas and creativity is your intellectual property. This can include books, films, software, music.
IPR	Intellectual Property Rights are the rights you have to control the use and copying of your own intellectual property.
Open source	Open source software is provided not just as an "executable file" but also as source code, written in a high-level programming language. The user can edit and change the code.
Plagiarism	Using somebody else's words or other intellectual property, and claiming that it is your own.
Public domain	The person who puts a product "in the public domain" has relaxed their intellectual property rights, and given permission for people to use their work. There may be some restrictions still in place though, so check carefully.

Project work

On page 173, you were given the task of reading a book or watching a film about hackers and the ethics or practice of breaking into computer systems. Write a review of the book or film. Explain the ethical stance set out by the writer and whether you agree or disagree with it.

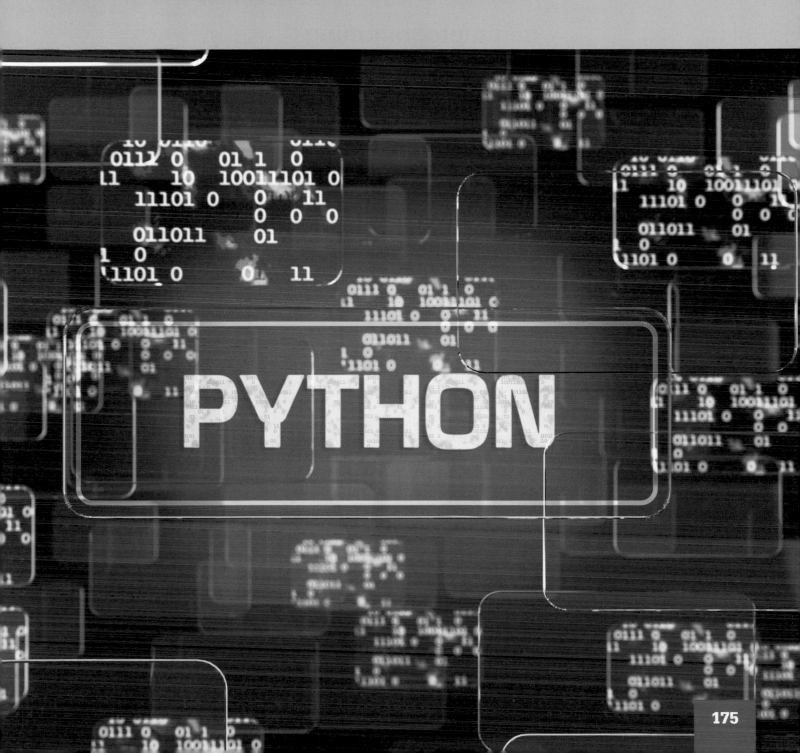

8 Programming

Syllabus reference

8.1 Introduction to programming

Learners are advised to try out solutions to a variety of different problems on a computer using a language of their choice.

See also:

Chapter 5 Software

8.1 Introduction to programming

Introduction to Python

> **Introduction**
>
> In this chapter you will learn to program using the Python programming language. This section is an introduction to Python.

Begin programming

In this section you will learn about programming. The Python programming language is used as an example. There are many other programming languages. The features you will learn about are found in almost all languages.

So, for example, you will learn how to "declare a variable" or "add a loop" to a program. You will learn how to do these things using Python. But remember that you could have used any other language.

To extend your understanding of programming you could work independently to learn about an additional language and see how it compares to Python. However this is not essential.

What is Python?

Python is a programming language. Here are some ways to describe Python using terms you have already learned:

- Python is a high-level language.
- Python is an interpreted language.
- Python is open source software.
- Python is free software.

If you cannot remember what all these terms mean, look back at pages 144–145 and 170–171. Python is developed under an open source licence, making it free to use.

Free software

Python is free, so you can download it onto your own computer at home. You do not have to pay. That means you can practise programming outside of classroom time.

To download Python go to the main Python website:

> https://www.python.org/

Choose "Downloads" from the menu.

Versions

There are several versions of Python. Some start with 2, for example 2.7.10. Some start with 3, for example 3.5.3. In this book we use the type that begins with 3 (version 3), but you can use either type. Any differences between the versions will be explained.

Integrated development environment

Like many program languages, Python comes with an integrated development environment (IDE). The Python IDE is called IDLE.

An IDE is similar to a word processor. An IDE lets you type up your program and save it like a document. A typical IDE has extra features you don't find in a word processor. IDLE:

- uses colour to show different features of the program code
- lets you run the code (execute the program)
- gives you guidance about errors in your code.

Start IDLE

When you start IDLE you will see a window like this. It says "Python Shell" at the top. Open the menu as shown in the picture:

Choose "New Window". A second window will open. It looks like this:

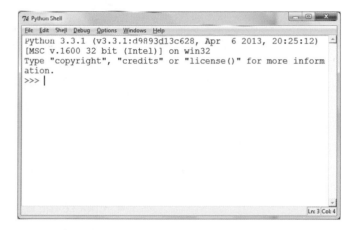

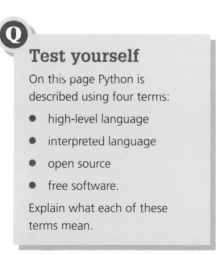

↑ Open the file menu and choose new window

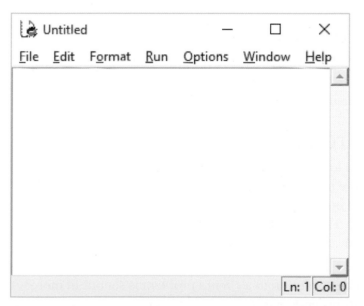

↑ The second window is where you will enter the Python code

Whenever you use Python you will see two windows like this. The new window you opened is where you write the program. Then you can run the program. The results will appear in the "Python Shell" window.

The new window has a menu bar across the top. The "File" menu will let you save the programs you make, and open saved programs. The "Edit" menu will let you cut, copy and paste.

Q **Test yourself**

On this page Python is described using four terms:

- high-level language
- interpreted language
- open source
- free software.

Explain what each of these terms mean.

Q **Learning activity**

Start up Python IDLE and open a new window as shown in this section. Investigate the menu bars.

Syllabus reference

**2.1.1 Flowcharts and
pseudocode**

Learners should be able to: use
flowcharts and pseudocode;
produce an algorithm for a given
problem (either in the form of
pseudocode or a flowchart).

See also:

Chapter 9 Solution development

Algorithms

Introduction

Flowcharts and pseudocode are ways of setting out the logic of a program. This is called making an algorithm. In this section you will start to learn about algorithms.

Algorithm

An algorithm describes a set of steps to solve a problem. For example, a recipe is a simple algorithm. Algorithms are used in mathematics to describe how to solve problems.

For programmers the term "algorithm" describes the logical structure of a program. An algorithm sets out all the actions that the program will carry out. It is a way of describing a program before you start work on it.

An algorithm is not written in a particular programming language. Turning an algorithm into a program is called coding.

Why do programmers use algorithms?

Why do programmers spend time setting out an algorithm instead of starting work by writing code? There are several reasons. Setting out an algorithm helps them to:

- plan their approach to the problem and check it makes sense before they begin

- choose the right way to solve the problem

- describe their solution to others, including people who use a different programming language

- keep a record of the logic of their solution.

Plan backwards from results

All programs are written for a purpose. Typically, the programmer works for a client. The client pays the programmer to make a program. The programmer talks to the client to find out what the client needs. This will be the output or result of the program. The programmer plans backwards from this final output. The programmer must make sure the program provides the results the client has asked for.

The process of developing a solution to a client's problem is set out in more detail in *Chapter 9 Solution development*.

Flowchart

A flowchart is a type of diagram. It uses boxes connected by arrows to show the logic of a program. The boxes stand for actions. Different shapes of box stand for different actions. The boxes are connected by arrows. The arrows show the flow or sequence of the program.

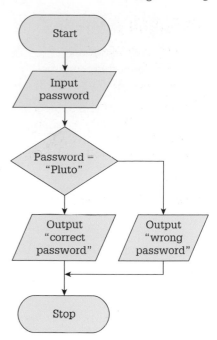

Pseudocode

Pseudocode is a different way of setting out an algorithm. It uses words instead of boxes and arrows.

Pseudocode is not exactly like any particular programming language but it is similar to program code. There are many different types of pseudocode. In this book you will learn a particular one that is somewhat similar to Python.

Example

This pseudocode represents the same algorithm as the flowchart shown above:

```
READ Password
IF Password = "Neptune" THEN
   PRINT "Correct password"
ELSE
   PRINT "Wrong Password"
ENDIF
```

This program checks whether a password is right. What do you think the right password is?

Advantages and disadvantages

There are advantages to each way of making an algorithm:

- A pseudocode algorithm uses less space than a flowchart. Pseudocode is similar to normal program code. It is easier to write neat pseudocode than drawing a flowchart. You don't need special graphics software.

- A flowchart algorithm is often easier for an ordinary person to understand than a pseudocode algorithm: a flowchart algorithm is more accessible and readable.

In this book you will learn both.

Q Test yourself

1. A programmer said: "When I plan a program the most important thing is that the program produces the right outputs". Explain this answer. Do you agree with her?

2. What is an algorithm? Why do programmers create algorithms before they start to write program code?

3. What features of a flowchart help the programmer to describe an algorithm?

4. What are the advantages and disadvantages of using pseudocode compared to a flowchart?

Q Learning activity

Using any graphics package, create the flowchart shown on this page.

Syllabus reference

**2.2.1 Programming: use
  predefined procedures/
  functions**

Learners should be able to use
predefined procedures/functions

8.2 | Begin coding

Output

> ### Introduction
> You have learned that a programmer works for a client. The program that
> is designed for the client must produce the output that the client wants. In
> this section you will learn how to produce output from a program.

Python output

The main output of a simple Python program is on-screen display. To make
Python display output on the screen you use the command "print". You
must type the command in lower case letters:

```
print("....")
```

Whatever is inside the brackets and quote marks will appear on the screen
when you run the program. A set of characters inside quote marks is called a
string (or sometimes called a literal). Python will display the string exactly as
you type it inside the quote marks. You can use single or double quote marks.

To print a blank line you enter this code:

```
print("\n")
```

**NOTE: If you are using Python version 2, you leave the brackets out of
the print command. This is the main difference between the two versions
of Python.**

Function

A function is a special type of command that makes the computer transform
or use a value. "print" is a function.

Every function uses or transforms a value. The value is shown in the brackets
after the function name. This value is called the parameter of the function.

The print function includes a parameter, inside brackets. The print
function will display the parameter on the screen.

Predefined function

Most functions are made by programmers when they write their program
code. However, "print" is a predefined function. This means it comes as part
of the standard Python code.

Python comments

Comments are lines of code that the computer will ignore. Comments are
used by programmers to add explanatory notes for anyone who looks at the
program and wants to understand it.

In Python any text that follows the hash symbol (#) is ignored by the computer. It is treated as a comment.

Example program

Here is an example of a Python program using `print` and comments.

IDLE uses colour as follows to show the different types of code you have entered:

- the function name is shown in purple
- the string is shown in green
- the comments are shown in red.

If you make a mistake you may spot the colours are wrong.

What is the error in this example?

```
# Program name: myfirst
# Code written by: Alison Page
# This program demonstrates use of the print command


print("===========================")
print("          W E L C O M E          ")
print(" This is my first program ")
Print("===========================")
```

Save and run

Python is an interpreted language. When you run the code, Python will read the lines one at a time. It will turn the line of program code into machine code. The machine code will go to the CPU. The CPU will carry out the commands on that line. This is how you save and run the program code:

- To save the program code choose "Save" from the file menu and enter a name for the program. Pick a name that reminds you what the code does.
- To run the program code open the "Run" menu. Choose "Run Module". If you try to run without saving, Python will remind you to save first.

The output of the program will appear in the "Python Shell" window.

Syntax errors

"Syntax" means the rules of a language. If you make a mistake in the program code, this is a syntax error. The code will not run. An error message appears in the "Python Shell" window.

```
>>>
===========================
          W E L C O M E
 This is my first program
Traceback (most recent call last):
  File "C:/Python33/myfirst.py", line 9, in <module>
    Print("===========================")
NameError: name 'Print' is not defined
>>>
```

The error message tells you what error it found, and in what line of the code. Go back to the code. Correct the error. Save and run the program again. It is OK to make mistakes in code. All programmers do this.

Learning activity

Invent a name for a new computer game. Produce a Python program that displays a welcome screen for the game. Save and run the program.

Test yourself

1. What is a string?
2. What does the computer do with comments added to a program?
3. Explain the syntax of a `print` command. What goes in the brackets?
4. Describe what happens when you run a Python program.

Syllabus reference

2.2.1 Programming concepts

Learners should be able to understand and use the concept of sequence.

2.1.2 Pseudocode

Learners should be able to: understand and use OUTPUT (for example PRINT); understand and use standard flowchart symbols to represent these statements, commands and structures.

Sequence

Introduction

In the previous section you created a simple Python program. In this section you will use that program to demonstrate the concept of sequence. You will produce algorithms that show the same sequence.

Sequence

The sequence of commands in a program means the order in which they are carried out. You have made a simple program with a series of `print` commands. The commands are simply carried out in the order they appear in the program, starting with the first line and working down the screen.

In *8.4 Repetition* you will learn about alternative sequences, for example loops, where commands are repeated several times.

Pseudocode

Pseudocode uses a print command similar to Python, but there are some differences. The word **PRINT** is written in upper case letters. There are no brackets.

Here is a pseudocode version of the Python program from the previous page:

```
PRINT "==========================="
PRINT "    W E L C O M E"
PRINT "This is my first program"
PRINT "==========================="
```

You can use single or double quotes in pseudocode print commands. Look at the Python program you wrote and compare it with the pseudocode version.

Sequence in pseudocode

The sequence of a pseudocode program is easy to understand. Each line is carried out in the order in which it is written.

Flowchart

Every flowchart has one start and one end. Start and end are shown by boxes with rounded corners. A typical flowchart goes down the page. The sequence of commands is shown by an arrow.

Outputs are shown using a box like the one below.

The value to be output is shown inside the box. Strings are shown in quote marks, just as in Python or pseudocode.

Flowchart diagram (left margin):

START → Output "--------" → Output "Welcome" → Output "This is my 1st program" → Output "--------" → END

Simplifying a flowchart

When you are making a flowchart you have a choice. You can:

- show every output in a separate box, giving the full details
- simplify output into a single box, which summarises the output.

Here is an example of a flowchart that simplifies the algorithm.

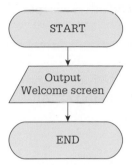

This example does not show every output in a separate box. It summarises all the output. This saves space and time when the algorithm is created. The disadvantage is that when you turn it into a program, you will need to turn one box in the flowchart into many lines of code.

Test yourself

1. What is the difference between the syntax of the print command in pseudocode and Python?

2. This page shows the same algorithm in pseudocode and as a flowchart. Which do you prefer? Give reasons for your answer.

3. In Python, comments are not carried out by the CPU. Why don't we need to use comments in pseudocode?

4. Draw a flowchart for a program that would output your name.

5. A programmer summarised program output to simplify the algorithm. What are the advantages and disadvantages?

Learning activity

In the previous learning activity you made a Python program. Make a pseudocode algorithm and a flowchart to match the program you made.

Syllabus reference

2.2.1 Programming concepts

Learners should be able to: use predefined functions; declare and use variables.

Input

Introduction

Every computer system has input and output. You know how to write a Python program to make output. Your Python programs should take input from the user. In this section you will learn how to write code that accepts user input.

Input

The input command is a predefined Python function similar to print. An input command looks like this (all in lower case):

```
input("...")
```

The text inside the brackets is called the prompt. It is a message telling the user what they need to input. When you run the program, the computer will display the prompt, and wait for the user to type something. For example:

```
input("Enter the password")
```

Variable

The command you just learned asks the user to type something. This is input to the computer. Usually you want the computer to save the user input. The saved input will be held in the memory of the computer while the program is running. *an area in computer memory that stores a value while the program is running*

If you want to save user input, you must give the computer a memory location to use:

- If you were writing a program in machine code or assembly language you would have to give a memory address in RAM. You would use a hexadecimal number.

- In a high-level language such as Python you give the memory location a name. This is much more convenient. A named memory location is called a variable. It is called a variable because the data stored in the location can vary.

Remember that the contents of RAM are volatile, so the variable will go out of computer memory when the program stops.

Example command

This command will take the user input and store it as a variable called Password:

```
Password = input("Enter the password")
```

This variable is called Password. Whatever input the user types will be stored in the variable.

Naming variables

You can choose any name for a variable, but it is important that the name you choose reminds you of what data the variable stores. This will make your program easier to write and easier for other people to understand. When choosing a variable name:

- The name must not include spaces. Use only letters, numbers and the underscore character (_).
- Whether you use upper or lower case letters is your own decision. Many Python programmers use all lower case. In this book variables start with a capital letter to make them stand out.

Declaring variables

In some programming languages you have to make the variable before you can use it. This is called declaring the variable. In Python you do not need to declare a variable before you use it. The variable is declared when you first use it.

To summarise, the Python command shown here does two things:

- It declares a variable called `Password`.
- It puts the user input into the variable.

Output a variable

You can output a variable using the `print` command. Here is an example that will output the value stored in the memory location:

```
print(Password)
```

When you output a variable you do **not** put quote marks round the variable name. You don't want the computer to print the word "Password". You want it to show the data that is stored in that memory location.

You can combine a string and a variable in the same output command. Put a comma in between them:

```
print("Your password is", Password)
```

Example

This program uses all the commands you have learned so far.

Notice that IDLE shows the variable name in black text.

```
# Program name: myfirst
# Code written by: Alison Page
# This program demonstrates use of print command


print("===========================")
print("      W E L C O M E        ")
print(" This is my first program ")
print("===========================")

Password = input("Enter the password")
print("Your password is ", Password)
```

Test yourself

1. An input command includes a prompt. What is the purpose of a prompt?

2. If you enter an input command without a variable, what happens to the user input?

3. If you enter an input command with a variable, what happens to the user input?

4. An input command in Python both declares and uses a variable. What does "declare" mean?

5. Explain the difference between these two commands in Python:

```
print("User
Name")
```

```
print(UserName)
```

Learning activity

You have created a program to display the welcome screen to a computer game.

1. Add a line that asks the user to choose a character name and then stores it using a suitable variable.

2. Add a line that says "Get ready to play" and then displays the name of the character.

Syllabus reference

2.2.1 Programming concepts

Learners should be able to: declare and use variables and constants; understand and use basic data types: integer, real, char, string and boolean.

See also:

1.3 Data storage

Assign a value

Introduction

In the previous section you learned how to pass user input to a named memory location. The memory location is called a variable. In this section you will learn how to store other values in variables. This is called assigning a value to the variable.

Assign a value

Storing a value in a variable is called assigning a value to the variable. The equals sign is used to assign a value.

To assign a value to a variable, you use code with this structure:

- the name of the variable
- an equals sign
- the value you want to assign to the variable.

Name of variable	=	Value

Example

This program has several lines that assign values to variables.

```
# Program name: assign
# Program by:    alison page
# this program shows assignment commands

Name = "Alison"
Age = 99
FaveColour = input ("enter your favourite colour: ")
```

1. In the first line a string is assigned to a variable. Strings are shown using quote marks.

2. In the second line a number value is assigned to a variable. Number values do not have quote marks.

3. In the last line, user input is assigned to a variable.

Constants

Some programming languages have constants as well as variables. The value of a constant is typically set early in the program code. Once the value has been set it cannot be changed. That is why it is called a constant.

In Python, if you want to store a value that does not change, you can use a variable. You can set the value early in the program code. Then do not alter the value and it will remain constant.

Calculated values

You can tell the computer to assign the result of the calculation to a variable. Find out more about this on pages 188–189.

Data types

In Chapter 1 you learned that the computer stores all data as binary code. It uses different methods to store different types of data. For example, text is stored using ASCI or Unicode.

When you create a variable, the computer has to decide what type of storage to use, depending on what type of data it is. These are some important data types:

- Integer – an integer variable will store a whole number, with no decimal point.
- Real – a real variable will store a number with a decimal point. In Python this data type is called float.
- String – a string variable stores a string of text characters. It uses Unicode to store the characters.
- Boolean – a boolean variable stores a True or False value. It uses a binary digit to store it.
- Char – short for "character", a char variable stores a single text character. This variable type in not used in Python.

In some programming languages you have to tell the computer what data type to use. You do that when you declare the variable. In Python you do not need to tell the computer what data type to use. The computer picks a suitable data type when you assign a value to the variable:

- If you assign a whole number it will make an integer variable.
- If you assign a decimal number it will make a float variable.
- If you assign a string it will make a string variable.

There is one exception – a variable that stores user input. The computer does not know what type of data the user might type in. In this case the computer always uses a string variable.

Test yourself

1. In the example in this section, values are assigned to three variables. What are the names of the variables?
2. What data type will the computer use for each of the variables?
3. What is the difference between a constant and a variable?
4. Why must the computer choose a data type for each variable it uses?
5. What data type would the computer use in the example shown below?

```
Age = input("enter your age")
```

Learning activity

Open the computer game program you have created. Create a variable called `HitPoints`. Assign a number value to this variable. Output the variable using a suitable `print` command.

Calculated values

Introduction

You have learned how to assign a value to a variable. In this section you will learn how to assign a calculated value to a variable. This lets you write a program that works out the answers to calculations.

Assigning calculated values

You have learned that you assign a value to a variable using the equals sign. Using this method you can assign the result of a calculation to a variable.

| Name of variable | = | Calculation |

For example, this line will work out 240 + 270 and assign the result to a variable called Cost:

```
Cost = 240 + 270
```

The variable Cost now stores the result of the calculation. If you output the variable you will see the result of the calculation:

```
print("The cost is", Cost)
```

Arithmetic operators

Calculations in Python use symbols to stand for the main mathematical processes.

These symbols are called arithmetic operators. Here is a short program that uses the four arithmetic operators.

Symbol	Action
+	plus
–	minus
*	multiply
/	divide

⬆ Arithmetic operators

```
# program: arithmetic
# program by: Alison
# demonstrates the four main arithmetic operators

Value1 = 20
Value2 = 5

print("The two values are ", Value1 , " and ", Value2)

Times = Value1 * Value2
Add = Value1 + Value2
TakeAway = Value1 - Value2
Divide = Value1 / Value2

print("Here are the results of...")
print("Multiplying: ", Times)
print("Adding     : ", Add)
print("Subtracting: ", TakeAway)
print("Dividing   : ", Divide)
```

When you run the program you will see these results.

```
The two values are  20  and 5
Here are the results of...
Multiplying:  100
Adding     :  25
Subtracting:  15
Dividing   :  4.0
```

Data types

The first three results are of integer data type. The computer uses the integer type if it is adding, subtracting or multiplying integers. The fourth variable is of the float data type. This is because a division sum can produce a decimal fraction. The float data type can store decimal fractions.

Only number data types can be used in calculations. Strings cannot be used in calculations.

Using input in calculations

In the previous example the values of the two variables were assigned within the program as follows:

```
Value1 = 20
Value2 = 5
```

It would be more interesting to let the user input the values of the variables;

```
Value1 = input("Enter the first value")
Value2 = input("Enter the second value")
```

However, there is a problem. Input variables are always string data type. String data type cannot be used in calculations.

Changing data type

If you want to use an input variable in a calculation you must change it from string to a numeric data type. You can change it to float or integer.

This command will convert `Value1` to integer data type:

```
Value1 = int(Value1)
```

This command will change `Value2` to the float data type:

```
Value2 = float(Value2)
```

You must convert any input variable to integer or float data type before you use it in a calculation.

Example

This program demonstrates all the skills you have learned in this section.

```
# program: arithmetic
# program by: Alison
# demonstrates the four main arithmetic operators

print("SHOWING THE ARITHMETIC OPERATORS")
print("\n")

Value1 = input("Enter the first value: ")
Value2 = input("Enter the first value: ")
print("\n")

Value1 = int(Value1)
Value2 = int(Value2)

print("The two values are ", Value1 , " and ", Value2)
print("\n")

Times = Value1 * Value2
Add = Value1 + Value2
TakeAway = Value1 - Value2
Divide = Value1 / Value2

print("Here are the results of...")
print("Multiplying: ", Times)
print("Adding     : ", Add)
print("Subtracting: ", TakeAway)
print("Dividing   : ", Divide)
```

Test yourself

1. Describe the meaning of the four arithmetic operators.

2. Dividing an integer by an integer produces a value of the float data type. Explain why.

3. Why do we always need to convert the data type of an input variable before using it in any calculation?

4. Explain the difference in the way a whole number is displayed if it is of the integer data type, or if it is of the float data type.

Learning activity

Produce these programs to practise coding.

1. Copy the program shown in the final picture on this page. Run it and see what results you get.

2. Change the program so that the input variables are converted to the float data type. What is the difference in the final results you get?

3. Produce a program where the user enters any number and the computer shows the "times table" for that number, from 1 to 12.

Variables in pseudocode

Introduction

You have learned to create Python programs that use input, output and variables. In this section you will see how to work with variables in pseudocode.

Pseudocode

Pseudocode means "pretend code". Pseudocode is not a programming language despite looking a lot like one. Pseudocode cannot be converted into an executable file.

We write pseudocode to set out the logic of a program. The pseudocode describes the algorithm. For this reason, we include variables when we write pseudocode. Of course they are not real variables. They do not stand for real memory locations. We just use them to plan the program before we write it.

One good thing about pseudocode is we do not have to worry about data types when writing it.

Store input using a variable

Pseudocode lets you take user input and store it as a variable. To input a value to a variable you use the word READ, for example this command:

```
READ Password
```

This command will read user input and assign it to a variable called Password.

Choose the names of variables in pseudocode in the same way that you would choose variable names in Python:

- Choose a name that reminds you what data is stored.
- The name must be one word, with no spaces.
- You can use upper or lower case.

One difference between working with variables in pseudocode and Python is you do not need to give a prompt when using pseudocode.

Assign a value

To assign a value to a variable you use an arrow. The arrow points from the value to the variable:

```
Age ← 15

Name ← "Alison"
```

The arrow has the same function as the equals sign in Python. The arrow shows the value going into the variable.

Calculate a value

Pseudocode uses the same arithmetic operators as Python. You can assign any calculated value to a variable, just as you can in Python:

```
Price ← 120 + 90
```

You can calculate using variables:

```
Cost ← 200

Profit ← 20

Price ← Cost + Profit
```

What is the value of the variable `Price` at the end of this code?

Output a variable

Pseudocode uses the word `PRINT` to stand for output.

You can output a string. Remember to include quotation marks:

```
PRINT "I can write pseudocode"
```

You can output a number value. No quotation marks appear:

```
PRINT 99
```

You can output a variable. No quotation marks appear:

```
PRINT Age
```

Example

This pseudocode program puts together the different commands shown on this page:

```
READ Value1

READ Value2

Result ← Value1 * Value2

PRINT "The two numbers multiplied together make"

PRINT Result
```

Test yourself

1. What is an arrow symbol used for in pseudocode?

2. Explain how to use pseudocode to input a value to a variable.

3. Write the pseudocode line that will print a variable called `MyName`.

4. Write one line of pseudocode that will add 40 to 60 and store the result in a variable. Choose any name for the variable.

Learning activity

Write the following programs in pseudocode.

1. A program that inputs two numbers and produces the result of dividing one by the other.

2. A program that inputs the price of two meals in a restaurant and outputs the total bill.

3. A program that adds a 10 per cent service charge to the restaurant bill. Remember that calculating 10 per cent is the same as dividing by 10.

Syllabus reference

2.1.2 Flowcharts

Learners should be able to understand and use standard flowchart symbols.

Variables in flowcharts

Introduction

You have learned how to create a variable in Python. You have made a variable to store user input. You have also learned how to assign a value to a variable. In this section you will see how to describe these actions when you work with flowcharts.

Input value

Remember that an input value is stored in a variable. The flowchart box that stands for "input" is the same shape as the output box.

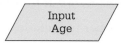

Inside the box you show the word "input" and the name of the variable.

You can show every input in a different box. If many different variables are all input at once, the flowchart may summarise all the inputs into a single box.

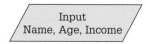

This simplifies the flowchart.

Assign value

As well as inputting a value to a variable you can assign a value to a variable. In pseudocode you use an arrow. In Python you use an equals sign.

The flowchart box to assign a value to a variable is an ordinary rectangle.

Cost = 200

Inside the box you show the variable and the value. Use an equals sign as in Python, or an arrow as in pseudocode.

Calculate value

You can assign the result of a calculation to a variable. To do this you use one or more of the arithmetic operators.

Calculating a value uses the same box as assigning a value. You must show the variable name inside the box. You must show the calculation inside the box. The familiar arithmetic operators are used.

Profit =
Income – Expenses

Output value

You have already learned that the output box is used to output strings, numbers and variables. Make sure you include the word "output". Otherwise you can't tell input and output apart. They both use the same shape of box.

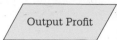

Example

This flowchart uses all the flowchart symbols you have learned so far.

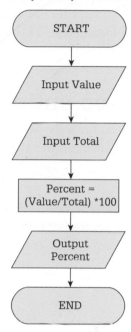

What algorithm is described by this flowchart? What calculation is carried out?

Test yourself

1. What shape of box is used to represent input?

2. How can you tell the difference between a box used for input and output?

3. Which of the arithmetic operators are used in flowcharts?

4. What shape of box is used to represent a calculation?

Learning activity

Draw flowcharts to represent the following algorithms.

1. A program that inputs two numbers and outputs the result of dividing one by the other.

2. A program that inputs the price of two meals in a restaurant and outputs the total bill.

3. A program that adds a 10 per cent service charge to the restaurant bill. Remember that calculating 10 per cent is the same as dividing by 10.

Syllabus reference

2.2.1 Programming concepts

Learners should be able to understand and use the concept of selection.

2.1.2 Flowcharts

Learners should be able to understand and use standard flowchart symbols.

8.3 Selection

Logical decision

Introduction

You have learned that a program is written to make an output the client wants. You have learned to write a program that makes output. In this section you will learn how the computer can produce different outputs depending on the results of a logical test. This is called selection or a conditional structure.

Select between two options

The programs you have written so far have been based on a simple sequence of commands. There is one path through the algorithm. A more complex type of program has a branching structure. There are two paths and the computer selects one of the paths.

In order to select the right path, the computer carries out a logical test. A logical test is a test that gives an answer of either True or False. If the test result is True the computer takes one path. If the test result is False the computer takes the other path.

Logical test

A logical test compares two values. Remember that the answer to a logical test is always True or False.

To compare two values you use a relational operator. Here are the main relational operators.

Operator	Meaning
=	equal to
<>	not equal
<	less than
>	more than

Here are some logical tests made using relational operators.

Logical test	Meaning
Age > 17	Age is more than 17
Price = 9.99	Price is equal to 9.99
Name <> "Leon"	Name is not Leon

When the computer sees a logical test like these it does the comparison. For example, it compares the variable Age with the value 17. Is Age bigger than 17? The answer will be yes or no (True or False). That is a logical test.

Decision box

In a flowchart a logical test is shown inside a box called a decision box. A decision box is diamond shaped.

One arrow goes into the decision box. Two arrows come out of the box. The arrows are labelled YES and NO. This is how it works:

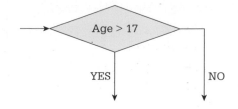

- If the answer to the logical test is YES you follow the YES arrow.
- If the answer to the logical test is NO you follow the NO arrow.

It is normal in flowcharts for the YES arrow to go straight down. The NO arrow goes out to one side. This is so common that sometimes the labels YES and NO are left out.

Example

In this example, the algorithm decides whether you are old enough to go to college.

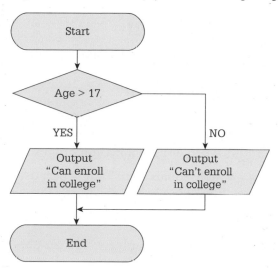

The user inputs his or her age. If the age is over 17, the computer outputs a message saying "Can enrol in college". If the result of the test is NO the computer outputs a message saying "Can't enroll in college".

Program code

In this section you have looked at flowcharts that use a logical test. In the next section you will write program code that uses a logical test.

Test yourself

1. In an algorithm with two paths, how does the computer choose which path to take?

2. List the four most common relational operators, giving the meaning of each one.

3. How are relational operators used to make logical tests?

4. Draw the flowchart symbol used to represent a decision. Label the YES and NO arrows.

Learning activities

1. Copy the flowchart shown on this page.

2. Create a flowchart for a program where the user inputs a password. If the password is "Outstanding99" the computer will output the message "You entered the correct password". If the answer to the test is NO the computer will output the message "Wrong password. Goodbye".

Syllabus reference

2.2.1 Programming concepts

Learners should be able to understand and use the concept of selection.

Python `if...`

Introduction

In the previous section you learned about the concept of selection, using a logical test. In this section you will see how logical tests are used in Python programming.

Example

In this section you will create part of a program to sell tickets for a ride on the Nightmare Roller Coaster. This is an extreme ride. You must be age 15 or over to ride on it. You will write the code to check the age of someone who wants to buy a ticket.

Logical test in Python

There are special rules in Python about relational operators and data types.

Relational operators in Python

Operator	Meaning
==	equal to
!=	not equal
<	less than
>	more than

⬆ Relation operators

The relational operators in Python programming are slightly different from those you saw in the previous section (used in flow charts). Make sure you use these relational operators when writing a Python program.

Equal is shown using a double equals sign. That is because a single equals sign already has a use in Python: to assign a value to a variable. Not equal is shown as an exclamation mark plus an equals sign.

Data type and comparison

In Python different data types can be used for different logical tests:

- "Equal to" and "not equal to" operators can be used with variables of any data type including strings.
- "Less than" and "more than" operators can only be used with numerical values (integer or float).

Collect the comparison data

Every logical test uses a comparison. Before you can apply the logical test you must collect the data for comparison. Before we can decide if the person is old enough to ride on the roller-coaster we must find out their age.

```
# program: show_if
# code by: Alison
# purpose: show how the 'if' structure works

print("Buy a ticket for the Nightmare Roller Coaster")
print("You must be 15 or over")

Age = input("Please enter your age: ")
Age = int(Age)
```

In this program the data is input by the user and stored in a variable called Age. Next the variable Age is converted to integer data type. Remember that a "bigger than" comparison can only be carried out with a numerical value.

if...

The code which uses a logical test to select between two commands is called a conditional statement or an if statement. In Python an if statement has this structure:

- the word "if" (lower case)
- the logical test
- a colon (two dots, like this ":").

if	logical test	:

In this section you will create part of a program to sell tickets for a ride on the Nightmare Roller Coaster. If you are younger than 15 years old you cannot buy a ticket. The logical test is Age < 15 (age is less than 15).

Following the if statement, you enter the command or commands that you want the computer to carry out if the logical test result is True.

In this example, the program will output the message "sorry come back when you are older". It will only show this message if the logical test result is True.

```
print("Buy a ticket for the Nightmare Roller Coaster")
print("You must be 15 or over")

Age = input("Please enter your age: ")
Age = int(Age)

if Age < 15:
    print("sorry come back when you are older")
```

Use of indentation

"Indentation" means that there is empty space at the start of a line of code. The line is set in from the left margin. Indentation is very important in Python. If you get the indentation wrong, your program will not work properly.

The if statement you typed ends with a colon. The colon tells Python that the next line you type must be indented. The indentation shows that the line "belongs inside" the if statement. There might be one indented line, or there might be many indented lines. However many lines are indented, they all "belong inside" the if statement.

The lines inside the if statement will be carried out if the logical test is true. If the test is false they will not be carried out. Indentation shows which lines will be carried out.

If you do not want a line of code to be indented, press "backspace" to delete the empty space at the start of the line. This turns the indentation off. The next lines you type will not be indented.

Use TAB key to indent

You have learned that Python adds indentation automatically.

But you can also use the TAB key on your keyboard to add indentation. Press TAB before you start typing a line of code. This adds an indentation at the start of the line.

To remove indentation, you can delete the tab, using the backspace or delete key on your keyboard.

Q Test yourself

1. What is the final symbol on the first line of an if statement?

2. What does indentation show in an if statement?

3. Where does a logical test appear in an if statement?

4. In the example on this page, why was the Age variable converted to integer data type?

Q Learning activities

1. Copy the program shown on this page and make sure it works properly.

2. Create a program that checks a user password for a computer game. Choose the correct password. If the user enters the correct password display the message "Welcome to the game".

Syllabus reference

2.2.1 Programming concepts

Learners should be able to understand and use the concept of selection.

Python `if... else...`

Introduction

In the previous section you learned to write Python code using an `if` statement. The commands inside the `if` statement are carried out if the logical test result is True. In this section you will extend the `if` statement to include commands carried out if the logical test result is False.

Algorithm

In the previous section you wrote a program that asked for the user's age. The logical test was age less than 15. If the age was less than 15 the message "sorry come back when you are older" appeared. On the left of this page is a flowchart that matches that structure.

Now we will extend the program. We will add a second message. This message will be output if the logical test is False. Here is a flowchart that shows the structure of the extended program.

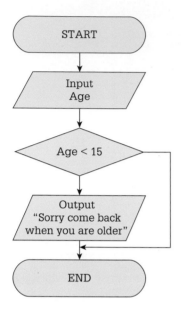

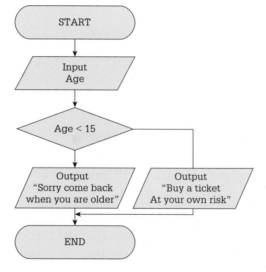

`if... else...`

In Python you can make the computer choose between two different actions. You use an `if` statement, then you use the word `else`:

- The indented code that follows the `if` statement is carried out if the test result is True.

- The indented code that follows the word `else` is carried out if the test result is False.

Using this code we can extend the Nightmare Roller Coaster example.

```python
print("Buy a ticket for the Nightmare Roller Coaster")
print("You must be 15 or over")

Age = input("Please enter your age: ")
Age = int(Age)

if Age < 15:
    print("sorry come back when you are older")

else:
    print("you can buy a ticket at your own risk")
```

Here is the extended program. Can you work out what this code does?

Use of indentation

Indentation shows which code belongs "inside" the `if` statement:

- The `if` statement and the `else` statement are not indented.
- The lines that follow the `if` statement and the `else` statement are indented.

The indented lines that follow the `if` statement will be carried out if the test result is True. The indented lines that follow the `else` statement will be carried out if the test result is False.

Example

This program carries out a calculation for the user:

- The user enters two numbers. They are stored as the variables `Num1` and `Num2`.
- Then the user chooses what calculation to do. This input is stored as the variable `Choice`.

The computer chooses an action using `if… else`.

```
# program plusminus

print("Plus/Minus. A calculation that does addition and subtraction.")

Num1 = input("enter a number: ")
Num2 = input("enter another number: ")

Num1 = int(Num1)
Num2 = int(Num2)

choice = input("Type + to add the numbers together (else subtract)")

if choice == "+":
    answer = Num1 + Num2
else:
    answer = Num1 - Num2

print("The answer is :", answer)
```

Read through the program code and think about what it does. Now try typing in the program and using it to see what happens. Did the program do what you expected?

Test yourself

Answer these questions about the example program.

1. Why are the variables `Num1` and `Num2` converted to integer data type in this program?
2. What does the computer do if the user types +?
3. What does the computer do if the user presses the Enter key with no typing?
4. This program uses whole numbers such as `99`. What happens if you type a decimal number such as `99.9`? Try it and see.
5. How would you change the program so it allows decimal numbers?

Learning activities

1. Enter and run all the examples of code shown on these two pages.
2. On page 185 you created a program that checks a user password. Extend the program to show an appropriate message if the user types the wrong password.
3. Adapt the calculation program so it accepts decimal values.
4. Make a calculation program that selects multiply or divide.
5. Adapt the calculator program so it outputs the question as well as the answer.

Syllabus reference

2.2.1 Programming concepts

Learners should be able to understand and use the concept of selection.

Python `elif`

> ## Introduction
>
> In the previous section you learned how to use `if` and `else` to select between two options. In this section you will learn a more complex form of selection. The Python command `elif` lets the computer select between more than two options. In this section you will learn how to use `elif`.

What is `elif`?

You have learned to use `if... else...` in Python. By using `if` and `else` you can make the computer choose between two different actions. The computer makes the choice based on the result of a logical test. A logical test has only two results: True or False.

Python has a more complex structure called `elif`. The `elif` structure lets you use a series of logical tests. That means the computer can select from more than two options.

Use of `elif`

`elif` is useful when you need to write a program where the user can choose from several different options. In many programs you need to give the user a simple yes/no choice. If that is what you need, you can use `if... else...`.

In other cases you need to give the user more options than a simple yes/no choice. For example, some computer programs offer the user a menu of choices. If you want to give the user more than two options to choose from, you can use `elif`.

Structure of `elif`

The structure of `elif` is based on the `if... else...` structure you already know.

Begin `elif`

You begin with a normal an `if` statement like this:

```
if test:
    command
```

Of course instead of *test* you include a logical test. Instead of the word *command* you put an indented line of code. This line of code will be carried out if the test result is True.

Indentation

Remember that indentation shows the lines that are linked to the logical test.

Continue `elif`

By using the word `elif` you can extend the `if` statement. You can add more logical tests. Just type the word `elif` and a test. Each elif statement works like an if statement. There can be as many elifs as you want. For example:

```
if test:
    command
elif test:
    command
elif test:
    command
```

The computer will carry out all the tests in order until it finds a test that is true. Then it will carry out the commands that go with that test. Once a computer has found a "true" test and carried out the commands that go with it, the elif command is finished. The computer will go on to the next part of the program.

Finish `elif`

The computer might get through all the tests and not find a single one that is true. You can finish the elif statement with "else". The lines that follow "else" will be carried out if none of the tests were true.

Here is the final structure:

```
if test:
    command
elif test:
    command
elif test:
    command
else:
    command
```

Review `elif`

Here are the rules about `elif`:

- It starts with a normal if statement
- You can use the word `elif` as many times as you want to.
- Each `elif` is followed by a logical test and a colon.
- Each elif is followed by indented lines. These lines will be carried out if the logical test is True.
- You don't have to use `else` at the end, but sometimes it is helpful.

Example

It might be easiest to see this structure by looking at an example. This program lets you choose one of the four arithmetic operators, then it carries out the calculation.

```
print("This program works as a calculator")

Num1 = input("enter a number: ")
Num2 = input("enter another number: ")

Num1 = int(Num1)
Num2 = int(Num2)

choice = input("choose the operator (+ - / *): ")

if choice == "+":
    answer = Num1 + Num2
elif choice =="-":
    answer = Num1 - Num2
elif choice == "*":
    answer = Num1 * Num2
elif choice == "/":
    answer = Num1 / Num2
else:
    print("you didn't choose a valid operator")
    answer = 0

print("The answer is :", answer)
```

There are four choices, so there are four logical tests.

Q

Test yourself

1. How many times are you allowed to use an `elif`?

2. What is each `elif` followed by?

3. If the test that follows an `elif` is true, what does the computer do?

4. If none of the tests is true, what does the computer do?

Q

Learning activities

1. Copy the program shown on this page. Try running the program. See what happens when you enter different choices.

2. Create the code for one scene from a computer game. The user must type "north", "south", "east" or "west". The computer displays a different danger or challenge for each of these four options.

Syllabus reference

2.1.2 Pseudocode

Learners should be able to use the following conditional statements:
IF..., THEN..., ELSE..., ENDIF;
CASE..., OF..., OTHERWISE...,
ENDCASE.

Selection in pseudocode

Introduction

You have learned to use if, else and elif in Python. Pseudocode has similar structures. In this section you will learn to understand and use pseudocode selection structures.

Selection

In pseudocode, selection is done using logical tests. The way this is done is very similar to the way it is done in Python. If you have learned to use if, else and elif in Python you will find it easy to use similar structures in pseudocode.

In Python command words are shown in lower case. In pseudocode the words are shown in upper case.

IF... THEN... ELSE... ENDIF

The structure of a pseudocode IF statement looks like this:

```
IF test THEN

    commands

ELSE

    commands

ENDIF
```

There are many similarities to the if structure in Python. Remember that when you write the logical test, you should compare two values using a relational operator, just as in Python.

There are some differences between pseudocode and Python:

- The command words are in upper case.
- Instead of using a colon, the end of the first line is shown by the word THEN.
- The end of the whole IF statement is marked by the word ENDIF.
- You can put all the code on a single line of pseudocode instead of spreading it out over several lines.

Example

Here is a pseudocode version of the roller coaster program you made in on page 197:

```
READ Age
IF Age < 15 THEN
    PRINT "sorry come back when you are older"
ELSE
    PRINT "you can buy a ticket at your own risk"
ENDIF
```

If you understand Python and you can use If in Python then you will understand programs set out in pseudocode.

CASE

In Python we use `elif` to carry out lots of tests in a row. In pseudocode a CASE statement is used for this. If you learn other programming languages you will find that "case" is a very common command word in programming – but it is not used in Python.

All the tests in a CASE statement are carried out using the same variable. You begin by saying what the variable is:

```
CASE Variable OF
```

Then you list all the different values for that variable, and the command that goes with each test. A colon separates the value and the commands:

```
Value: Commands
Value: Commands
Value: Commands
```

In Python `else` is used for the final command. The computer carries out this final command if all the other tests are false. In pseudocode the word OTHERWISE is used.

The CASE statement ends with the word ENDCASE.

Example

On page 201 you made a calculator program using Python. Here is exactly the same program made using pseudocode:

```
READ Num1
READ Num2

PRINT "choose the operator (+ - / *):"
INPUT Choice

CASE Choice OF
"+": answer ← Num1 + Num2
"-": answer ← Num1 - Num2
"*": answer ← Num1 * Num2
"/": answer ← Num1 / Num2

OTHERWISE
  PRINT "you didn't choose a valid operator"
  answer ← 0

ENDCASE
PRINT answer
```

Python does not have a CASE command, though it is found in many other computer languages. If you need something like the CASE statement in Python, you would use `elif`, though the two commands are not exactly the same.

Test yourself

1. What are the similarities between the IF statement in pseudocode and the `if` statement in Python?

2. What are the differences between the IF statement in pseudocode and the `if` statement in Python?

3. Explain why you would use the CASE statement when a user has to pick from a menu of different choices.

4. Look at the second pseudocode program on this page. When is the variable answer set to value 0?

Learning activity

You have completed several Python learning activities. You have created a series of Python programs. Create a pseudocode version of every Python program you have made.

Syllabus reference

2.2.1 Programming concepts

Learners should be able to understand and use the concept of repetition.

2.1.2 Flowcharts

Learners should be able to understand and use standard flowchart symbols.

8.4 Repetition

Loops

> ### Introduction
> Programs use loops. Loops are sections of a program that repeat over and over again. In this section you will look at loops in flowcharts.

What is a loop?

You have learned about program sequence, which is when commands are carried out in order. You have learned about program selection, which is when the computer uses a logical test to choose between different options. In this section you will learn about program repetition.

A loop is a section of code that is repeated. The program loops back on itself. Using loops makes programs much more powerful. Just a few lines of code can make a program that will run for a long time.

Exit condition

Every loop must have an exit condition. The exit condition is a logical test. The exit condition tells the computer when to stop repeating the loop.

When you are using a loop, it is important that there is a way to stop the loop. You must make sure that the exit condition can come true. Otherwise, the loop will never stop.

Types of loop

There are two types of loop:

- counter-controlled loop
- condition-controlled loop.

The two types of loop have different exit conditions.

Counter-controlled loop

In a counter-controlled loop the computer counts up how many times the loop repeats. When it reaches a set number, the loop stops. You use a counter-controlled loop when you know exactly how many loops you need in the program. A counter-controlled loop uses a variable called the counter. The counter goes up by 1 every time the loop repeats. When it reaches a maximum value the loop stops. Learn more about counter loops on pages 206–207.

Condition-controlled loop

In a condition-controlled loop you set a logical test. The result of the test tells the computer whether to repeat the loop. The loop might repeat once, or a million times. You use the condition-controlled loop when you do not know how many times you need to repeat the loop. Learn more about condition-controlled loops on pages 208–209.

Flowchart loop

In a flowchart the exit condition is shown using a decision box. A decision box has a logical test inside it. A decision box has two arrows coming out of it. The loop that comes out of the side of the decision box goes back up the page. It rejoins the main arrow that shows the flow of the program.

Example

This flowchart shows an algorithm. The program asks a mathematics question and checks the user's answer.

Note these important features:

- The exit condition uses a variable called "Answer".

- A box inside the loop lets the user change the value of the variable "Answer".

Look at the flowchart structure. When will the program stop looping?

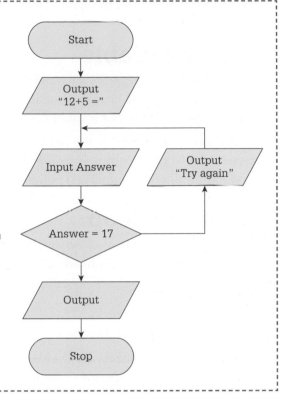

Key words

Two key words are very useful when talking about loops:

- "Increment" means increase a value by one.

- "Iterate" means perform a loop one time.

Test yourself

1. What is an exit condition?

2. What does "increment" mean?

3. There are two types of loop. Explain how they differ by contrasting the exit conditions for each type.

4. A teacher wrote a program to process the results of exactly 100 student tests. What type of program loop does she need?

5. A student wrote a condition-controlled loop. The exit condition checked a variable called finish. She forgot to include a command inside the loop to change the value of finish. What happened when she ran the program?

Learning activity

1. Draw the flowchart shown on this page.

2. Draw a flowchart for a program that asks for a password. It loops until the user gives the correct password. You can choose what the correct password is.

Syllabus reference

2.2.1 Programming concepts

Learners should be able to understand and use the concept of repetition.

for **loops**

> ## Introduction
>
> You have learned there are two types of loop: counter-controlled and condition-controlled loops. In this section you will learn how to make a counter-controlled loop. In Python this is called a `for` loop.

Counter variable

A counter-controlled loop uses a variable as the counter. The counter variable will increment (go up by 1) every time the loop iterates (repeats). When the counter reaches the maximum value the loop will stop.

You can choose any name for the counter variable. Some programmers call it `counter`, but the most common name is `i`. This name is quick to write, and understood by all programmers. It is the name we will use.

Python `for` loop

In Python a counter-controlled loop is called a `for` loop. Here are some examples of `for` loops. In each case the counter is called `i`:

```
for i in range (1, 100):
for i in range (0, 5):
for i in range (4, 8):
```

The two numbers in brackets are the start and stop values for the counter. The program will count from the lower number to the higher number. It will stop just before it reaches the higher value. For instance, in the first example the program will count from 1 to 99, then stop.

If you do not specify a start value, Python will start at 0.

You do not need to write any code to increment the counter variable. Python will do that on its own.

Indented lines are repeated

You have learned that indentation is important in Python. Indentation is added automatically by Python after you type a colon. Or you can add indentation yourself using the TAB key.

Indentation shows which lines belong inside the loop. There might be one indented line, or more. The indented lines will be repeated.

How many times will these lines be repeated? The computer will count the iterations until it reaches the right number. Then the loop will stop.

Complete structure

The Python structure looks like this:

```
for i in range (start, stop):
    command
```

The indented commands will be repeated.

Example

Here is an example Python program with a `for` loop.

```
# program forloop
# demonstrates the 'for' loop in Python

for i in range(1, 5):
    print("count number ", i)

print("now the loop has stopped")
```

Inside the loop there is a command to print the counter variable. This is what you see when you run the program.

When you run the program you will see the counter variable. The computer will print the counter variable every time the loop repeats. The value will be bigger each time. When the counter variable reaches the stop value, the loop stops.

```
count number   1
count number   2
count number   3
count number   4
now the loop has stopped
```

Input the stop value

In this program the user can choose the number of iterations. The user inputs a number. User input is stored as a variable called `howmany`. The program loops until it reaches that value.

```
# program forloop
# demonstrates the 'for' loop in Python

howmany = input("how many loops do you want?")
howmany = int(howmany)

for i in range(1, howmany+1):
    print("count number ", i)

print("now the loop has stopped")
```

These are features of this program:

- The user inputs a value. It is stored in the variable `howmany`.
- Input variables are always string data type. So the next line converts the variable to an integer.
- The variable `howmany` is used as the stop value of the for loop.
- The stop value for the loop is set at `howmany + 1`. This is because the `range` exits the loop at the stop value, so the loop stops 1 before this value.

Step count

Typically the Python `for` loop command will count up in increments of 1. However, a different step size can be used. You simply add the step size you want to use as a third number inside the brackets. The command:

```
for i in range (0, 100, 10):
```

will count up from 0 to 100 in increments of 10.

You can even use a negative number and Python will count backwards:

```
for i in range (100, 0, -10):
```

Q

Test yourself

1. If the start and stop values of a Python loop are set at 1 and 11, how many times will the loop iterate?

2. How does Python know which commands to repeat inside the for loop?

3. In the second example program on this page the user sets the number of iterations for the loop. In your own words explain the reason for this command:

   ```
   howmany -
   int(howmany)
   ```

Q

Learning activity

1. An example of a Python program where the user sets the number of iterations of the loop is given above. The user does this by setting the upper value of the counter range. Create a new version of this program so the user sets the upper and lower value of the counter range.

2. Create a program so the user enters a number value and the program shows the value of that number multiplied by 1, by 2, by 3 and so on up to 12.

Syllabus reference

2.2.1 Programming concepts

Learners should be able to understand and use the concept of repetition.

`while` **loops**

> ## Introduction
>
> You have learned there are two types of loop: counter-controlled and condition-controlled loops. In this section you will learn how to make a condition-controlled loop. In Python this is called a `while` loop.

Loop while a test result is true

There are many different types of condition-controlled loop used in programming. Python uses just one – the `while` loop. These are key facts about the `while` loop:

- A `while` loop starts with a logical test.
- If the test is result is True, the loop iterates.
- If the test result is False, the loop stops.

Other types of loop are used in different programming languages but not in Python. You can learn about other types of loop on pages 206–207.

Loop structure

The first line of a `while` loop is very easy to write. It consists of:

- the word `while`
- a logical test
- a colon (":").

The line or lines that follow this are indented. The indented commands will be carried out while the logical test result is True. The indentation shows you which lines belong inside the loop. The indented lines will be repeated.

Test variable

As a reminder, if the logical test result is True the loop will repeat. If the logical test result is False, the loop will stop, and the rest of the program will continue.

You must make it possible for the loop to stop. To use the `while` loop, remember these rules:

- The logical test at the top of the loop must have a variable in it.
- There must be a line inside the loop that can change the value of that variable. Otherwise, the loop will never stop.

Example

On this page you will make a computer game made using a single `while` loop. The game is called "The Maze of Doom". Here is how it starts.

```
# program mazeofdoom
# this program is a game where the user has to escape from a maze
# it demonstrates the 'while' loop in Python

print("GAME: The Maze of Doom")
print("You are surrounded by thick hedges. You cannot see over them.")
print("You can go North, South, East or West. Which do you choose.?")
print("\n")
Direction = input("Type one letter: N, S, E, W: ")
```

This program starts with introductory comments. Then there are five lines of code. These lines are not indented. They only happen once, at the start of the game. They do not loop. Then the player is asked to input a letter that stands for north, south, east or west. User input is stored in a variable called `Direction`.

Add a loop

Now we will extend the program, using a `while` loop.

```
# program mazeofdoom
# this program is a game where the user has to escape from a maze
# it demonstrates the 'while' loop in Python

print("GAME: The Maze of Doom")
print("You are surrounded by thick hedges. You cannot see over them.")
print("You can go North, South, East or West. Which do you choose.?")
print("\n")
Direction = input("Type one letter: N, S, E, W: ")

while Direction != "W":
    print("The hedges continue on either side of you.")
    print("You are getting tired and hungry")
    print("Which direction do you want to go?")
    Direction = input("Type one letter: N, S, E, W: ")
    print("\n")

print("You see the way out ahead of you.")
print("WIN: you have escaped the Maze of Doom")
```

Start the loop

The loop starts with a logical test. It looks like this:

```
while Direction != "W":
```

The logical test is `Direction != "W"`. The variable is called `Direction`. The relational operator `!=` means "does not equal", so the loop will repeat while the variable `Direction` does not hold the value "W".

Inside the loop

Then there are five indented lines. These five lines will repeat with each iteration of the loop. There are three lines that tell the player that he or she is still stuck in the maze. Then there is a line that takes user input:

```
Direction = input("Type one letter: N, S, E, W: ")
```

This is the line that lets the user change the value of the variable `Direction`. This is how the user can stop the loop.

After the loop

There are a few lines at the end that are not indented. They are not inside the loop. They will be carried out only once, after the loop has stopped.

Learning activity

1. Enter the program shown on this page. Run the program and try playing the game.

2. Create a different game. The player must escape from a lion. The only way to escape is to get a feather and tickle the lion. Give the player several choices. When the player picks "tickle with a feather" the lion will run away.

3. Use the `while` loop to create a password system. The program will loop unless the user enters the correct password.

Test yourself

Answer these questions are about the game "The Maze of Doom".

1. How many lines are inside the loop?

2. What would happen in this game if the user entered w right away?

3. What would happen if the user entered a lower case w?

4. You want to change the game so that typing w makes the loop continue and anything else makes the loop stop. Which line would you change, and how would you change it?

Syllabus reference

2.1.2 Pseudocode

Learners should be able to understand and use pseudocode, using the following loop structures: FOR..., TO..., NEXT; WHILE..., DO..., ENDWHILE; REPEAT...UNTIL

Loops in pseudocode

Introduction

You have learned to make counter-controlled and condition-controlled loops in Python. In this section you will see how the same loops are made in pseudocode.

FOR loop

A counter-controlled loop in pseudocode has a similar structure to Python. In this example the counter variable is shown as i:

```
FOR i ← start TO stop

    commands

NEXT i
```

There are some differences from Python:

- Command words are shown in upper case.

- An arrow is used to point to the counter variable.

- The structure ends with NEXT i.

- In Python the loop stops before it reaches the stop value. In pseudocode it stops when it reaches the stop value.

To make a FOR loop you must put numbers in place of *start* and *stop*. Remember that in pseudocode the FOR loop counts up to the stop value. The final iteration uses the stop value. Indent the lines that you want to repeat inside the loop. Here is an example:

```
READ Value

FOR i ← 1 TO 5

  PRINT Value * i

NEXT i

PRINT "The loop has stopped"
```

If the user entered the value 10, what output would be produced by this loop? Remember that in pseudocode, on the first iteration the counter value will be 1, and on the final iteration it will be 5.

WHILE loop

A WHILE loop in pseudocode has a similar structure to a while loop in Python. A logical test comes at the top of the loop. If the test result is True the loop will continue:

```
WHILE test DO

    commands

ENDWHILE
```

To use a WHILE loop in pseudocode, replace the word *test* with an actual test, using a logical variable. Enter commands inside the loop. The structure ends with the word ENDWHILE. Here is an example:

```
PRINT "You are stuck in a maze"
READ Direction
WHILE Direction <> "W" DO
   PRINT "You are still in the maze"
   READ Direction
ENDWHILE
PRINT "You have escaped!"
```

The test comes at the top of the loop, so:

- You have to set the value of the test variable before the loop starts.
- If the test result is False the commands inside the loop will not be carried out even once.

REPEAT... UNTIL loop

A REPEAT loop is a different type of loop. It has different rules from a WHILE loop:

- The test comes at the end of the loop.
- If the test result is True the loop will stop.

The pseudocode structure looks like this:

```
REPEAT
   commands
UNTIL test
```

Here is the game "The Maze of Doom", made using a REPEAT loop:

```
REPEAT
   PRINT "You are stuck in a maze"
   READ Direction
UNTIL Direction = "W"
PRINT "You have escaped!"
```

The test comes at the bottom of the loop. So:

- You do not have to set the test variable before the loop starts.
- The commands inside the loop are carried out at least once before the test.

Q

Test yourself

1. You want to make a loop, with the test at the top of the loop. What type of loop would you use?

2. You want to make a loop that stops when the test result is True. What type of loop would you use?

3. You want to make a loop that repeats 100 times. What type of loop would you use?

4. Explain the main differences between the WHILE and REPEAT loops in pseudocode.

Q

Learning activities

1. Write an algorithm in pseudocode that prints out the 17 times table.

2. Write an algorithm for a password login, using the WHILE loop.

3. Write an algorithm for a password login, using the REPEAT loop.

Syllabus reference

2.2.2 Data structures; arrays

Learners should be able to declare and use one-dimensional arrays, show understanding of the use of one-dimensional arrays.

8.5 | Data structures

Lists and arrays

> ### Introduction
>
> You have learned to use a variable to store a single data value. In this section you will learn about a new kind of variable called a list. This lets you store a list of different values.

Make a list

A teacher made a Python list to store the names of her students. Here is the command:

```
Studentlist = ["caspar", "soolin", "ali", "roberto", "priti"]
```

The full list is shown in square brackets. In this example it is a list of five names. The different items in a list are called elements. The elements in a list are separated by commas. There are five elements in this list. The elements are of string data type.

You can also make a list of numbers. A scientist made a list to store the result of an experiment each day for a week. Here is the command:

```
Resultslist = [2.3, 2.2, 4.5, 6.6, 1.9. 8.7, 6.0]
```

Numerical values do not have quotation marks. How many elements are there in this list? Which data type is used in this list?

Features of a list

A list is a variable that stores multiple elements. Each element in the list has its own name. The name of an element is the name of the list plus an index number. The numbering starts at 0:

```
Studentlist[0] contains "caspar"

Studentlist[1] contains "soolin"

Studentlist[2] contains "ali".
```

(The list will continue in this way.) The index number tells you the position of the element in the list. The index number is in square brackets.

Working with elements

Once you have made a list you can work with the elements. Each element in a list can be treated as a variable in its own right. You can print a list element:

```
print(Studentlist[0])
```

You can assign the value to another variable:

```
ClassLeader = Studentlist[0]
```

You can use a list variable in logical tests:

```
if Studentlist[0] == "caspar":
```

Working with the full list

You can also work with the full list. For example, with a single command you can print the entire list:

```
print(Studentlist)
```

This will print the whole list, showing all the elements, including the square brackets, the commas, and the quote marks. The output will look like this:

['caspar', 'soolin', 'ali', 'roberto','priti']

Example

This program shows the commands you have learned.

```
# python studentlist
# shows how to use a list in python

studentlist = ["caspar", "soolin", "ali", "roberto", "priti"]

print("student number 0 is")
print(studentlist[0])

print("student number 1 is", studentlist[1])

print("now I will print the whole list")
print(studentlist)
```

Comparison to other programming languages

In this section you have learned to use a Python list to store values. Similar data structures are available in other programming languages, but there are differences.

List or array?

In most other programming languages this type of variable has a different name. It is called an array. When programmers talk about an array they are referring to the equivalent of a Python list.

Declare or use?

In many programming languages, "declare" means to define the name of a variable and the data type it contains. You have to declare an array, or a list, before you can use it. In Python, you do not need to declare a list. You use it and the computer works out the right data type, and the number of elements in the list.

Test yourself

1. What symbols mark the start and end of a list?

2. How are the elements of a list separated?

3. What is the index number of the first element in a list?

4. Give the command to create a list called Rainbow with seven elements. Choose the values you would store in this list.

5. Give the command to print the second element in the list called Rainbow.

6. Give the command to print the whole list called Rainbow.

Learning activites

1. Enter the program shown on this page. Run the program and see what happens.

2. A soccer team has 11 players. Create a program that stores the names of 11 players in a list called Team. You can use real soccer players, and make your dream team, or just make up names.

3. Add lines to the soccer program so it prints out the names of the first three players.

Syllabus reference

2.2.2 Data structures

Learners should be able to use a variable as an index in an array; read or write values in an array using a FOR..., TO..., NEXT loop.

See also:

8.4 Repetition (for loops)

Output a list

Introduction

You have learned to make a list. You know how to print a single element from the list, or print the whole list. In this section you will learn how to use a `for` loop to print all the elements in a list one by one.

Example

In this section we will use an example list: `Rainbow`. Here is the command to create the list:

```
Rainbow = ["red", "orange", "yellow", "green",
          "blue", "indigo", "violet"]
```

Print an element

The command `print(Rainbow)` will print the whole list including square brackets, commas and quote marks. Or you can print a single element:

```
print(Rainbow[3])
```

This will print the word `green` with no square brackets or quote marks.

Print all elements

There are seven elements in the list. To print all the elements one by one would take seven lines of code. A bigger list would need more lines. It would be a lot of work to write all the lines of code. However, there is an easier way. We can use a counter-controlled loop. The loop will count through the elements of the list, printing each one in turn.

Counter variable

A counter-controlled loop needs a counter variable. We will use the variable `i` as the counter variable.

- Every time the loop iterates, the counter variable will increment by 1.
- We will use the variable `i` as the list index number. Every time the loop iterates, the list index number will count up by 1.

Start and stop values

Every counter-controlled loop has a start and stop value. The start value is 0, because the first element on a list is number 0. The stop value is the number of elements in the list. This list has seven elements, so we will use 7 as the stop value.

Example

This program will count through all the elements in the list. It will print the counter variable. It will print the element with that index number.

```
# program Rainbow
# shows how to print the elements of a list
# using a counter-controlled loop


Rainbow = ['red', 'orange', 'yellow', 'green', 'blue', 'indigo', 'violet']

for i in range(0,7):
    print(i, Rainbow[i])
```

The output looks like this.

The list stops at 6. A counter loop stops just before the stop value. This program prints elements 0–6: all the elements in the list.

```
0 red
1 orange
2 yellow
3 green
4 blue
5 indigo
6 violet
```

How many iterations?

In the previous example the stop value was 7 because the list had exactly 7 elements. We can adapt the program so it works for a list of any length.

Find length of list

This command will find the length of the list called `Rainbow`. It counts how many elements there are in the list:

```
len(Rainbow)
```

This command will store the value in a variable called `Listlength`:

```
ListLength = len(Rainbow)
```

Use length of list as the stop value

Now we can use the variable `ListLength` as the stop value of the counter-controlled loop. Here is the first line of the loop:

```
for i in range (0, ListLength):
```

This means the counter will increment from 0, up to the length of the list. Then it will stop.

Example

Here is a program that uses all the commands you have learned.

```
# program Rainbow
# shows how to print the elements of a list
# using a counter-controlled loop

Rainbow = ['red', 'orange', 'yellow', 'green', 'blue', 'indigo', 'violet']

ListLength = len(Rainbow)

for i in range(0, ListLength):
    print(i, Rainbow[i])
```

Test yourself

1. Give the single-line command which will print the whole of the list called `Rainbow`, inside square brackets.

2. A programmer wanted to print all the elements in a list. She did not write a different line of code to print each element. Instead she used a counter-controlled loop. Why do you think she did this?

3. A programmer used a counter-controlled loop to print the elements of a list. The start value was 0. Explain why he used 0 instead of 1 as the start value.

4. A programmer used a counter-controlled loop to print all the elements in a list. He did not know how many elements there were. Explain how he found the right stop value to use.

Learning activities

1. Copy the `Rainbow` program shown here, and run it to see what the result is.

2. On page 213 you created a list for a soccer team. Use the skills you have learned on this page to print the name of every player in the soccer team.

Syllabus reference

2.2.2 Data structures

Learners should be able to use a variable as an index in an array; read or write values in an array using a FOR..., TO..., NEXT loop.

See also:

8.4 Repetition (for loops; while loops)

Add elements to a list

Introduction

In the previous section you learned how to use a counter-controlled loop to output all the elements of a list. In this section you will learn how to use a counter-controlled loop to input elements to a list.

Append

Adding an element to a list is called appending. The new element is added at the end of the list. Here is an example. This command will add the element "Ultra Violet" to the list called `Rainbow`:

```
Rainbow.append("Ultra Violet")
```

You enter the name of the list, then a dot, then the word "append". You end the command with the element you want to add, in brackets.

Append to an empty list

The simplest way to put elements in a list is to start with an empty list. Then append as many elements as you want.

Create an empty list

You can make a list with no elements in it. Here is an example. This makes an empty list called `Rainbow`:

```
Rainbow = [ ]
```

You can give the list any name.

Counter loop

Next you use a counter-controlled loop to append elements to the empty list. The start value of the loop is 0. The stop value of the loop depends on how many elements you want to add. In this example we will add seven elements:

```
for i in range (0,7):
```

You can use any number for the stop value.

Get a new value and append to the list

There must be two commands inside the loop. The first command will get the new value from the user. The second command will append it to the list.

We use a variable to store the input from the user. In this example the variable is called `NewValue`:

```
NewValue = input("enter the next element of the list")
Rainbow.append(NewValue)
```

Example

Here is the completed program, using the commands from this page.

```
# program Rainbow
# append to a list

Rainbow = [ ]

For i in range(0, 7):
    NewValue = input("enter the next element of the list: ")
    Rainbow.append(NewValue)
```

Choose how many elements

If you are a confident programmer, try this extension activity. You can let the user choose how many elements to add to the list:

- Input the value and store it as a variable.
- Convert the data type to integer.
- Use the variable as the stop value of the `for` loop

Here is a program showing these commands.

```
# program Rainbow
# append to a list

Rainbow = [ ]

HowMany = input("How many elements in the list? ")
HowMany = int(HowMany)

for i in range(0, HowMany):
    NewValue = input("enter the next element of the list: ")
    Rainbow.append(NewValue)
```

You can add extra lines at the end of the program to print out all the elements of the list.

```
print("\n")
print("The elements of this list...")

for i in range(0, HowMany):
    print(i, Rainbow[i])
```

while loop

Here is an extension activity for the most confident programmers. Write a program that uses a `while` loop to add elements to an array. After adding an element, the user is asked if he or she wants to add another. If the user inputs "Y" the loop iterates.

Add extra lines at the end of the program to print all the elements of the list.

Q Test yourself

These questions are about creating a list called `Months`. It has 12 elements: the names of the months.

1. Write the command to make an empty list called `Months`.
2. Write the command to append the value `January` to the list `Months`.
3. Write the first line of a counter-controlled loop that will let the user add 12 elements to the list.
4. Write two lines that will (a) take user input and (b) append that value to the list.

Q Learning activities

1. Make the program shown on this page, that inputs values to the list called `Rainbow`.

2. Make a program that lets you input the names of 12 months to make a list.

3. Use the `Months` program to input the names of the months in a different language, such as French.

3. Add lines to your `Months` program so that the list of months is printed using a counter-controlled loop.

4. Complete one or both of the extension activities.

Review

Key terms

Algorithm   A method for solving a problem set out as a series of step by step instructions with one start and one end.

Arithmetic operator   A symbol that represents an operation in mathematics, The operation completes a calculation. The main operators are +, −, *, /.

Condition-controlled   A loop in a program. The number of times it repeats depends on the results of a logical test.

Counter-controlled   A loop which repeats a set number of times.

Flowchart   A diagram which sets out an algorithm.

Logical test   A test using a relational operator which has the result True or False.

Loop   A program construct where a section of code is repeated several times: it can be condition-controlled or counter-controlled.

Pseudocode   A way of writing out an algorithm using words and symbols which are similar to program code.

Relational operator   A symbol which compares two values. The result of the comparison is either True or False. The main relational operators are =, <>, >, <.

Variable   A named area of computer memory which can be used to store a value while a computer program is running.

Project work

In Chapter 1, you learned about hexadecimal numbers. Write the following programs using this knowledge:

1. A program where the user inputs a denary number, and the program loops until the user enters a number smaller than 16.

2. Building on program 1: A program where the user inputs a denary number from 1-15 and the computer outputs the hexadecimal equivalent.

HINT: "if" and "elif" will help you to find numbers bigger than 9 and turn them into their hexadecimal equivalent.

If you have found these programs quite easy to make, create a range of programs which convert between binary, hexadecimal and denary.

9 Solution development

Syllabus reference

2.2.1 Programming concepts

Learners should be able to understand and use the concept of counting; work out the purpose of a given algorithm; explain standard methods of solution; produce an algorithm for a given problem (either in the form of pseudocode or flowchart).

2.1.2 Pseudocode

Learners should be able to show an understanding of counting (for example Count ← Count + 1).

2.1.2 Flowcharts

Learners should be able to understand and use standard flowchart symbols to represent the above statements.

See also:

Chapter 8 Programming

9.1 Worked examples

Count how many

> ### Introduction
>
> In the last chapter you learned programming methods. In this chapter you will put your skills to use. You will learn about how programmers use their coding skills to produce solutions to problems. In this section you will learn how to use a program to "count how many".

Worked examples

This section will show you examples of common programming solutions. You will learn to produce those solutions in Python. You will also look at the algorithms as flowcharts and pseudocode. In the following sections you will **not** learn how to program. It is assumed that you know how to do tasks such as assign a value to a variable, and make loops. If you cannot remember how to do these tasks, go back to *Chapter 8 Programming* and revise those skills.

To make the most of these worked examples, do the following:

1. Write the algorithm in pseudocode.
2. Draw the flowchart.
3. Create a working Python program.
4. Learn and understand the program.
5. Be able to recognise future examples.
6. Write new Python programs based on this code.

Count how many

This program will "count how many". You could adapt the program for many different uses. For example, it could count how many marathon runners cross the finishing line, or count how many cars are produced by a car factory.

The basic program has this structure:

● Create a variable called Count. Value is 0.

● Create a variable called CarryOn. Value is "Y".

● Start a condition-controlled loop. It will loop while CarryOn = "Y"

● Every time you want to count up by 1, you press "Y".

● Count goes up by 1 with each loop

● When the loop stops, the value of Count is printed.

In pseudocode

Here is that structure shown as pseudocode:

```
Count ← 0

CarryOn ← "Y"

WHILE CarryOn = "Y"

        Count ← Count + 1

        PRINT "Type Y to continue"

        READ CarryOn

ENDWHILE

PRINT Count
```

Which line of the pseudocode increases Count by 1? Which row lets you input "Y" to carry on?

Flowchart

In the right margin you can see the same algorithm shown as a flowchart.

When you are drawing a flowchart it is simplest to show the test (the decision box) at the bottom of the loop.

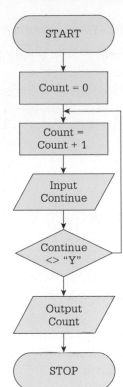

In Python

Here is the completed Python program.

```python
## WORKED EXAMPLE
# Count how many

print("begin count")
Count = 0
CarryOn = "Y"

while CarryOn == "Y":
    Count = Count + 1
    print("Count so far: ", Count)
    CarryOn = input("Do you want to continue (Y/N):")

print("count ended")
print("you counted :", Count)
```

Make this program for yourself and check that it works.

Learning activity

Using the example on this page create a Python program for at least one of the following. If you are confident make sure you do activity 3: Stretch and challenge.

1. Write a program for an official at a marathon to use to count the runners as they cross the finishing line.

2. Write a program for a farmer so he can count how many new lambs are born in his flock.

3. **Stretch and challenge:** Write a program to control a car park barrier. It must count how many cars go into the car park. In this example the loop will stop if the number in the car park reaches 100. At this point, no more cars can enter.

Test yourself

1. What are the names of the two variables used in the Python program?

2. What are the data types of the two variables?

3. What is the exit condition of the loop? In other words, what makes the loop stop?

4. Explain why we use a condition-controlled loop and not a counter-controlled loop in this program.

Syllabus reference

2.2.1 Programming concepts

Learner should be able to: understand and use the concept of totalling; work out the purpose of a given algorithm; explain standard methods of solution; produce an algorithm for a given problem (either in the form of pseudocode or flowchart).

2.1.2 Pseudocode

Learners should be able to understand totalling (for example Sum ← Sum + Number).

2.1.2 Flowcharts

Learners should be able to understand and use standard flowchart symbols to represent the above statements.

See also:

Chapter 8 Programming

Calculate a total

Introduction

In the previous section you learned a standard algorithm and code to count how many times something happened. It used a loop. In this section you will learn how to create a program that calculates a total by adding values together.

Sum total

In this section you will create a program to add up a series of values. This is a very useful basic program structure. You can adapt the program structure for many different needs. For example, you could use it to add up the bill in a shop or restaurant; add up the total score a student gets in an exam; or add up the total production of a factory.

In everyday speech we use the word "sum" to refer to any calculation, for example: "I am good at doing sums". In mathematics "sum" is used to mean the total you get by adding up a list of numbers. We will use the word in that sense.

Which type of loop to use

Should you use a condition-controlled loop or a counter-controlled loop to calculate a sum total? It depends on the following:

- Sometimes you know in advance exactly how many values you will need to add together. For example, if you are adding up the marks a student has gained for the questions in an exam, you know exactly how many questions there are, so you know how many items (values) need to be added together. In this case, you would use a counter-controlled loop.

- Sometimes you do not know how many values you need to add together. For example, if you are adding up customers' bills in a shop, every customer could buy a different number of items. You would not know in advance how many values you would need to add together, so you would use a condition-controlled loop.

The worked example in this section uses a condition-controlled loop.

Program structure

Here is the basic structure of a program to add up the sum total of a series of numbers:

- Create a variable called Sum. Set its value to 0.
- Make a loop (it can be a condition-controlled or counter-controlled loop).
- Every time the loop increments, the user enters a value.
- Every time the loop increments, the input value is added to the variable Sum.
- When the loop stops, the value of Sum is printed out.

In pseudocode

Here is the sum total algorithm shown in pseudocode. This example uses a condition-controlled loop:

```
Sum ← 0

CarryOn ← "Y"

WHILE CarryOn = "Y"

        READ Number

        Sum ← Sum + Number

        PRINT "Type Y to continue"

        READ CarryOn

ENDWHILE

PRINT Sum
```

Flowchart

In the right margin you can see the same algorithm shown as a flowchart.

The flowchart loop will increment until the user enters any value except "Y".

In Python

Here is the completed Python program.

```python
## WORKED EXAMPLE
# Sum (Add together)

print("begin to add up the total")
Sum = 0
CarryOn = "Y"

while CarryOn == "Y":
    Number = input("enter the next value to add: ")
    Number = int(Number)
    Sum = Sum + Number
    CarryOn = input("Do you want to continue (Y/N):")

print("Adding up completed")
print("The total was :", Sum)
```

Enter this program yourself and check that it works.

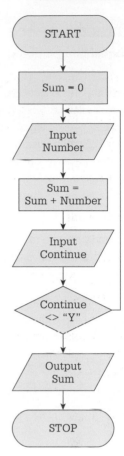

Learning activity

Create Python programs for at least one of the following. These activities increase in difficulty from the first to the fourth. Make sure you do at least the first one.

1. Make a program for a shopkeeper that will enter the cost of each purchase and display the total customer bill.

2. Adapt the shop program so that the user can enter and add up decimal number values.

3. Make a program for a teacher to add up the marks from ten questions to give a total test mark. It must be counter-controlled.

4. Make a program for a mathematician. The mathematician will enter a series of numbers. The computer will calculate the product.

Test yourself

1. Explain the reason for this line in the Python program:

   `Number = int(Number)`

2. Create a pseudocode algorithm using a counter-controlled loop to add up exactly ten values.

3. You have learned that the sum of a series of numbers is calculated by carrying out a series of additions. If instead you use a series of multiplications, the result is called a product. Create a flowchart that calculates the product of a series of numbers.

223

Syllabus reference

2.2.1 Programming concepts

Learners should be able to understand and use the concept of counting and totalling; work out the purpose of a given algorithm; explain standard methods of solution, produce an algorithm for a given problem (either in the form of pseudocode or flowchart).

2.1.2 Pseudocode

Learners should be able to understand totalling and counting.

2.1.2 Flowcharts

Learners should be able to understand and use standard flowchart symbols to represent the above statements.

See also:

Chapter 8 Programming

Calculate an average

Introduction

In the last two sections you learned how to use program methods to count up and to add up. By combining these two methods you can create a program that works out an average. This is a good way to practise your programming skills.

Average (mean)

This program will calculate an average. The mathematical term for an average is a "mean".

The mean value is calculated as follows.

1. Count how many values there are (the count).
2. Add up the total of the values (the sum).
3. Divide the sum by the count to give the average.

Which type of loop to use

Should you use a condition-controlled loop or a counter-controlled loop for this program? Once again, it depends whether you know the number of values in advance. The worked example in this section uses a counter-controlled loop.

Program structure

You have seen two examples using a condition-controlled loop. In this section for a change we will use a counter-controlled loop.

Here is the program structure:

- Create a variable called Sum with the value 0.
- Create a variable called Count, which stores a number input by the user.
- Start a counter-controlled loop: the start value is 0, the stop value is Count.
- Every time the loop increments, the user enters a value. The input value is added to the variable Sum.
- When the loop stops, Sum is divided by Count to give the average.

In pseudocode

Here is the structure shown in pseudocode. It uses a counter-controlled loop:

```
Sum ← 0
PRINT "How many values do you want to enter?"
READ Count
FOR i ← 1 TO Count
        READ Number
        Sum ← Sum + Number
NEXT i
Average ← Sum / Count
PRINT Average
```

Flowchart

In the right margin you will see the same algorithm shown as a flowchart.

This shows what a counter-controlled loop looks like in a flowchart.

In Python

Here is the completed Python program.

```
## WORKED EXAMPLE
# Mean (Average)

Count = input("How many values will you enter? ")
Count = int(Count)
Sum = 0

for i in range(0, Count):
    Number = input("enter a value: ")
    Number = int(Number)
    Sum = Sum + Number

print("Adding up completed")
Mean = Sum/Count
print("The average was :", Mean)
```

Enter this program for yourself and check that it works.

Test yourself

1. Which line in the pseudocode starts the counter-controlled loop?

2. What is the name of the counter variable in all these examples?

3. What variable sets the upper range of the counter loop?

4. Which boxes in the flowchart are inside the counter loop?

5. List all the variables in the Python program, and explain what they are used for.

Learning activity

Create Python programs for at least one of the following. Make sure you do at least the first one.

1. Make a program for a scientist that adds up the weight of six eggs in grams, and gives the average weight. A typical egg weighs 50–75 grams. Use integer values.

2. A marathon has 15 competitors. Make a program that records the number of minutes each runner took to complete the race and calculates the average time taken. A typical time would be 250 minutes. Use floating point values.

3. Adapt the marathon program to use a condition-controlled loop. You can use this program to work out an average when you don't know how many runners will complete the race.

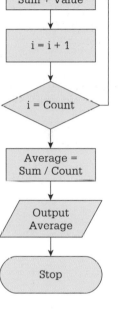

Syllabus reference

2.1.1 The need for verification

Learners should be able to: understand the need for verification checks to be made on input data; explain standard methods of solution; comment on the effectiveness of a given solution.

See also:

Chapter 8 Programming

Verification

> ## Introduction
>
> In this section you will learn to use programming methods to check input. You will also see why it is important to include error checks in a program.

Error checks

A program will go wrong if the user enters the wrong data. If the input is wrong then the output of the program will definitely be wrong. Sometimes wrong data can cause the program to crash, or get stuck in an endless loop.

For this reason many programs include input checks. User input is checked before it is used in the program. Typically, the procedure is as follows.

1. Input from the user is stored in a temporary variable.
2. The content of the temporary variable is checked.
3. If the input passes the error check, then the value is used in the program.

Error message

Typically, if the input is wrong there is an error message. This tells the user what he or she has done wrong. Sometimes the user is given a chance to enter the data again.

Types of check

There are two types of check:

- verification
- validation.

Learn about verification in this section. Learn about validation on pages 228–229.

Verification

Verification means entering the data twice. The two attempts will be stored as two different variables. The computer will check that the two variables match. If they do not match then there has been a mistake in data entry.

A verification check is often used when you change your password on the computer. You have to enter the new password twice. That is because it is very important that you don't make a mistake that would lock you out of the computer.

Use selection or repetition

You can use either selection (`if... else...`) or repetition (`while` loop) for verification.

Selection

One way to verify an input is to use an `if... else` structure, as follows.

1. The user enters a value and it is assigned to a variable.
2. The user enters the value again, and it is assigned to a second variable.

3. An `if` statement is used to compare the two variables.

   If the two variables match, the input has passed the verification check, so you can use it in the rest of the program.

4. If the two variables do not match, `else` will show an error message.

The disadvantage of this method is that the user only gets one chance to enter the right data.

Repetition

An alternative method is to use a condition-controlled loop. It will loop until the input is correct.

1. The same data is entered twice and stored in two variables.

2. A `while` loop is used. It will loop if the two values do not match.

3. Inside the loop the user is given a chance to re-enter the data.

4. When the two values match, the loop will stop.

The advantage of this method is that it gives the user several chances to get the value right.

Example
Selection: Use `if... else`

Here is an example of a Python program using `if... else` for password verification.

```
## WORKED EXAMPLE
# Verification

Try1 = input("enter new password  : ")
Try2 = input("enter password again: ")

if Try1 == Try2:
    Password = Try1
    print("Password has been reset")
else:
    print("The two passwords do not match")
```

Make this program yourself and check that it works.

Repetition: Use a `while` loop

Here is an example of a Python program using a `while` loop for verification.

```
## WORKED EXAMPLE
# Verification with loop

Try1 = input("enter new password  : ")
Try2 = input("enter password again: ")

while Try1 != Try2:
    print("The two passwords do not match")
    Try1 = input("enter new password  : ")
    Try2 = input("enter password again: ")

Password = Try1
print("Password has been reset")
```

Enter this program yourself and check that it works.

Test yourself

1. List the three variables used in these Python programs. What data type is each one?

2. Explain the purpose of each of the three variables in the program.

3. Which of the two programs is the most useful for password input? Explain your answer.

Learning activity

Create pseudocode and flowchart algorithms to match the two Python programs shown on this page.

Validation

Syllabus reference

2.1.1 The need for validation

Learners should be able to understand the need for validation (which could include range checks, length checks, type checks and check digits); explain standard methods of solution; comment on the effectiveness of a given solution.

See also:

2.1 Data transmission (Check digit and checksum)
8.3 Selection (Python `elif`)

Introduction

You have learned why error checks are important. Many programs include error checks. In this section you will learn about a type of error check called validation.

Validation

Validation means checking that data is valid. That means the input data is sensible in context. In general, when making a program we know what sort of input data to expect. Data that is not what we expect can crash the program or produce incorrect results. Validation blocks this data.

Validation criteria

Validation criteria are rules about what data can be accepted by the program. When data is entered it is checked against the validation criteria. If data does not meet the criteria it is not used in the program.

Selection or repetition?

In this section you will look at examples of validation in programming. As with verification, we can use either selection or repetition. The advantage of using repetition is that it gives the user many chances to enter the right data.

Validation checks

Validation checks data using criteria. There are many different types of validation criteria:

- Range checks are only used with numerical variables. The number must be within a valid range. For example, a teacher may need to enter the age of a student at a secondary school where the age could not be below 12 or above 18 years.

- Length checks are used mainly with text variables, particularly code numbers. The right number of characters must be entered. For example, a mobile phone number may need to have exactly 11 digits.

- Type checks can be used with all variables. You have learned that every variable must have a data type. A type check makes sure that input is of the right data type. For example, if you are entering an age it must be a number value; if you are entering a name it must be made of letters of the alphabet and so on.

- Check digits (in *2.1 Data transmission* you learned about the use of check digits): a check digit is calculated from a long number using a mathematical formula. The check digit is entered along with the number. The computer uses the same formula to calculate the check digit. The two check digits should match. Otherwise, there has been a mistake in data entry.

Examples

There are many different ways of making validation checks in Python and in other programming languages. We will look at some examples.

This Python program has a range check. The user inputs how much money she wants to take out of her bank account. If the value is below 0, the number is rejected.

```
## WORKED EXAMPLE
# Range check

Balance = 1000.00
Money = input("How much money do you want from your bank account: ")
Money = float(Money)

if Money < 0:
    print("You cannot withdraw less than 0")
else:
    print(Money, " has been withdrawn from your account")
    Balance = Balance - Money

print(Balance, " remains in your account.")
```

Here is the same program with extra range checks built in. This program uses `elif`.

```
## WORKED EXAMPLE
# Range check

Balance = 1000.00
Money = input("How much money do you want from your bank account: ")
Money = float(Money)

if Money < 0:
    print("You cannot withdraw less than 0")
elif Money > Balance:
    print("You do not have that much money")
elif Money > 250.00:
    print("You cannot withdraw more than $250.00 a day")
else:
    print(Money, " has been withdrawn from your account")
    Balance = Balance - Money

print(Balance, " remains in your account.")
```

Finally, this program uses a loop to repeat the input until the data is in the right range.

```
## WORKED EXAMPLE
# Range check

Age = input("How old are you: ")
Age = int(Age)

while Age < 0:
    print("You cannot be less than 0")
    Age = input("How old are you: ")
    Age = int(Age)

print("Age data accepted")
```

Q

Learning activities

1. Enter the Python programs shown on this page and try them out to see what happens.

2. Create a program for a bank cash machine. It has two loops in it. Base the program on the following:

- Include a variable called `Balance` with a starting value of 1000.

- The user inputs a four-digit password. The program loops until the user enters the number 9080.

- The user inputs the amount he or she wants to withdraw from their account. The program loops until this is smaller than `Balance`.

Q

Test yourself

1. What variables are used in the first program and what are their data types?

2. Explain the range checks used in the program above that uses `elif`.

3. What is the error message in the third program (the one with the loop)?

4. Describe the four types of validation check you have learned.

5. Explain the difference between validation and verification.

Syllabus reference

2.1.1 Test data

Learners should be able to suggest and apply suitable test data.

9.2 Testing and evaluation

Test data

Introduction

Testing a program means trying it out. A programmer will always test a program to make sure it works properly. If there are problems or errors they will be fixed. In this section you will learn about how to design good tests with suitable test data.

Input and output

A completed program that runs on a computer is an example of software. You have learned that software is made for clients or customers. Software has input and output:

- Input is the data the user enters into the computer.
- Output is the result the computer gives to the user.

The client needs the output of the software. That is why people buy software. Programmers must know what the output should be. They must make software that produces the right output.

Testing

Before software is passed to the client it must be tested. To test software:

- Try out different inputs to the software.
- Check what output you get.

The output you get should match the output the client wants:

- If the output matches what the client wants, the software has passed the test.
- If the output does not match the client's requirements, the software has failed the test. The programmer must fix the software.

Programmers will plan a whole series of tests. They will record every test and what the results are. They will analyse test results to make sure the software is working properly.

Test data

To test software you must input data. That is called the test data. To carry out a full range of tests you must try many different types of test data.

As a rule, you should try three different types of test data:

- Normal data – this is the normal input that you would expect users to enter when they use the software in real life. You must make sure that in normal use the software works as expected and accepts the input.

- Extreme data – test the limits of your software by entering large or small numbers that are at the upper and lower limits of the acceptable range. The program should accept these inputs.

- Abnormal data – this is data that should not be entered, for example when a user enters letters instead of numbers, or presses the Enter key at the wrong time. We use these tests because users sometimes make mistakes and we must check what happens when they do. The best result is for the data to be rejected and an error message to be shown.

Example

A programmer made a program to add up the bill in a coffee shop. The user enters the cost of drinks and the software shows the total amount.

The program was tested. Here are some of the values that were input as test data:

- the prices of two ordinary cups of coffee

- a very big order with 100 different coffees

- the number 1 000 000

- letters of the alphabet instead of numbers.

Can you work out which of these are normal, extreme and abnormal data?

Test yourself

1. What is test data: the input, the program code or the output?

2. Explain why programmers test a program before they pass it to the client.

3. An input prompt says "enter a four digit number". The test data was the letter "X". Explain why.

4. An input prompt was enter your age. The test data was 999. Explain why.

5. A test produced the expected results. What does that tell the programmer?

6. A test produced output that was different from what the client wanted. What must the programmer do?

Learning activity

A voice recognition program records samples of human speech and shows the words as text on the screen.

1. What are the inputs and outputs of this software?

2. Design some tests for this program. Say what test data you would use, and what results you expect.

Syllabus reference

2.1.1 Test data

Learners should be able to: suggest and apply suitable test data; comment on the effectiveness of a given solution.

Evaluation

Introduction

You have learned that software is made for clients. The client needs the output of the software. The programmer must make software that produces the right output. In this section you will learn how to evaluate effectiveness by looking at the outputs.

Effective

A good program is effective, which means that the program produces the right effect. It produces the right outputs. Programmers need to decide whether each program they have made is effective.

The programmer needs to know what outputs the client wants. The outputs are the client's requirements. The program is effective if it:

- produces all the client's requirements
- produces outputs with no errors in them
- works in a way the client likes.

If the program is effective the programmer can give it to the client. If the program is not effective the programmer must make changes and improvements.

Test effectiveness

After the program is completed it is tested. Testing checks the outputs of the program. The outputs of the program are compared with the client's requirements.

Examples

The client wanted a program that would input five numbers and output the largest number. A programmer made this program. Then the programmer had to test the program.

Test plan

The programmer planned tests. Each of the client's requirements had to be tested with normal, extreme and abnormal data.

The test plan is set out in a table. For each test we need to know the purpose of the test, the test data and the expected output. The expected output is what we would see if the program worked without any problems.

Here is an example test plan. This plan shows three tests. In real life the programmer would do more tests than this.

Test number	Purpose of test	Test data	Expected output	Actual output	Analysis
1	Test with normal integer values	1, 3, 5, 7, 9	9		
2	Test with normal decimal values	1.4, 1.5, 1.6, 1.7, 1.8	1.8		
3	Test with impossible values (text)	A, B, C, D, E	Error message "Enter numbers only"		

Record test results

Test results are recorded in the table. They are recorded in the "Actual output" column.

Here is an example. The first test produced the expected outcome. The next two tests did not produce the expected result.

Test number	Purpose of test	Test data	Expected output	Actual output	Analysis
1	Test normal use	1, 3, 5, 7, 9	9	9	
2	Test decimal numbers	1.4, 1.5, 1.6, 1.7, 1.8	1.8	1	
3	Invalid inputs	A, B, C, D, E	Error message "Enter numbers only"	Program crashes	

Analyse test results

The programmer compared the actual results to the expected outcomes. If the actual and expected outputs are the same, no action is needed. If the actual and expected outcomes are different, further action is needed.

The results of this analysis are shown in the final column of the test table.

Test number	Purpose of test	Test data	Expected output	Actual outcome	Analysis
1	Test normal use	1, 3, 5, 7, 9	9	9	No action needed
2	Test decimal numbers	1.4, 1.5, 1.6, 1.7, 1.8	1.8	1	Use float data type
3	Invalid inputs	A, B, C, D, E	Error message "Enter numbers only"	Program crashes	Include a validation check

Report on effectiveness

Finally, you can sum up the effectiveness of the solution. You will summarise the findings of all the tests. You will explain whether the solution works. Is the program effective? Does it produce the results the client wants? Does it always produce the correct outputs? Is more work needed?

Q

Test yourself

1. Why did the test data include letters as well as numbers?

2. What outcome would you expect from the input 11, 12, 13, 14, 15?

3. Explain the analysis of test 2.

4. Explain the analysis of test 3.

Q

Learning activity

You have produced many Python programs. Carry out tests on one or more programs. Record your test results. Comment on the effectiveness of each program.

Syllabus reference

2.1.1 Trace tables

Learners should be able to use trace tables to find the value of variables at each step in an algorithm.

See also:

8.1 Introduction to programming (Algorithms – flowcharts and pseudocode)

9.1 Worked examples (Calculate a total)

9.3 Developing algorithms

Trace tables

Introduction

We have looked at how a programmer tests and evaluates a program. Now we will explore ways to test and evaluate algorithms. In the next few sections you will look at examples of flowcharts and pseudocode. In this section you will learn a method of testing algorithms that uses a short trace table.

Test an algorithm

You have learned that algorithms are used to set out the logic of a program. An algorithm is made before the programmer starts to write code. It is a good idea to test the algorithm before you make the program.

This section explains how you can test an algorithm. An algorithm is not working software. You cannot run it and see what happens. Instead you use a trace table. A trace table records the values of each variable in an algorithm.

1. The table has a column for each variable in the algorithm.

2. The table has a row for every line of the algorithm.

3. You go through an algorithm line by line.

4. You record the value of each variable at every line.

Examples

Here is a pseudocode algorithm for a simple program that carries out an addition or subtraction sum. It uses the `IF` structure.

When you make a trace table, start by numbering every line of the algorithm:

```
1.   READ Num1

2.   READ Num2

3.   PRINT "Enter plus or minus"

4.   READ PlusMinus

5.   IF PlusMinus = "+" THEN

6.       Answer ← Num1 + Num2

7.   ELSE

8.       Answer ← Num1 - Num2

9.   ENDIF

10.  PRINT Answer
```

Make the trace table

There are four variables in this algorithm. They are `Num1`, `Num2`, `PlusMinus` and `Answer`. We make a trace table with a column for every variable.

Test data

Just as when you are testing a program, to test an algorithm you must choose test data. The test data will be the input to the algorithm. In this example we will choose the test data:

20   15   +

Line	Num1	Num2	PlusMinus	Answer
1.				
2.				
3.				
4.				

Count through the lines

Now you count through the lines of the algorithm. At each line you show the values of the different variables:

- Line 1: user input is assigned to variable Num1. Look at the test data. The first value is 20, so put 20 in the "Num1" column of the trace table.

- Line 2: user input is assigned to variable Num2. The test data is 15. This goes in the "Num2" column of the trace table.

- Line 3: an output line. There are no changes to variables.

- Line 4: user input of a plus or minus sign. Our test data is + and that goes into the "PlusMinus" column of the trace table.

This is what our trace table looks like so far.

If a value is entered into a variable, it stays in that variable for all the lines that follow. The value in a variable column only changes if the algorithm changes it.

Line	Num1	Num2	PlusMinus	Answer
1	20			
2	20	15		
3	20	15		
4	20	15	+	

Complete the trace table

The next line of the algorithm is line 5. This line has a logical test. The test is:

PlusMinus = "+"

The test result is true, so the algorithm moves to line 6:

Answer ← Num1 + Num2

Num1 + Num 2 makes 35. The value 35 is assigned to the variable Answer.

The algorithm finishes with line 10, which is an output line. The completed trace table looks like this.

Line	Num1	Num2	PlusMinus	Answer
1	20			
2	20	15		
3	20	15		
4	20	15	+	
5	20	15	+	
6	20	15	+	35
10	20	15	+	35

What is the output of this algorithm?

Q Test yourself

1. The trace table has a column for each...?

2. What should be entered into each row of a trace table?

3. Explain two ways that a value can be assigned to a variable.

4. A trace table normally counts down line by line – but not always. Why not?

Q Learning activity

Create trace tables for the algorithm shown on this page. Use these sets of test data:

20   30   –

100   99   *

-19   -15   +

Syllabus reference

2.1.1 Trace tables

Learners should be able to use trace tables to find the value of variables at each step in an algorithm.

See also:

9.1 Worked examples
9.2 Testing and evaluation

Trace tables (loops)

Introduction

In the previous section you created a short trace table. In this section we will create a trace table for an algorithm with a loop in it.

Example

Here is the algorithm we will test. The lines are numbered to help us make the trace table:

```
1. Largest ← 0

2. CarryOn ← "Y"

3. WHILE CarryOn = "Y" DO

4.    READ Number

5.    IF Number > Largest THEN Largest ← Number ENDIF

6.    PRINT "Type Y to continue"

7.    READ CarryOn

8. ENDWHILE

9. PRINT Largest
```

What does this algorithm do?

Test data

We will test the algorithm by entering the following test data:

```
Number = 10

CarryOn = "Y"

Number = 5

CarryOn = "N"
```

We will see what output we get.

Shortening the trace table

The trace table could get very long. To make the trace table shorter we will only include lines where a value is assigned to a variable.

Trace table

Here are the first few lines of the trace table. In the first two lines, values are assigned to the variables `Largest` and `CarryOn`. In line 4 input is entered and assigned to the variable `Number`.

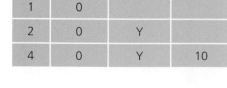

Line	Largest	CarryOn	Number
1	0		
2	0	Y	
4	0	Y	10

Logical test

Line 5 has a complete `IF` statement on one line:

```
5. IF Number > Largest THEN Largest ← Number ENDIF
```

The `IF` statement includes a logical test. The test is `Number > Largest`. Check the values in the trace table:

```
Number = 10
Largest = 0
```

Number is bigger than Largest. Therefore, the command is carried out:

```
Largest ← Number
```

The value of the variable Number is assigned to the variable Largest.

Line	Largest	CarryOn	Number
1	0		
2	0	Y	
4	0	Y	10
5	10	Y	10

Loop

Now the algorithm goes around a loop. Let us trace this carefully line by line:

- Line 6 is an output. There are no changes to variables.
- In line 7 the test data Y is entered into the CarryOn variable. This does not change the value of the variable.
- Line 8 marks the end of the loop. We go back to the top of the loop. We go back to line 3.
- Line 3 is a logical test. The test result is True, so the loop continues.
- Lines 4–7 are carried out again, using the next lot of test data.

Here is the completed test table, following the loop.

In line 7 the value N is entered. We go back to the top of the loop. Line 3 is:

```
3. WHILE CarryOn = "Y" DO
```

This test result is False. The loop stops. The algorithm goes to line 9. The variable Largest is printed out. It has the value 10.

Line	Largest	CarryOn	Number
1	0		
2	0	Y	
4	0	Y	10
5	10	Y	10
7	10	Y	10
4	10	Y	5
5	10	Y	5
7	10	N	5

Test yourself

1. What does the algorithm on this page do?

2. Create a trace table for the algorithm shown on this page. Use the test data below. What is the output?

```
50, Y, 20, Y, 99, Y, 55, N
```

Learning activity

In *9.1 Worked examples* you created a series of different algorithms:

- count
- total
- average (mean)
- verification
- validation.

In *9.2 Testing and evaluation*, you learned how to choose suitable test data.

Your challenge in this section is to test the algorithms you made.

1. Pick one of the algorithms you made in *9.1*. *Write out the algorithm*. Number every line.

2. Choose suitable normal test data for this algorithm.

3. Produce a trace table showing the value of every variable at every line of the algorithm.

If you are confident, produce trace tables for all the algorithms you have made.

Syllabus reference

2.1.1 Trace tables

Learners should be able to use trace tables to find the value of variables at each step in an algorithm.

See also:

9.1 Worked examples

9.2 Testing and evaluation

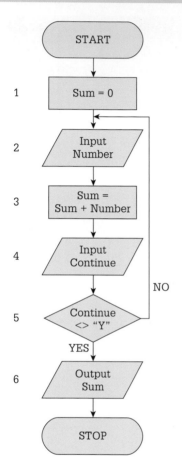

Trace tables (flowcharts)

Introduction

You have created trace tables for algorithms made in pseudocode. In this section you will learn to create a trace table for a flowchart algorithm.

Example

An example of a flowchart is shown on the left. Every box in the flowchart is numbered. This helps us make the trace table.

Before we begin the trace table, can you work out what this algorithm does?

Test data

We will use this test data:

```
Number = 7
Continue = Y
Number = 8
Continue = N
```

Make the trace table

There are three variables in this algorithm. They are called Sum, Number and Continue. We make a trace table with a column for each of these variables.

The trace table has a row for each box in the flowchart:

- In box 1: Sum is given the value 0.
- In box 2: data is input to the variable Number. The test data is 7.
- In box 3: the values of Sum and Number are added together and assigned to the variable Sum.
- In box 4: data is input to the variable Continue. The test data is Y.

The trace table shows these changes.

Box	Sum	Number	Continue
1	0		
2	0	7	
3	7	7	
4	7	7	Y

Loop

Box 5 is a decision box. Like every decision box it shows a test. The test is:

```
Continue <> "Y"
```

That means "The value in the variable Continue is different from Y". This test result is False, so we take the NO arrow out of the decision box. The NO arrow goes off to the right of the decision box. It loops back up the algorithm. We end up above box 2.

Now we go down the algorithm again:

- In box 2: data is input to the variable Number. The test data is 8.
- In box 3: the values of Sum and Number are added together and assigned to the variable Sum.
- In box 4: data is input to the variable Continue. The test data is N.

Line	Sum	Number	Continue
1	0		
2	0	7	
3	7	7	
4	7	7	Y
2	7	8	Y
3	15	8	Y
4	15	8	N

Finish

Box 5 is a decision box. Like every decision box it shows a test. The test is:

```
Continue <> "Y"
```

That means "The value in the variable Continue is different from Y". This test result is True, so we take the YES arrow out of the decision box. The YES arrow goes down. We have gone out of the loop.

The final box is box 6. The variable Sum is output. It has the value 15. That is the result of the algorithm.

Test yourself

1. What calculation is carried out by the algorithm on this page?

2. Suggest some different test data you could use to test this algorithm.

3. How does numbering the flowchart boxes help us to make the trace table?

4. How do we decide how many columns there should be in the trace table?

Learning activity

You have created flowcharts for these other algorithms:

- count
- average (mean)
- verification
- validation.

Create a trace table for at least one of these flowcharts. Choose suitable test data.

Syllabus reference

2.1.1 Purpose of algorithms

Learners should be able to work out the purpose of a given algorithm.

See also:

9.1 Worked examples

Analyse algorithms

Introduction

You have made algorithms using pseudocode and flowcharts. You have used trace tables to test the algorithms. In this section you will put all your skills together to help you to analyse and understand any algorithm.

Purpose of an algorithm

You have learned that an algorithm takes data and processes it to produce information. For example the flowchart on page 223 took a series of numbers as input. The output was the sum (total) of the numbers.

The purpose of an algorithm is to turn input data into output information. To describe the purpose of an algorithm you must describe the relationship between input and output values.

In this section you will learn some methods for understanding the purpose of an algorithm, including:

- spotting familiar algorithms
- reflecting on variable names
- noticing what calculations are used
- noticing the structure of the algorithm
- using a trace table if you still cannot work it out.

Familiar algorithms

You may recognise a familiar algorithm from your learning activities. Look back at *9.1 Worked examples*. Learning to recognise these common algorithms will make you a better programmer.

Naming conventions

A well-designed program or algorithm will have sensible variable names. The name of the variable will tell you its purpose and help you to understand the algorithm. For example, on page 236 the variable is called `Largest`. On page 223 the variable is called `Sum`. These names help you to understand what each algorithm does.

However, variable names do not always give you all the information you need. For this reason, you need to consider other elements.

Calculations

Algorithms nearly always include calculations. In pseudocode, calculations use the arrow symbol to assign a calculated value to a variable:

```
Sum ← Sum + Number
```

Flowcharts use a rectangular box. The calculation is shown inside the box.

Calculations are a key way that data is transformed into information. Look at the calculations in the algorithm. Which arithmetic operators are used?

```
Sum =
Sum + Number
```

Describe in words what you see. This will help you to understand the purpose of the algorithm.

Structure

Look at the structure of the algorithm. There are two important structural features to look at:

- Are there any IF structures?
- Are there any loops?

Describe in words the structure of the algorithm. This will help you understand what it does.

IF structures

Look at the IF structure of the algorithm. Answer the following questions.

1. What is the logical test?
2. What actions are carried out if the test result is True?
3. What actions are carried out if the test result is False?

Loop structures

Look at the loop in the algorithm. Answer the following questions.

1. Is it a counter-controlled or a condition-controlled loop?
2. What actions are carried out inside the loop?
3. What is the exit condition of the loop?

Trace tables

It can take some time to make a trace table for an algorithm. You need to choose suitable test data. You may need to do several trace tables, using different test data.

Try the simpler analysis methods first, but if you are still stuck use a trace table. Thorough testing using a trace table will help you to understand any algorithm.

Learning activity

This algorithm uses a calculation called MOD. MOD gives you the remainder of an integer division. For example:

```
Remainder ← Number MOD 2
```

Here the variable Number is divided by 2. The remainder from the division is assigned to the variable Remainder:

```
1. Even ← 0
2. FOR i ← 1 TO 5
3.     READ Number
4.     Remainder ← Number MOD 2
5.     IF Remainder = 0 THEN Even ← Even + 1 ENDIF
6. NEXT i
7. PRINT Even
```

What does this algorithm do?

Test yourself

1. How will naming conventions help you understand an algorithm?
2. What symbol is used in a pseudocode calculation command?
3. What flowchart symbol is used for the exit condition of a loop?
4. Explain two ways in which logical tests are used in algorithms.

Syllabus reference

2.1.1 Identify and fix errors in algorithms

Learners should be able to identify errors in given algorithms and suggest ways of removing these errors.

See also:

Chapter 8 Programming
9.2 Testing and evaluation

Find errors in algorithms

Introduction

You have learned how to test algorithms and work out the purpose of algorithms. In all the examples so far the algorithms have been well designed and free of errors. In this section you will learn how to work with algorithms that have errors. You will find out how to identify and correct the errors.

Types of error

There are three types of error you can find in an algorithm or computer program:

- syntax errors
- run-time errors
- logical errors.

Syntax errors

"Syntax" means the rules of a language. This includes the rules of pseudocode. The lines of pseudocode must exactly match the rules of the language.

Syntax errors occur when the programmer has not entered the commands in the correct way. For example, the first line of a pseudocode counter loop is written like this:

```
WHILE CarryOn = "Y" DO
```

If you omitted the word DO, this would be a syntax error.

Correcting syntax errors

When you write program code, the compiler or interpreter will tell you if it spots a syntax error. The program will halt. When you write in pseudocode you need to spot your own errors. You have to learn the rules of the language and remember them.

It is usually easy to correct a syntax error. You retype the line to match the rules of the language.

Run-time errors

Run-time errors do not break the rules of the language. The program code will run, but when you run the program, it will go wrong. Common run-time errors are:

- endless loop
- divide by 0.

Endless loop

Every loop must have an exit condition. The exit condition is a logical test. It tests the value of a variable. If the test result is True the loop will stop. There must be a way to stop the loop. There must be a command inside the loop that changes the variable.

If you cannot make the variable match the exit condition, the loop will never stop. To correct it you must add a command inside the loop that lets you stop the loop.

Divide by 0

It is mathematically impossible to divide by 0. If you try to do this, your program will crash. This is a danger if you have a calculation using division in your program. Use validation to prevent the user from entering a 0 in this case.

Logical errors

A program without syntax or run-time errors can still have logical errors. A logical error means the program works properly, but it does not do the right thing. For example, a programmer wrote a program to add a service charge to a bill. He used the minus sign instead of the plus sign. The program worked, but it gave the wrong result.

Find logical errors

To find logical errors you must:

- have a clear statement from the client about what the program is supposed to do
- carry out a wide range of tests
- compare the results of the tests with what the client wants.

If there are logical errors, the test results will not show the right values. You must change the program to make it do what the client wants.

Learning activity

Find three errors in this pseudocode algorithm. The lines are numbered to make it easier to discuss the structure:

```
1. Product ← 1
2. Continue = "Y"
3. WHILE Continue = "Y" DO
4.      READ Number
5.      Product ← Product * Number
6. ENDIF
7. PRINT Product
```

1. Answer these questions.

   a Identify the line or lines where each error occurs.

   b Say whether each error is a syntax, run-time or logical error.

   c Explain the error.

2. Write a corrected version of the algorithm and explain what it does.

Test yourself

1. What is a syntax error?

2. What command must you find inside a condition-controlled loop?

3. What do you call an error that produces output that does not match the client's needs?

4. Explain how testing will help you spot errors in an algorithm.

Syllabus reference

2.1.1 Produce an algorithm for a given purpose

Learners should be able to produce an algorithm for a given problem (either in the form of pseudocode or flowchart).

Create an algorithm

Introduction

You have learned how to analyse algorithms to find out their purpose and to remove errors. In this section you will learn how to create a new algorithm to perform a task.

Understand the requirement

An algorithm processes inputs to create outputs. To plan an algorithm you must:

- be clear about what outputs are required
- work backwards from the required outputs
- know what processing is needed to make the output.

Make sure you have a clear statement of the purpose of the algorithm before you start work. This needs to include:

- what values will be input
- what calculations and other processes will occur
- what output is required.

Re-use and adapt

If you are lucky you will already know an algorithm that matches the requirement. Good programmers will know many different algorithms. They will know algorithms they have made themselves. They will know the work of other programmers. This makes their job much easier and quicker.

In other cases you might know an algorithm that is almost right for the purpose. You may have to adapt the algorithm slightly, but this is still much easier than making a new algorithm.

For example, a programmer made an algorithm to calculate the charge for a meal in a restaurant. Later, she adapted it to work out the entrance fee for a cinema. With a few changes the algorithm worked, saving the programmer a lot of work.

Create an algorithm

Sometimes you will need to create an algorithm starting from nothing. Here are some tips.

Inputs, outputs and variables

Think about the client's requirements. Think about all the inputs and outputs you need, then:

- add lines to enter input and store it as a variable
- add an output statement at the end of the algorithm to show the result.

Calculation

Consider what calculations will be required to turn inputs into outputs. Think about what arithmetic operators you will need, then:

- between the input and output lines, add any calculations that are needed.

Selection

Selection means the use of IF in pseudocode, or a decision box in a flowchart. An algorithm with these features has a logical test. It chooses between two different actions. You need to:

- state the logical test
- state the actions to take if the test result is True (and other actions if it is False).

Repetition

If the algorithm processes a series of numbers (or other data), you may need to use a loop. Remember:

- If you know how many items of data there are, use a counter-controlled loop.
- If you do not know how many items of data there are, use a condition-controlled loop.
- Decide which lines of your algorithm go inside the loop.
- Make sure the loop has an exit condition.

Test yourself

An algorithm was needed to find the smallest of 1000 values. Answer the following questions.

1. Which algorithm that you have worked on already might help you with this task?

2. What type of loop would you use in this algorithm?

3. How many variables do you need? Suggest names for them.

4. What logical test will you include in the algorithm?

5. Using the answers to these questions, create an algorithm for the stated purpose.

Learning activity

Create an algorithm that will count the number of teenagers entering a youth club. The person at the door will record "M" for male, "F" for female and "X" when the club closes. The output will be the number of male and female teenagers who visited the youth club.

Syllabus reference

2.1.1 Systems made of sub-systems; top-down design

Learners should be able to show understanding that every computer system is made up of subsystems, which in turn are made up of further sub-systems; use top-down design.

9.4 Development methods

Top-down programming

Introduction

You have learned to write computer programs and algorithms. You have learned about the development process including trace tables, testing and evaluation. In this section you will look at how programmers use these methods in real life to produce software for their clients. On this page we will look at how a software development task is broken down into smaller programs.

Creating software applications

An algorithm produces a solution to a given problem. For example, it may loop until the correct password is entered, or it may produce the average from a group of numbers.

A real-life software system will include many different sub-systems. For example, the software system for a small business may include sub-systems to:

- keep track of the items in stock
- record profit and loss
- pay staff wages.

To create a software system, a programmer must produce lots of smaller sub-systems. Each sub-system does a different task. The sub-systems combine to make software that does all the work needed by the client.

Top-down programming

In top-down programming we begin by analysing the software system into sub-systems. Then we break those sub-systems down into even smaller components. For example, the software to pay staff wages may be broken down further into systems to:

- record staff hours
- calculate pay by multiplying hours by pay per hour
- work out tax and other deductions
- print pay slips.

The programmer will work on these components one at a time. When they are all finished they will be fitted together to make the complete payroll system.

Choice of method

Most programmers nowadays work in teams. The task of making the software is split between different people. Each person creates a different sub-system, then the sub-systems are fitted together.

Advantages

Top-down programming has many advantages:

- It lets you plan the task in full before you begin programming.

- It breaks a big difficult task down into smaller and easier tasks.

- The different tasks can be given to different people, so the work is done more quickly.

- Each sub-system can be tested and perfected before all the sub-systems are fitted together.

Disadvantages

Some programmers do not like using top-down programming. They identify some disadvantages:

- Using top–down design means that coding cannot be the first task – programmers have to start with planning.

- Sometimes the different sub-systems do not work well together and the program goes wrong.

Top-down analysis

You have learned that every computer system:

- starts with input data

- ends with output information.

If you decide to use top-down programming, you must begin by breaking this overall system into sub-systems. For each sub-system you must decide what are its data inputs and information outputs.

Typically, the output from one sub-system will become the input for the next sub-system. A top-down plan must state:

- what all the different sub-systems are

- the inputs and outputs of each sub-system.

A structure diagram shows the different sub-systems and how they relate to each other. Learn more about structure diagrams on pages 248–249.

Test yourself

1. Top-down programming helps with team work. Explain why.

2. Why is testing easier when you use top-down programming?

3. A programmer planned a system by defining sub-systems. What information is included in the plan?

4. A programmer thinks she might be able to break a sub-system down into even smaller sub-systems. Discuss the advantages and disadvantages of this approach.

Learning activity

A programmer wanted to develop a software application to help students keep track of what homework they had to do. What sub-systems might be needed in this software application? Describe the inputs and outputs of each sub-system.

Syllabus reference

2.1.1 Systems made of sub-systems, top-down design

Learners should be able to show understanding that every computer system is made up of sub-systems, which in turn are made up of further sub-systems; use top-down design, structure diagrams.

Structure diagrams

Introduction

You have learned that computer systems are made of sub-systems. Structure diagrams show these sub-systems. In this section you will learn to understand structure diagrams and to draw them.

Structure diagram

A computer system is made of smaller sub-systems. When you plan the computer system you decide what the sub-systems are. This is top-down programming.

A structure diagram is a drawing of the computer system. It shows the sub-systems. The first stage of top-down programming is planning the sub-systems. The structure diagram lets you show the plan in visual form.

The structure chart will be used to:

- plan the work that needs to be done
- tell the program team about the plan
- check the work when it is completed.

Basic structure

A structure diagram looks like a family tree. Every system and sub-system is shown as a box. At the top of the tree is a box with the name of the whole system in it. For example, it may be a payroll system.

Think of the main tasks that must be performed by the system. These tasks are shown in the level below. In this example the payroll system has to record the hours people work, calculate their pay, transfer the money to them, and give them a payslip.

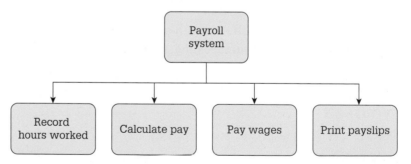

To make sure your structure diagram is correct, you must check the following:

- Have you included every task? There must be nothing missing from the system.
- Are the tasks distinct from each other? There must be no overlap between tasks.

Each task will be assigned to a programmer or a team of programmers. Later, the different sub-systems will be fitted back together to make the finished software system.

Further breakdown

Each of the sub-systems can be broken down into even smaller sub-systems. You carry on with this analysis until you have broken the task down into its smallest components. Each component takes input and processes it to make output.

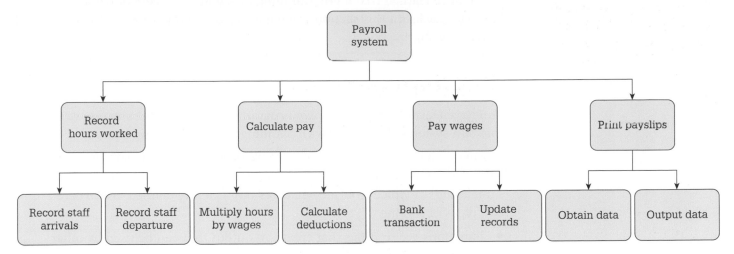

Each of the components can be assigned to a different programmer or team. Each component is small enough that a simple program will produce the required output.

Test yourself

1. Explain why your structure chart must include every task carried out by the software.
2. Explain why the different sub-systems must be distinct, with no overlap between them.
3. How would you know that the structure chart is completed?
4. Name a software package that you could use to make a structure chart.

Learning activity

Here is some information about a software system. Create a simple structure chart for this software system:

- The stock control system must record all deliveries to the warehouse. It must record all the stock that goes out of the warehouse.

- It must calculate how much stock is left in the warehouse. The software will print out an alert if the level of stock gets too low.

Here is some more information about the stock control system. Use this information to expand the structure chart:

- When stock arrives the system will record the time of arrival from the computer clock. The stock details will be entered by hand. Each item of stock will be given a barcode.

- When stock goes out of the warehouse the barcode will be scanned. The stock records will be updated automatically.

Syllabus reference

2.1.1 Predefined functions; library routines

Learners should be able to: use library routines and sub-routines; use predefined procedures or functions.

Code libraries

> ## Introduction
>
> You have learned that a programming task will be broken down into smaller tasks. In this section you will learn how programmers help each other by sharing code.

Sub-routines

You have learned about top-down programming. Software systems are split up into sub-systems. This helps with planning, development and testing.

In top-down programming, programs are broken down into sub-programs. A sub-program is also called a routine or a sub-routine (all these terms mean the same thing). A typical routine will carry out a clearly defined task. There are two types of routine:

- Functions are routines that create an output that can be used by other routines.

- Procedures or sub-procedures are routines that carry out tasks but do not supply any output to other routines

In Python, functions and procedures are created in the same way. In some programming languages different methods are used to create functions and procedures.

Predefined functions

Some functions are so useful that they come as part of the main Python package. These are called predefined functions. You have used two predefined functions:

- `print()`
- `input()`

These functions are very important. You have used these functions in every program you have written.

Data-type conversion is carried out by predefined functions. You have learned two of these:

- `int()`
- `float()`

There are many other predefined functions in the Python programming language: search the web for "Python predefined function" to see a full list.

Re-usable routines

Programmers will also make their own sub-routines as they complete programming projects. They may re-use these sub-routines in later programming projects. This has important advantages:

- It saves time because programmers can use code that is ready made.

- The programmers have used the code before so they have tested it and know it works.

For example, you made a program that checked a password. This could be used as a sub-routine in other projects. Any time you need a password you could re-use the code you have already made.

Code libraries

Since Python was developed, programmers have written many useful sub-routines. Programmers are helpful and support each other. Programmers will share many of the useful sub-routines they have made. This makes the programming language easier to use. It speeds up program development.

The sub-routines are stored in files called modules. The Python code library stores all the modules that are available. Here is part of the Python code library.

To use these stored modules in a program, you type the word "import" and the name of the module you want to use. From then on you can use any of the procedures and functions from that module in your program.

Can you see the module called "random"? You will use this module now.

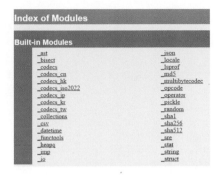

↑ Part of the Python code library

Example

The module called "random" includes many useful sub-routines that create random numbers. To use these sub-routines enter this line of code into a program:

```
import random
```

We will use one of the sub-routines in this module. The sub-routine is called `randint`. This subroutine creates a random integer. The following command will create a random integer between 0 and 100:

```
random.randint(0, 100)
```

Here is the function in use in a program. A random integer is assigned to a variable called `example`:

```
example = random.randint(0, 100)
```

Here is a simple program that uses the random module to make a random number, and then shows it on the screen.

```
## make a random number

import random

example = random.randint(0, 100)

print("the random number is ", example)
```

Q Learning activity

1. Introductory activity: create a Python program that generates ten random numbers.

2. Developmental activity: create a Python program that prints out a random mathematics question, using two random numbers.

3. Stretch and challenge: create a Python program that prints out a random mathematics question, gets an answer from the user and tells the user whether the answer is right.

Q Test yourself

1. What is the difference between a procedure and a function?

2. What predefined functions have you used in your programming?

3. What are the advantages of re-using code you wrote for a different program?

4. What does the command "import random" do?

Review

Key terms

Code library	A set of stored sub-routines which can be used in lots of different programs to make work easier.
Effective	A program which produces the effect that was intended.
Logical error	A program error where the program will be translated into machine code, and the machine code will run, but the program does not work effectively. It does not do what it is supposed to do.
Run-time error	A program error that means that the program can be translated into machine code, but the machine code will not run properly: for example, it crashes or gets stuck in an endless loop
Sub-routine	A section of program code which carries out a single well defined action. A sub-routine is typically given a name which identifies its purpose. Procedures and functions are sub-routines.
Syntax error	A program error which breaks the rules of the computer language in which the program was written. The program cannot be translated into machine code.
Top-down design	A program development method where a large problem is broken down into manageable parts
Trace table	A table showing the value of a variable at different stages of an algorithm
Validation	An error check method where the input data is evaluated using validation criteria. If the data does not meet the criteria an error message is displayed.
Verification	An error check method where the same data is entered twice. The two versions are compared and they should match.

Project work

Write a program with the following features:

1. The user inputs a series of numbers. The numbers are stored as a list. The program loops until the user types X.

2. The user then sees a menu which gives them the following choices:

    A: Count

    B: Total

    C: Average

3. The user enters one of the three choices. The program then prints out the entire list, plus the count, total (sum) or average (mean) of the list.

If you complete this easily then add validation checks so all inputs to the list must be numbers from 1–100.

10 Databases

Syllabus reference

2.3.1 Single-table database from given data storage

Learners should be able to define a single-table database from given data storage requirements.

See also:

1.3 Data storage

10.1 Database design

Records and fields

Introduction

You have learned that the computer holds data. Data is organised to make useful information. A database is an organised collection of data. In this section you will learn about the structure of a database.

Data and information

Data is a collective term for facts and figures. Computers are machines that process data to make information.

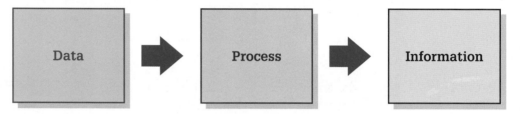

⬆ Data is processed to make information

A database is a way of storing data in an organised way.

Entities

Data means facts and figures. The facts must be about something. For example, they may be facts about:

- people (such as name or age)
- objects (such as weight or cost)
- places (such as address or country)
- events (such as date and time).

The people, object, places, events, etc. that are described by the data are called entities.

Tables

Every database is made of one or more tables. A table is a grid of data. In this book we will look at databases with just one table.

Here is an example of a data table. It shows data about best-selling music. The entities are albums.

Code	Artist	Title	Sales (millions)
MUSIC001	Taylor Swift	1989	6.0
MUSIC002	One Direction	Four	3.2
MUSIC003	Ed Sheeran	X	4.4
MUSIC004	Coldplay	Ghost Stories	3.7
MUSIC005	AC/DC	Rock or Bust	2.7
MUSIC006	Michael Jackson	Xscape	1.7
MUSIC007	Pink Floyd	The Endless River	2.5
MUSIC008	Sam Smith	The Lonely Hour	3.5
MUSIC009	Katy Perry	Prism	1.2
MUSIC010	Beyoncé	Beyoncé	1.4

Records

In a database a record means all the data about a single entity. A record is shown as a row of the database table. In this example, the information about "The Lonely Hour" by Sam Smith is one record of the table.

Code	Artist	Title	Sales
MUSIC008	Sam Smith	The Lonely Hour	3.5

This table has ten records. A typical computer database may have thousands or even millions of records.

Fields

A database stores the same facts about each entity. Each fact is called a field. A field is shown as a column of the database table. In this example, the title of the album is a single field.

This table has four fields. They are called:

- Code
- Artist
- Title
- Sales.

Title
1989
Four
X
Ghost Stories
Rock or Bust
Xscape
The Endless River
The Lonely Hour
Prism
Beyoncé

Each record in the database includes the same fields, always in the same order.

Test yourself

A student made a database to store information about every lesson he attended at college in one week. The database had one table.

1. What are the entities in this data table?

2. If you made a data table like this how many records would it have?

3. State three different facts you would record about each lesson in your weekly timetable.

4. Make a data table with information about your lessons.

Learning activity

Pick a subject you are interested in, and create a data table made of records and fields. Here are some suggestions:

- football teams in a league, such as the Premier League
- members of a club or society you belong to
- tracks on your MP3 player
- computer games you have played.

Include at least ten records in your table. You must decide what fields to use.

Syllabus reference

2.3.1 Suitable data types

Learners should be able to choose and specify suitable data types.

See also:

1.3 Data storage
8.2 Begin coding

Data types

Introduction

You have learned that data tables are made of records and fields. Every field must have a data type. In this section you will learn how to choose the right data type for each field in a data table.

Data storage

You have learned that the computer uses different methods to store different types of data. When you store data you must choose a data type. The data type tells the computer what storage method to use. In programming, you learned that each variable has its own data type.

When you make a data table you decide what fields you need. Each field stores one fact. For each field, you should choose:

- the name of the field
- the data type.

The field name should tell you what data is stored in that field. The field name goes at the top of the table column. In some databases the field name must be a single word.

Data types

The main data types to choose from are text, character, Boolean and numerical.

Text data type:

- can store any text data including letters, symbols and numbers
- cannot be used in numerical calculations.

Character or char data type can store no more than one text character.

Boolean data type can just store Yes/No (or True/False) data.

Numerical data type:

- can only store number data
- include integers and decimal numbers
- can be used in arithmetic calculations.

In some database applications you must specify whether numerical fields are integer or decimal data types. Integer fields can store whole numbers only.

There are two other common data types: dates and times. The exact format used for date and time data depends on the database software.

Choose data type

To decide which data type to use, consider the following:

- Look at the data you want to store – is it purely numerical or does it have other characters in it?

- Think about what you want to do with the data – will it be used in calculations?

Sometimes data can be made of digits, but it is not a numerical field. For example, phone numbers are made of digits, but you would store them as text data. This is because you cannot use phone numbers in numerical calculations. It wouldn't make sense to do that. Code numbers and ID numbers are stored as text data.

A good rule is: only use a numerical data type if the field stores a quantity (that is, something that you can count).

Example

There are four fields in this table. *Code*, *Artist* and *Title* are text fields. *Sales (millions)* is a numeric field. It is not integer data type because it includes a decimal point.

Code	Artist	Title	Sales (millions)
MUSIC001	Taylor Swift	1989	6.0
MUSIC002	One Direction	Four	3.2
MUSIC003	Ed Sheeran	X	4.4
MUSIC004	Coldplay	Ghost Stories	3.7
MUSIC005	AC/DC	Rock or Bust	2.7
MUSIC006	Michael Jackson	Xscape	1.7
MUSIC007	Pink Floyd	The Endless River	2.5
MUSIC008	Sam Smith	The Lonely Hour	3.5
MUSIC009	Katy Perry	Prism	1.2
MUSIC010	Beyoncé	Beyoncé	1.4

In this table you can see that Taylor Swift's album is called 1989, but it is not the numeric data type: 1989 is not a quantity. This data is in the Title field, which has been defined as text.

Test yourself

Answer these questions, referring to the data table about best-selling albums.

1. A programmer wanted to extend the database. He wanted a new field to show the cost of each album. Pick a name and data type for this field.

2. Explain in your own words why sales are shown as a numeric data type.

3. Explain in your own words why Taylor Swift's album called 1989 is text data not numeric data.

4. Think of a date field you could add to this table.

Learning activity

In the previous section you made a data table on the subject of your choice.

1. List the fields in your table. For each field give the field name and data type.

2. Expand your table to include at least one field of each of the main data types.

3. Enter the data from your field into a spreadsheet and format it as a table using the spreadsheet features.

Syllabus reference

2.3.1 Single-table database from given data storage requirements

Learners should be able to define a single-table database from given data storage requirements.

2.3.1 Suitable primary key for a database table

Learners should be able to choose a suitable primary key for a database table.

Primary key

Introduction

You have learned that a data table is made of records and fields. Every field has a data type. One of the fields in the data table is used for identification. This is the primary key. In this section you will learn to choose a field to be the primary key.

Design a data table

When you design a data table, you must decide what the entities are. The entities may be objects, people, places, events, etc. In a library table the entities might be books. In a travel agents they might be holidays. Each entity has a single record in the data table. A record makes one row of the table.

Next you must decide what the fields are. The fields are the facts that you will store about each entity. Every fact must have its own field. The fields are the columns of the data table.

In a well-designed data table:

- each field stores only one fact
- each fact is contained in only one field
- each fact is stored only once.

Another rule is that one field must be the primary key.

Identify records

A primary key is a unique field. That means the data in this field is different for every record in the data table.

Imagine a teacher who keeps records of students. Student name is not a primary key because you could have two students with the same name. Date of birth is not a primary key, because two students could have the same birthday. There is a danger that students' records could get mixed up. For this reason the teacher might give every student a code number. The number given to each student would be unique to that student. The records would never get mixed up.

The primary key is whatever field is used to identify each record in the database. Having a primary key is even more important in a big data table.

For example, a bank might have millions of customers. It is very likely that some customers will have the same name or the same birthday. It is important not to get their records mixed up, so every bank customer has a customer code.

Select a primary key

Almost all data tables include a primary key. It is usually a code and is usually the first field in the table. The code field is filled in when a record is added to the data table. As explained above, the primary key is different for every record in the table.

A code field can include letters or other text characters. It can be just numbers. However, a code field is always the text data type. It is not a numerical data type. A code number does not represent a quantity.

Some database software is set up to generate the primary key automatically. When you add a record to the data table, the computer automatically gives it a unique code number.

Relational database

Some databases have more than one table. For example, a holiday company might have:

- a table of customers
- a table of hotels
- a table of plane flights.

Each table will have a code field. When a customer books a holiday the computer will take the customer code, the hotel code and the flight code. The combination of these will make a holiday booking record.

In this way primary keys are used to make links between tables. This is called a relational database.

Test yourself

1. Look at the data table of best-selling albums on page 257. What is the primary key?

2. Do you have a student code number? Do you know what it is?

3. Ask your parent or another relative to show you his or her bank card. Can you see the primary key? How many numbers are there in that primary key?

4. Give an example of a code number you have found in everyday life. It could be on a library book, on a train ticket or a till receipt.

Learning activity

You have created a data table. Add a primary key to the data table.

Syllabus reference

2.3.1 Query-by-example from given search criteria

Learners should be able to perform a query-by-example from given search criteria.

10.2 Database queries

Select fields

Introduction

You have seen how data can be stored in data tables. In many cases you will not want to look at the whole data table. A data query is a way of picking out the records and fields that you want to look at. In this section you will learn how to make database queries.

Query

A data table can store a lot of data. It is rare that you want to look at all the data. Usually you want to pick out facts of interest.

For example, when you get money out of a cash machine, the bank computer looks up your record in the data table. It checks how much money you have got. It does not need to look at information about other customers. Similarly, when a teacher fills in a register she only wants to see the names of the students in that class, not all the students in the school.

A query is a computer command that picks out only the records and fields that you want to see.

Query-by-example

A query-by-example is a method of making a query. You say what fields and records you want to see. The computer will display data that matches your query.

On these two pages you will learn how to pick what fields to display. On pages 262–263 you will learn how to pick what records to display.

Example

We will make a query to go with the table of best-selling albums we used before.

Code	Artist	Title	Sales (millions)
MUSIC001	Taylor Swift	1989	6.0
MUSIC002	One Direction	Four	3.2
MUSIC003	Ed Sheeran	X	4.4
MUSIC004	Coldplay	Ghost Stories	3.7
MUSIC005	AC/DC	Rock or Bust	2.7
MUSIC006	Michael Jackson	Xscape	1.7
MUSIC007	Pink Floyd	The Endless River	2.5
MUSIC008	Sam Smith	The Lonely Hour	3.5
MUSIC009	Katy Perry	Prism	1.2
MUSIC010	Beyoncé	Beyoncé	1.4

Select fields

Imagine that a manager in the music business wanted to know which artists had sold the most albums. She only wanted to see two fields in the database:

- Artist
- Sales.

Here is a query-by-example.

	Code	Artist	Title	Sales
Table	ALBUMS	ALBUMS	ALBUMS	ALBUMS
Show		✓		✓
Sort				

This query sets out the four fields. Two of the fields are ticked. The computer will show these fields only. All the fields are from the same table. In a database with more than one table you could choose fields from several different tables.

Sort

The query-by-example also gives you the option to see the list sorted into order. The type of sort depends on the field type:

- Text fields are sorted in alphabetical order (A, B, C…, etc.).
- Numerical fields are sorted by numerical value (1, 2, 3…, etc.).

You can choose to sort in ascending order (with numbers getting bigger) or descending order (with numbers getting smaller). In this example we will use descending order, so the biggest sales go at the top of the list.

Here is the finished query-by-example.

	Code	Artist	Title	Sales
Table	ALBUMS	ALBUMS	ALBUMS	ALBUMS
Show		✓		✓
Sort				DESCENDING

Result

Here is the result of that query-by-example:

Artist	Sales
Taylor Swift	6.00
Ed Sheeran	4.40
Coldplay	3.70
Sam Smith	3.50
One Direction	3.20
AC/DC	2.70
Pink Floyd	2.50
Michael Jackson	1.70
Beyoncé	1.40
Katy Perry	1.20

This output shows the two fields that were chosen. It is sorted in descending order of sales.

Test yourself

1. Write a query that would produce a list of artists and titles, sorted in alphabetical order of album title.

2. Show the output you would expect from this query.

3. In a query-by-example, how do you tell the computer what fields to display?

4. What are the two ways of sorting a text field?

Learning activity

You have made a data table on a subject of your own choice. Produce a query-by-example to accompany that data table. What display would you see from this query?

Syllabus reference

2.3.1 Query-by-example from given search criteria

Learners should be able to perform a query-by-example from given search criteria.

See also:

3.2 Logical processing

8.3 Selection

Select records

> ## Introduction
>
> You have learned how to make a query-by-example. It tells the computer what fields to display. In this section you will learn to create a query that tells the computer what records to display.

Select records

A query can select one or more records from the data table. Only the selected record or records will be shown. This is very useful. Many data tables are very large and you may not need to see all the records.

Look for a match

The simplest way to select records is using a match. You enter text into the query table. This is called the search criteria. The computer will find all records that match the search criteria.

Here is an example:

	Code	Artist	Title	Sales
Table	ALBUMS	ALBUMS	ALBUMS	ALBUMS
Show	✓	✓	✓	✓
Sort				
Criteria			= "Prism"	

This query will show the record that has "Prism" in the Title field. It will show no other records. Here is the result of that query.

Code	Artist	Title	Sales
MUSIC009	Katy Perry	Prism	1.20

Combine criteria

You can combine more than one criteria. To do this you add more rows to the data table. Each new row starts with a logical connector such as AND, OR and NOT. Here is an example:

	Code	Artist	Title	Sales
Table	ALBUMS	ALBUMS	ALBUMS	ALBUMS
Show	✓	✓	✓	✓
Sort				
Criteria		= "Taylor Swift"		
OR		= "Katy Perry"		

This query will find records where the artist is Taylor Swift OR Katy Perry. Here is the result of that query:

Code	Artist	Title	Sales
MUSIC001	Taylor Swift	1989	6.00
MUSIC009	Katy Perry	Prism	1.20

Other comparisons

As well as looking for matches you can use relational operators such as < and >. The query below will find every album that has sold more than 3 million copies. The list will be sorted in ascending order.

	Code	Artist	Title	Sales
Table	ALBUMS	ALBUMS	ALBUMS	ALBUMS
Show	✓	✓	✓	✓
Sort				ASCENDING
Criteria				> 3

Here is the result of that query:

Code	Artist	Title	Sales
MUSIC002	One Direction	Four	3.20
MUSIC008	Sam Smith	The Lonely Hour	3.50
MUSIC004	Coldplay	Ghost Stories	3.70
MUSIC003	Ed Sheeran	X	4.40
MUSIC001	Taylor Swift	1989	6.00

Test yourself

1. Write a query-by-example that would print a table showing title and sales of all albums selling less than 3 million, sorted in alphabetical order of Title.

2. Write a query-by-example that will produce a table showing all data for albums with the title "Four" or "X".

3. State the output you would expect for this query.

4. For Q2 you wrote a query by example using the logical operator OR. If you changed the operator to AND what output would the query produce? Explain your answer.

Learning activity

You made a data table on a subject of your own choice. Write a query-by-example to accompany that data table. Use either text matching or a relational operator.

State the output you would expect from the query.

Review

Key terms

Entity A thing, person or event. Each record in a database table stores data about one entity.

Field In a database table, a field is typically shown as one column of a table. A field stores a single item of data about an entity. Every record in the table has the same fields.

Primary Key A field which stores a unique value. Every record in the table has a different value in the primary key field.

Query An instruction to the computer to find and display information from a database. A query typically specifies which records to show, which fields to show from those records, and a sort order.

Record In a database table, a record is typically shown as one row of the table. A record stores all the data relating to a particular entity.

Table A collection of data records. All the records in the table should relate to the same type of entity. A database may have many different data tables.

Project work

This data table shows best-selling computer games. The table is called GAMES.

Game	Publisher	Sales (millions)	Released
Mario Kart DS	Nintendo	23.3	2005
Call of Duty: Black Ops	Activision	24.8	2010
Grand Theft Auto: San Andreas	Rockstar Games	27.5	2006
Super Mario Brothers Wii	Nintendo	27.8	2009
Wii Play	Nintendo	28.2	2007
Call of Duty: Modern Warfare	Activision	28.5	2009
New Super Mario Brothers	Nintendo	30.7	2006
Wii Sports Resort	Nintendo	32.6	2009
Mario Kart Wii	Nintendo	34.3	2008
Grand Theft Auto V	Rockstar Games	45.0	2013
Minecraft	Mojang	60.0	2009
Wii Sports Resort	Nintendo	82.9	2006

1. What are the entities in this data table?

2. How many records are there in this table, and how many fields?

3. Suggest suitable data types for the fields.

4. What is the output of this data query?

	Game	Publisher	Sales	Released
TABLE	GAMES	GAMES	GAMES	GAMES
Show	✓	✓	✓	
Sort			DESCENDING	
Criteria		NOT "Nintendo"		

5. Make a data query which will display all details of all games released since 2009.

6. Make a data query which will display the name and release year of all games selling more than 30 million.

Here are some more facts about best-selling computer games:

- Tetris has sold 143 million since June 6, 1984
- Pokémon has sold 270.8 million since February 27, 1996
- Super Mario has sold 297.88 million since September 13, 1985

7. Use this information to add three more records to the data table.

8. Create a data query-by-example table based on the extended table. Choose any query you like.

9. Pass the query to another student.

10. Another student has given you a data query. Produce an output in response to the query. Give the response back. Mark each other's work.

Index